MADOC

AND THE

DISCOVERY OF AMERICA

RICHARD DEACON

MADOC AND THE DISCOVERY OF AMERICA

*Some New Light on
an Old Controversy*

GEORGE BRAZILLER

New York

To

TREVOR T. PENNANT WILLIAMS

of Prestatyn,

an ardent Cambrian

CONTENTS

	Page
Preface and Acknowledgements	xi
1 'To Travel Hopefully'	1
2 In Quest of Madoc	11
3 The Age of Owain Gwynedd	32
4 Curraghs, Coracles and Square-Masters	43
5 Voyage with 'Ten Sailes'	56
6 Did Columbus know of Madoc?	70
7 Madoc the Sailor	82
8 The First Expedition	97
9 The Origins of the Welsh Indians Legend	108
10 'General' Bowles Goes to London	124
11 John Evans's Strange Quest	137
12 Reports from Travellers	151
13 Willem the Minstrel	164
14 Landfall in Alabama	179
15 In the Footsteps of the Welshmen	193
16 Mainly on the Mandans	207
17 A Language Conundrum	220
Bibliography and Sources	239
Supplementary Notes to Chapters	243
Index	259

ILLUSTRATIONS

facing page

Wales in 1100 (reproduced by kind permission of Faber &
  Faber from *Historical Atlas of Wales*)   34

A fifteenth-century impression of a twelfth-century British
  vessel (Radio Times Hulton Picture Library)   35

Dolwyddelan Castle, reputed birthplace of Madoc (from
  an engraving by Buck, by kind permission of the National
  Library of Wales)   35

Edward Williams (Iolo Morganwg) (reproduced from an
  etched portrait by Robert Cruikshank after Elijah Waring,
  by kind permission of the National Library of Wales)   50

Governor John Sevier of Tennessee   50

Remains of the old stone pier said to be the departure point
  of Madoc's first expedition (by kind permission of Mrs.
  Victor Wilde)   51

Marisco Castle on Lundy Island, departure point of Madoc's
  second expedition (Radio Times Hulton Picture Library)   51

Map of the world, 1482 (Radio Times Hulton Picture
  Library)   98

The commemoration marker of Madoc's landing erected by
  the D.A.R. at Mobile Bay   99

Mobile Bay from the air (by courtesy of Congressman Jack
  Edwards)   99

A section of John Evans's map, showing the Mandan villages (by kind permission of the Library of Congress, Washington, D.C.)   114

A sketch map of the ancient fortifications at Duck River, Tennessee   115

Plan of the remains of the 'Castle of the Sons of Owain' (Crown Copyright. Reproduced by kind permission of the Controller of Her Majesty's Stationery Office)   115

George Catlin, painter and student of the Mandans (from a portrait by William Fisk, by kind permission of the Smithsonian Institution National Collection of Fine Arts)   194

Mah-To-Toh-Pa, chief of the Mandans   195

Portrait of a Mandan woman   195

A Mandan Indian in full dress sketched by Catlin (Radio Times Hulton Picture Library)   210

Contemporary sketch of a Mandan koorig   211

Method of carrying a Welsh coracle (from a drawing by George de la Motte, by kind permission of the National Library of Wales)   211

LINE ILLUSTRATIONS IN TEXT

Genealogical tree of the House of Gwynedd   23

Map showing the probable course of Madoc's first expedition   101

Map showing the routes followed in U.S.A. by the 'Welsh Indians'   202

PREFACE
and
ACKNOWLEDGEMENTS

THE STORY OF Madoc ab Owain Gwynedd is one that has been sadly neglected by his own countrymen during the past hundred years. Welsh scholars have been much more sceptical of the claims that he discovered America in 1170 than many historians and geographers of other nations.

There have been good reasons for the scepticism. For very many years even Welsh experts had been completely fooled by Iolo Morganwg's forgery of ancient odes. Then an expedition in search of the reputed descendants of Madoc along tributaries of the Missouri River ended in dismal failure.

Nevertheless, the legend persists, and in the light of more recent evidence there are equally sound reasons for claiming that Madoc did reach the shores of the New World some 322 years before Columbus.

There is a special reason why this is an appropriate moment to investigate this story once more. A tablet commemorating the reputed landing place of Madoc in Alabama has been erected by the Daughters of the American Revolution, and this year exhaustive research has revealed what was his probable departure point from Wales – the remains of an old stone quay now converted into a flowering rockery.

I must confess that what gave me the necessary morale for this formidable task of research in the face of immense discouragement from many experts was the fact that I had myself sailed across the Atlantic Ocean in a small flat-bottomed landing-craft, which even the Americans who built it declared would never finish the trip.

Apart from all this, the investigation of the legend proved rewarding in the wide range of themes and fascinating sub-plots that it produced. On the purely literary side there are endless disputes about the correct translations of ancient odes and the authenticity of sources, the countless foreign references to Madoc, notably the almost unknown, sublimely romantic, yet factually based narrative of the elusive Willem the Minstrel of Holland.

I wish to express my warmest thanks to the many individuals and organizations in several countries who have helped me in my quest for the truth about Madoc. First of all I must pay tribute to the courtesy and helpfulness of the following:

The staff of the Manuscripts Room of the British Museum; Mr. G. R. Crone, Librarian of the Royal Geographical Society; Mr. D. G. Owens, Keeper of Mss. and Records at the National Library of Wales; Mr. E. D. Jones, Librarian of the National Library of Wales; Mr. E. Gwynne Jones, Librarian of University College, Bangor; Mr. T. Gwynfor Jones, Department of Welsh History, University College of South Wales; Dr. Iorwerth Peate, Curator of the Welsh Folk Museum. St. Fagan's Castle, Cardiff; Mr. George Naish, of the National Maritime Museum at Greenwich; Professor Idris Foster, of Jesus College, Oxford; Mr. N. S. E. Pugsley, City Librarian, Exeter; Mr. Merfyn Phillips, of St. Dogmaels, Cardigan (for much useful information about coracles) Mr. L. A. Hemelrijk, of Amsterdam; Mr. Clifford K. Shipton, Director of the American Antiquarian Society; Mr. Donald T. Schmidt, of Brigham Young University, Provo, Utah; Mr. William C. Sturtevant, of the Division of Cultural Anthropology, the Smithsonian Institution, Washington; Mrs. Alice P. Hook, Librarian of the Cincinnati Art Museum; Mrs. Frances H. Stadler, Archivist of the Missouri Historical Society (for permission to quote from the Mackay Indian Notes in the Clark Papers), St. Louis, Miss.; Mrs. Nancy C. Prewitt, Assistant Director of the Western Historical Manuscript Collection, University of Missouri Library, Columbia, Missouri.

I gratefully acknowledge permission for the use of copyright material from:

Mr. James N. Osborn and Professor Edwin B. Knowles, of the

Renaissance Society of America, for the quotations from the ms. of *Anatomie of Spayne*; the British Museum for extracts from the Cottonian Mss.; Mr. Arthur T. Halliday, of Baltimore, for the notes of his great-grandfather; Mrs. Grafton S. Porter, of Cincinnati, for extracts from the papers of J. Morgan Lewis and other material.

Professor David Williams and the University of Wales Press, for extracts from *John Evans & The Legend of Madoc*; Mr. Arthur T. Griffith, of Philadelphia, for extracts from his correspondence; Mr. Kinchen Exum and the Lookout Publishing Company, of Chattanooga, Tennessee, for extracts from Zella Armstrong's *Who Discovered America*; Faber & Faber, Ltd., for the reproduction of the twelfth century map of Wales from *Historical Atlas of Wales*; the Library of Congress, Washington, D.C., for John Evans's map; the Royal Commission on Ancient Monuments in Wales and Monmouthshire for the plan of the hill fort on Carn Fadrun; the Smithsonian Institution for the picture of George Catlin from a portrait by William Fisk.

I particularly wish to express my special gratitude to Mr. T. T. Pennant Williams, of Prestatyn, for much valuable advice on sources and many constructive suggestions; to Mrs. O. M. Wilde, of Rhos-on-Sea, and Mr. Norman Tucker, of Colwyn Bay, for great assistance in tracking down the site of the ancient port of Aber-Kerrik-Gwynyon; to the late Rev. E. F. Synnott, of Iden, who provided some invaluable clues as well as suggesting sources for maritime research; to M. Edouard Duvivier, of Poitier, for his fascinating contribution on Willem the Minstrel; and, finally, to that enthusiastic supporter of the Madoc claim, Mr. Hatchett Chandler, Curator and Historian of Fort Morgan, Alabama, whose *Little Gems from Fort Morgan* provided most interesting material on the environs of Mobile Bay and the ancient fortifications in Alabama and Tennessee.

R. D.

I

'TO TRAVEL HOPEFULLY'

IMAGINATION MORE THAN knowledge, romantic inspiration more than ability were the real driving forces behind the early explorers of this planet.

The urge to discover new lands, to seek, as did Alexander the Great, the 'earth's utmost verge', was something that was nurtured and fostered by our early story-tellers and the creators of pagan folk-lore and their symbolistic gods and goddesses. Some of these early explorers may have believed implicitly the legends which were spun about unknown lands far across the oceans, but many more must have regarded them with suspicion and plodded on very much in the spirit of Robert Louis Stevenson – that 'to travel hopefully is a better thing than to arrive'.

The New World was seeded in the minds of men long before it was actually sighted, and if there had been no legends about a lush and extensive continent waiting to be discovered, it might have taken longer before America was revealed as a fact. Thus in any careful examination of the claims of those alleged to be the first to discover the American continent one must investigate the legends before the facts.

Hanno, as far back as 800 B.C., was reputed to have sailed round the west coast of Africa and 'thirty days westwards of the Pillars of Hercules',[1] which caused a later scribe, Periplus, to suggest that he might have discovered a new land. There is no suggestion that he did, but his voyage may have paved the way for legend creators.

In 400 B.C. Plato followed up the story of Hanno's voyage by talking of 'the lost world of Atlantis', referring to 'an island in the mouth of the sea in the passage of those straits, called the Pillars of Hercules . . . larger than Libya and Asia, from which there was an easy passage over to other islands and from those islands to that continent which is out of that region. Poseidon settled in this island, from whose son Atlas its name was derived, and divided it among his ten sons'.

Plato's theory was that the inhabitants of Atlantis crossed over to Europe and Africa, subdued all Libya as far as Egypt and all Europe as far as Asia Minor, but that eventually the island sank beneath the sea.

Aristotle also mentioned the Carthaginians as having colonized a land 'many days' journey from the Pillars of Hercules', but he was no more precise than this in denoting the situation of the mythical 'New World'. Seneca wrote prophetically: 'The time will come when the ocean will loosen the chains of nature and we shall behold a vast country; a new Typhis shall discover New Worlds: Thule shall no longer be considered the last country of the known world.'[2]

So to the ancients, it is clear, the New World existed at least as a legend or as folk-lore, at best as the intuitive feeling of Greek intellectuals that there must be an outer world. Didorus Siculus in 100 B.C. was more precise: he decreed that the Phoenicians had discovered a 'large, sweet, fertile island opposite to Africa', and, by his description, it would appear that this island was about 10,000 furlongs from the African coast.

Atlantis may have been the will-o'-the-wisp as far as these ancient scribes were concerned, as for centuries there was confusion between the idea of Atlantis, a lost kingdom which disappeared under the sea – 'by a flood and earthquake destroyed', according to Plato – and America itself. Nor has history ever satisfactorily solved the mystery of Atlantis except to prove that Atlantis was certainly not America. Consensus of opinion still places this 'lost kingdom' as having been somewhere west of the Straits of Gibraltar, and Plato may have based his account of it on information obtained from Phoenician sailors about the Canary

Islands or the Azores. But equally Atlantis may have been a large and ancient island overwhelmed by an earthquake and sunk without trace in the Atlantic Ocean, or, a less popular but in some ways factually a greater possibility, it could have been situated in what are now the Hoggar Mountains of Southern Algeria at a time when the ocean washed over the Sahara Desert and the mountains were islands inhabited by the forefathers of the Touareg tribes. For the Touareg language is unlike Arabic, Swahili or any other African tongue, but resembles only one of the dialects spoken in the Himalayas.

Ptolemy's map of the world, originally drawn about A.D. 150 and reproduced in a printed edition in 1472, was remarkably accurate as far as it went in depicting the known world. Africa was shown as far south as Ethiopia, with unknown lands indicated to the south-east of that continent; the British Isles appear on the farthermost north-west corner of the map, which otherwise reveals only middle and southern Europe, the southern part of Russia, Arabia, India, Ceylon and what today would be Burma, Siam and Vietnam. This was the world as it was known to the Romans.

When Pytheas discovered Thule – Ultima Thule – six days' voyage north of Britain, close to 'the frozen ocean', the Greeks believed he had found the end of the world. Yet what was Thule? No one can be sure even today; it might have been Iceland, or the Faroes or the Shetlands. But for centuries the learned among the Greeks scoffed at Pytheas. Strabo, who wrote his geographical work about the beginning of the Christian era, regarded Pytheas as a liar and poured contempt on the idea of a vast New World, expressing the belief that the breadth of the habitable world was 3,000 miles and the length about 7,000. Yet the conception of a New World in its various forms – Atlantis, the Isles of the Blest, Paradise, the Land Beyond the Magic Mirror – persisted. Thus St. Brandon, emulating Ulysses, sailed away across the trackless seas in quest for the Island of the Saints, reported to be in the Western Sea. The account of this voyage can be described as at best mythical, but it is the first known attempt of any man to cross and explore the Atlantic Ocean, telling how Saint Brandon voyaged for seven years, discovering unknown islands.

If anyone travelled hopefully, it was Brandon. But the stories of this saint are important in establishing a link between early legend and the first discovery of America. Brandon, in the sixth century A.D., paved the way for later voyages, and if the abbot of an Irish monastery in this era could voyage so far there is little reason to doubt the feasibility of others besides Columbus tackling the Atlantic crossing between that date and the sixteenth century.

The craft in which Brandon set sail is described as 'an osier boat covered with tanned hides and carefully greased, provisioned for seven years'. Whether or not seven years' provisions was an exaggeration matters little. The chief island which Brandon discovered is still somewhat of a mystery; in Martin Behaim's map of 1492 Saint Brandon's Isle is depicted as being much farther south than was originally thought, on almost the same latitude as Cape Verde. It could have been Madeira, as legend has it that 'the isle was full of singing birds and all the trees were charged with ripe fruit'.

In 1959 Mr. Geoffrey Ashe, an authority on the Arthurian legends, conceived the idea of repeating St. Brandon's voyage by sailing a tiny boat across the Atlantic, expressing the belief that possibly St. Brandon discovered America. He was of the opinion that the sailor-priest voyaged in a square-sailed craft similar to a certain type of Cornish fishing boat still in use. 'I want to prove that if you sail from Ireland in a boat of that type – it could only go before the wind – you will finish up in Newfoundland forty days later,' declared Mr. Ashe.[3]

This is an interesting theory, but it is rather contradicted by contemporary reports which stated that St. Brandon sailed west and south-west.

It was not until the ninth century A.D. that a real advance was made in discovering something approximating to a New World. Then the Vikings, who loved and lived by the sea, set forth in their black-sailed ships and discovered first Iceland and then the Faroes. Gardar made Iceland a refuge for pirates and marauders, and from here the lawless Erik the Red sailed away in 985 and returned after three years with news of a territory with good fishing which he colonized and eventually called Greenland.

The question has been raised as to whether the theories of Theopompus and Plato, whether they be the 'island of immense extent' in the western ocean, or 'the island continent of Atlantis', were purely imaginative, or possibly developed from reports of Far Eastern explorers. It seems probable that they were simply imaginative sorties into the realms of geography, but if one examines Asiatic history one finds the Chinese historian, Li Yen, in A.D. 800 giving an account of early voyages made by Chinese to Kamchatka and an area which must now be the north-west coast of America. Geologists are sure that Asia and America were once linked by land in the north and it is now clear that the 'Indians' of America, at least in the north, came from Asia via the Aleutian Islands.[4]

In 1962 a Peking University professor, Chu Shien-chi, claimed that five Chinese, led by a Buddhist monk, sailed from China to Mexico in A.D. 459 claiming similarities of language, mythology, coinage and customs between the Aztecs and ancient China in support of his theory. This story, said to have been traced through the translation of ancient records, suggested that this voyage of discovery was made through the Kuriles and Aleutians.[5]

It has been argued effectively, but not conclusively, that there were insufficient contacts between Greece and the Far East for anyone to have heard reports of the discovery of America from across the Bering Straits. On the other hand Plato's writings on the subject were said to be based on an old story which Crantor claimed came from the priests of Sais. All that is certain is that, despite the many who opposed these theories, the idea of a New World far out in the Atlantic continued to inspire explorers from 800 B.C. until the advent of Columbus.

The recent discovery of a reputed ancient map of Vinland, while not strengthening the claims that the Norsemen led the way in exploring the Atlantic's northern reaches, does re-open the whole question of ancient reconnaissance of the New World. It seems fairly probable that on five occasions between A.D. 983 and 1030 the Norsemen found new lands. They were, however, honest enough to admit that the Irish had arrived in Iceland before them. But these voyages were in the main short trips from one stretch of land to another and not to be compared with a major transatlantic crossing. Bjarni Herjolfson, an Icelander, is credited with having landed on the mainland of North America – probably the ice-bound fringes of that continent – by accident on his way to Greenland in 985–6, and Leif, son of Erik the Red, claimed to have landed in what is now either Labrador, or Newfoundland, in 1002–3, naming the territory Vinland, or the Land of Vines. This name was used in the past as an argument against Erik's finding Labrador on the grounds that vines could not possibly have grown there. On the other hand it has been proved scientifically that the climate in that region in Erik's day was much warmer than now. The stories handed down from the Icelandic sagas of 'Vinland the Good', describing a country if not flowing with milk and honey at least prolific of grapes, may not be such a fantasy after all. The sagas tell of Leif's voyage to a fruitful land and a balmy climate, and modern climatologists assert that between 950 and 1200 there was clear evidence of greater warmth in both Iceland and Greenland than there is today. Colder weather did not set in permanently there until the thirteenth century.

The Vinland Map,[6] however, does not prove that Leif discovered America, despite Yale University's claims that the map was made some fifty years before Columbus's voyage in 1492. Controversy over this map still rages furiously. Count Eigil Knuth, the Danish Polar explorer, was one of the first to deny that it proved the Vikings discovered America before Columbus.[7]

The Vinland Map was examined by Mr. Thomas E. Marston, Curator of Medieval Renaissance at Yale University, and by Mr. R. A. Skelton, superintendent of the Map Room at the British Museum. The latter stated that the map has 'strong affinities with a circular world map in the 1436 atlas of Andrea Bianco in the Bibleoteca Nazionale Marciana at Venice'. Both maps, for example, place Mount Sinai and Basra in Africa. Mr. Skelton is convinced that the outlines of Iceland, Greenland and Vinland were drawn at the same time and by the same hand as the rest. The suggestion is that whoever drew this map must have worked on a master map – unheard of and now lost – based on the Norse voyages to America in the twelfth century. This is not a very plausible theory as the Norsemen were not known to make maps; they relied on the stars for their navigation. Also ties between Iceland and Greenland and Norse lands weakened in the fourteenth century, and by the middle of the fifteenth century detailed knowledge accumulated by the Norsemen about the lands in the west had passed out of European consciousness.[8]

It would seem that as these lands were alleged to have been discovered more than one hundred years before the writing of Icelandic history the outline of Vinland could only have been transmitted over the centuries by word of mouth. Professor Eva Taylor, an expert on medieval cartography, criticizing the Vinland Map says that if its version of Greenland is genuine, it is the only map before the nineteenth century which shows the whole of Greenland. All other evidence is that the north of Greenland was unexplored until then.

A Soviet geographer, Samuel Varshavsky, made the surprising claim in 1962 that America was discovered 130 years before Columbus by an English Carmelite friar, Nicholas of Lynne. Nicholas is known to have been alive in 1386, but the dates of his birth and death are unknown.

A small but extremely vocal body of American historians have been campaigning in recent years against the glorification of Columbus, and they have been investigating all other earlier claimants to the discovery of the New World. One of the claims they are examining is that made more than half a century ago by an obscure Somersetshire librarian, Arthur Hudd, who told the Clifton Antiquarian Society that the real credit for naming the New World belonged to a Bristol merchant, one Richard Amerycke.

Richard Amerycke, one-time High Sheriff of Bristol, was the principal sponsor of John Cabot's voyage of discovery to the North American mainland – then assumed to be an island off China. In 1896 Arthur Hudd found in the muniment room of Westminster Abbey the Customs Roll for Bristol, recording that it was Amerycke who personally handed to Cabot a Royal reward of £20. Hudd believed that Amerycke and not Amerigo

Vespucci gave the name of America to the New World. There is no documentary proof of this.

Nevertheless, though Columbus still takes pride of place as the best-known and authenticated discoverer of America, it seems even with a slight study of the history of this subject that other and lesser known explorers have equal claims to be considered. True, some of these claimants were impostors and some of their sponsors are either credulous or deliberately deceptive, but in examining the history of a period when records were rarely kept, or, if they were, frequently inaccurately, one must examine legends to seek facts and realize that quite often legends were built on fact.

Indeed the embellished and romantic legends of the ancient Greeks were sometimes based on fact. It is possible that both Plato's 'Atlantis' and Anaximander's theory that the world was round and not flat were originally born from the evidence of Phoenician sailors in the one instance and from some pilgrim from the East in the other.

Arabs, Basques, Catalans, Dutch, French, Germans, Hindus, Chinese, Japanese, Phoenicians, Polynesians, Portuguese, Romans, Turks and Welsh have all claimed for their respective nations the honour of being the first to discover America.

But in this book we are concerned solely with one proposition: the alleged discovery of America in A.D. 1170 by a Welshman, Prince Madoc ab Owain Gwynedd. Did he, unheralded and unknown to the writers of history, arrive in the New World 322 years before Columbus? Was he the first of the great transatlantic explorers? Or is this a faded myth from the mists of Celtic legend, or a gilded and faked piece of evidence fabricated at the behest of the Tudors through jealousy of Columbus?

Whether or not one takes the view in favour of the Madoc claim, this is in many ways the most fascinating story of exploration which legend and history have handed down to us – a veritable Kon-Tiki style saga of the twelfth century. It is a story calling for patience, unrelenting search, agility and some forensic ability in putting together the jig-saw puzzle of clues and contradictions, of false evidence and romanticism, of gems of truth and fact sometimes to be found in one continent, sometimes in the other.

So extraordinary is the tale, so imponderable many of its facets that I was in the beginning abashed by the immensity of the task of unravelling it. In all humility I felt that the best starting point was the hard route – the route followed by those who have discounted the Madoc legend. I quickly found that it was not just a case of a legend having been ignored, or airily dismissed by historians. Admittedly Sir J. E. Lloyd, in his *History of Wales*, the standard work on the Roman to Middle Ages period in Welsh history, made no mention of Madoc. But scholars have argued about it over the centuries. The Welsh people subscribed to send John Evans to America in the 1790s to examine the Madoc story, and in 1858 Thomas Stephens, a distinguished Welsh scholar, submitted an essay on the subject to the Llangollen Eisteddfod. The theme for the essay was 'The discovery of America in the twelfth century by Prince Madoc ab Owain Gwynedd', the prize being £20 and a silver medal.

There were six entries for the competition; five of the essays gave an affirmative view of the Madoc legend, while Stephens, a Merthyr Tydfil chemist who had applied a scientific and meticulous mind to the study of Welsh literature, refuted the theme in a lengthy, detailed and closely reasoned thesis. His essay was by common consent the best work presented, but the prizes were withheld because, contrary to the expectations of the adjudicators, Stephens had disproved the story. It was argued that the terms of reference of the competition were so worded that what was called for was an essay on the *discovery* of America by Madoc, and not a rebuttal. One of the judges resigned because Stephens was not given the prizes, while another refused to award it to any other than Stephens. Eventually it was decided to make no award.

Yet if the case against Madoc has been substantially developed, there are many authorities who support the claims that he discovered America. Such encyclopedias as Webster's and *Encyclopaedia Americana* support the story; so do such historians as Hakluyt, Purchas, Prescott in his *History of Mexico*, Ridpath in his *History of the World*, Vespucci and John G. Palfrey, while Benjamin F. De

Costa, probably the most respected authority of his time on pre-Columbian voyages to America, accepted the Madoc claim and retained his belief in it in his last book in 1901.

An interesting feature of the age-long arguments that have waxed and waned around the subject over the centuries is that most of those who have delved into it come down positively either for or against. Few take a dispassionate view, or assert that there is no proof one way or another. A notable exception was that extremely cautious and sceptical historian, Justin Winsor, who, though one would have expected him by instinct to come down firmly against the legend, preferred to make no judgement on the issue and allowed for its being quite possible that Madoc had made such a voyage.

Each age has taken a different view of the subject, and, to make the question even more controversial, when the authorities of one continent have tended to support Madoc, those on the other side of the Atlantic have concurrently pooh-poohed it. The Tudor historians were overwhelmingly pro-Madoc, a fact which made the later anti-Tudor historians reject the theory. In the seventeenth century reports from French and British sources of the discovery of Indian tribes who spoke a dialect similar to Welsh revived interest in the question; these reports were in their turn rejected when John Evans failed to find evidence in support on his journey across America. But though Stephens tried hard to damn the story for ever in 1858, countless authorities since have upheld it, and on November 10, 1953, the Virginia Cavalier Chapter of the Daughters of the American Revolution erected a memorial tablet at Fort Morgan, Mobile Bay, Alabama, bearing these words:

> '*In memory of Prince Madoc, a Welsh explorer,*
> *who landed on the shores of Mobile Bay in 1170*
> *and left behind, with the Indians, the*
> *Welsh language.*'[9]

2

IN QUEST OF MADOC

SOME HISTORIANS, Welsh scholars among them, have gone so far as to deny the existence of Madoc and to dismiss him as a legendary figure like Ulysses or Atlas. One argument is that there were ten persons of that name in the twelfth century and that, as a son of Owain Gwynedd was not among these, there is no reason to discuss the tradition. A reviewer of Thomas Stephens's book[1] on Madoc, writing in *Archaeologia Cambrensis*, stated bluntly that Stephens's methods had 'the merit of closing the subject for ever, and of adding another item to the already long catalogue of exploded popular beliefs'.[2]

What has been disputed at great length is the true identity of Madoc. It is apparent at the very beginning of any quest for the man that chroniclers throughout the ages have tended to confuse one Madoc with another, so that the identity of the son of Owain Gwynedd has on more than one occasion been attributed to another Madoc who, far from sailing across the Atlantic and discovering America, actually died in his own country without ever leaving it. Inaccurate assessment of history and carelessness in accepting verbal versions of the Madoc story handed down from one generation to another have played into the hands of such competent and painstaking detractors as Stephens.

There is no logical reason for examining all ten Madocs mentioned by that eminent Cambrian, Professor Lloyd, but one must first look at the Reverend Walter Davies's contemptuous assessment that Madoc was 'killed in his own country, which he never left'. Walter Davies was better known as the bard, Gwalltir Mechain; living in the latter part of Iolo Morganwg's lifetime, he became one of Iolo's bitterest critics, biting, in fact, the very literary hand which had guided him so effectively in his early days. He was not a great poet, even by Eisteddfod standards, but he gained a reputation for being a sound man of the Establishment who damned anything novel, including the French Revolution.

None the less Gwalltir Mechain was a formidable critic and one to be respected. For this reason one must first of all examine the possibility that if there was a man named Madoc he died a most unseemly landlubber's death.

During this period of Welsh history there were no less than six Madocs who might have been confused with a son of Owain Gwynedd. It therefore seems to be a useful precautionary exercise to examine the various accounts of these six and to see whether the alleged discoverer of America might after all not be the son of the illustrious Owain, but some obscurer Welshman on whom the earlier story-tellers had conferred a more impressive pedigree.

Three of the Madocs of this era (c. 1100–1300) were rulers of Powys. One of these was Madoc ab Gruffydd, son of Angharad, a daughter of Owain Gwynedd. He became ruler of Powys in 1197, but was considered to be a renegade in King John's pay, though he swung away from the English yoke towards the end of his reign. He died in 1236 and was buried in his own foundation, Vale Crucis Abbey.

Another Madoc was named in a Welsh newspaper in 1818 as 'Prince Madoc, son of Llewelyn Gwynedd . . . who left Wales in the year 1169 to explore the Western Ocean'.[3] This claim can very swiftly be dismissed: Madoc ab Llewelyn Gwynedd led an insurrection in 1294, more than a hundred years after the alleged discovery of America. He was arrested in 1295 after the collapse of his rebellion; nothing is known of him after that date, nor is there any record of his execution.

Madoc ab Meredydd, another Prince of Powys and also related through marriage to Owain Gwynedd, was a contemporary of

Madoc ab Owain Gwynedd. He ruled Powys from 1142 to 1160, when he died and was buried at Meifod. This Madoc's story is sufficiently documented to discount any possibility of his having discovered America, and, indeed, as can be seen, he died ten years before the reputed finding of that continent. Professor Barbier, in his work on *The Age of Owain Gwynedd*, has made considerable mention of Madoc ab Meredydd.[4]

Some scholars find significance in the fact that there is no record of Madoc in the works of Giraldus Cambrensis, but there are several explanations of this. In the first place Giraldus was only twenty-four years of age when Madoc is supposed to have sailed to America, and from about 1166–72 he was completing his education at the University of Paris. It is true that he hunted and fished on the lands of the Princes of Gwynedd, but he spoke no Welsh and would not have been able to acquire knowledge of bardic odes or purely domestic history. John Williams, writing in 1791, referred to legends that King Arthur had knowledge of America and said that this has been linked with the Madoc story.[5] He may have been thinking of George Abbott, who asserted that King Arthur had been told of a vast, distant land far out in the Atlantic and that a 'Prince of Wales had first found it'.[6]

This again is symptomatic of the ridiculous lengths to which some of the pro-Madoc school have gone to support their views; King Arthur's legendary possession of a magical omniscience became with some romantic scholars as much as an obsession as King Charles's head with Mr. Dick.

Two other Madocs are more obscure. One is mentioned by Stephens in a somewhat irrelevant manner in an effort to show that because he was said to have been murdered between 1160 and 1164, he could not have discovered America in 1170. Stephens appears to take the view that because this Madoc was mentioned by contemporary bards and the son of Owain Gwynedd was also lauded by these twelfth-century poets of the court, they were one and the same. If Stephens could have established clearly that the Madoc who was killed really existed and that there was no son of Owain Gwynedd of this name, he would have gone far towards demolishing the Madoc legend. But he cites no documentary evidence to make this Madoc any more than a shadowy figure. Gwelltir Mechain believed this ode proved that Madoc was killed in Wales, but there is no substantiation of this, nor is there any positive identification with the son of Owain Gwynedd. The only evidence of the assassination of a man named Madoc – and it was a common enough name in the Wales of this period – was an ode by Llywarch Prydydd y Moch, a contemporary bard who wrote verses in honour of the sons and grandsons of Owain Gwynedd. This 'Ode to the Hot Iron' was written in 1169:

> *From having with my hand and blade slain the blessed one,*
> *From having been accessory to a murderous deed,*
> *Good Iron exonerate me: that when the assassin*
> *Slew Madoc, he received not [the blow] from my hand.*

On the basis of this ode Stephens claimed that Llywarch was suspected of murdering Madoc and forced to undergo the traditional ordeal of the hot iron to prove or disprove his guilt. He presumed that Llywarch was acquitted on the grounds, first that there was no record of his being convicted, and secondly that he had written other odes after 1169.

But even Stephens has to admit that this was possibly 'not the same Madoc'. The *Myvyrian Archaiology* (London, 1801) states that he was, in fact, of unknown parentage.

The fifth Madoc is mentioned by the bard Cynddelw Brydydd Mawr as being a member of Owain Gwynedd's bodyguard and not a member of his family. Mr. E. D. Jones, the Librarian of the National Library of Wales at Aberystwyth, considers this is evidence that 'the only Madoc connected intimately with Owain Gwynedd in contemporary poetry was the member of his retinue [teulu], commemorated in a series of elegiac stanzas by Cynddelw Brydydd Mawr', arguing that there is no hint in this elegy that this Madoc was the son of Owain Gwynedd. Indeed, Mr. Jones goes further than this and claims that 'there is no contemporary evidence of even the existence of Prince Madoc as one of the sons of Owain Gwynedd.'[7]

One other query seemed worth while raising at this stage in the quest for Madoc: did he exist under another name, or another spelling of the name? As far as spelling is concerned in ancient Welsh the name Madoc could be and was spelt as 'Madog', 'Madauc', 'Madawch' and 'Madawg'. So that any change in spelling of the name would not mean it referred to another person. But I particularly raised the question of whether the discoverer of America might bear another name because the Mandan Indians of North America were said to be descended from Madoc. Could there be any other legendary figure in the Wales of the twelfth century from whom the name Mandan had been derived? To this query Mr. E. D. Jones replied in a letter: 'The only similar name I can think of is the much earlier Manawyddan of the Mabinogion, but I do not know that the name was current in the twelfth century except in the Mabinogion.'

This may seem a slow and tedious route to take in quest of Madoc, but the crossing of hazardous documentary hurdles and the verbal pitfalls of ancient Welsh in the early stages of this book is not without fascination for the literary athlete. It is a challenging and delightfully rewarding terrain that one must traverse in the quest for truth. So far five of the six Madocs have been scrutinized, and the first three can be dismissed as neither having been the sons of Owain Gwynedd, nor of having discovered America. Yet the other two – the least significant of the four – require a little further consideration before examining the case for the last of the six Madocs, i.e. the son of Owain Gwynedd.

Was the Madoc of whom Llywarch wrote the same as the Madoc mentioned by Cynddelw? If one accepts the Myvyrian version that Cynddelw's Madoc was one of Prince Owain Gwynedd's bodyguard, then it is possible that he tallies with the man of 'unknown parentage' in Llywarch's ode to the hot iron. They lived in the same period and there is also the fact that Cynddelw referred to the 'possible *obliteration* of Madoc'. It is not clear whether Cynddelw meant the 'murder' of Madoc, or his disappearance, or simply his removal from the public eye. What is strange is that Cynddelw, a court bard, should write odes honouring a mere retainer, and that Llywarch should refer to a man of unknown parentage as 'the blessed one', a mode of poetic address usually reserved for nobles. As the bards were apt to treat both death and assassination precisely and in detail it seems unlikely at first sight that the two Madocs were one and the same, and the phrase 'obliteration' more probably means that Cynddelw's Madoc mysteriously disappeared.

Ieuan Brechfa, the poet and historian who wrote on the subject in the middle of the fifteenth century, suggested that the 'Ode to the Hot Iron' was deliberately written by Llywarch to hide the disappearance of Madoc and to make people think he was dead.[8] As Ieuan Brechfa wrote about three of the contemporary Madocs, it is not absolutely clear whether he had confused Llywarch's Madoc with one of the others, but there is some support for his belief. 'Meiron', an eighteenth-century bard writing on Welsh poets, referred to one of the odes of Llywarch – that of 'The Hot Iron' – as being 'of great importance and arousing some historical curiosity: it is an invocation, as if he were undergoing the fiery ordeal to exonerate himself from having any knowledge of the fate of Madoc'.[9]

'Meiron' has expressed himself somewhat obscurely, but it is possible to translate his theory into a lucid proposition. Llywarch mourned the disappearance of this Madoc, and for some reason felt a degree of personal responsibility for it. He was, however, not responsible for Madoc's fate and had no knowledge of whence he had gone. In support of this theory there is evidence that bards sometimes invoked the 'hot iron' as a kind of oath for affirming an incident which was in dispute. Gwalchmai may be cited as having used this poetic device when he mourned the disappearance of another of Owain's sons.

These suggestions add an ingredient of mystery to the story, but so far they in no way help to decide whether the 'murder' was an invention of the bard. One's instinct is momentarily to leave question marks against both Llywarch's and Cynddelw's Madocs, for there remains the question whether the discoverer of America was not a son of Owain Gwynedd, but one of his bodyguard. If the answer is in the affirmative, then Cynddelw's Madoc must be re-examined. In seeking an answer to this question one is first faced with academic arguments over the translation of ancient Welsh. E. D. Jones, supporting the arguments of Stephens, insists that Cynddelw Brydydd Mawr describes Madoc as 'a member of Owain Gwynedd's retinue', and this ode, also written in 1169, is entitled in some versions *Teilu Ywein Gwynet*.

But Cynddelw wrote a great variety of odes about the family of Owain Gwynedd, and if we examined them closely it doesn't appear impossible that he sang the praises of more than one Madoc. Mr. E. D. Jones writes that Cynddelw's Madoc 'ranks as a soldier rather than a sailor, the substitution of *myr* (seas) for *mur* (a wall or bulwark) by Dr. William Owen-Pughe in quoting this stanza in his *Dictionary of the Welsh Language*, under the word *dygforth*, is entirely unwarranted'.

Here is a comparison between the rival translations of Cynddelw's verses:

> *Since Madoc, the bulwark of swelling rage,*
> *I mourn a helping friend:*
> *The virile one was fierce in the raging fight,*
> *An arrogant commander of the portal.*

Stephens not only accepted this most unimpressive translation, but quite unnecessarily wrote into it after the words 'swelling rage', the verb 'was slain'. From this Stephens proceeded to argue that, as this ode was written between 1164 and 1169, here is proof that Madoc was killed prior to 1169 and therefore could not possibly have discovered America in 1170.

But Dr. William Owen-Pughe, supported by others, took a very different view. Two other translations are:

> *Since Madoc, conqueror of the raging seas departed,*
> *I mourn a well-tried friend:*
> *The virile one was steadfast in adversity,*
> *Proud defender of the portal.*

and

> *Since Madoc, bulwark against the swelling torrent,*
> *I mourn a stout adherent:*
> *The virile one was fierce in the ceaseless fight,*
> *An arrogant commander of the prow.*

The first translation, let it be noted, depends on whether the vital word is *myr* or *mur*; the second accepts *mur*, but turns the phrase 'swelling rage' into 'swelling torrent'. And even Stephens did not deny that 'swelling rage', at best a clumsy if not downright inaccurate translation, might be construed as referring to the sea and not to Madoc's temperament. In any event what seems to clinch this argument in favour of the theory that Madoc was a man of the sea and not a soldier is another ode of Cynddelw in which he most clearly and unambiguously states:

> And is not Madoc by the whelming wave
> Lost? How I sorrow for the helpful friend.

The next witness for the existence of Madoc is the bard Llywarch ab Llewellyn who hinted at a conflict of two warring princes:

> Two princes of strong passions broke off in wrath;
> The multitude of the earth did love them;
> One on land in Arvon, allaying of ambition,
> And another, a placid one in the bosom of the vast ocean,
> In trouble great and immeasurable,
> Prowling after a possession easy to be guarded,
> Estranged from everyone for the sake of a country.

True, there is no mention of Madoc here, but there is a hint of a prince, fond of the seas, pictured like the Flying Dutchman, doomed to rove the seas for a lifetime, yet always seeking a new land. This version is admittedly somewhat obscure and capable of being interpreted in a variety of ways. Stephens insists the ode was addressed to Rhodri, son of Owain and that Madoc is not a subject of the poem. 'Dafydd and Rhodri were the two princes,' he says; 'the one on land in Arvon [Caernarvonshire] **was** Dafydd, and the one of the bosom of the great sea was Rhodri . . . the possession easy to be guarded was not America, but Anglesey.'[10]

Rhodri was 'Lord of Anglesey' in 1188; he died in 1193 and was buried on the island. As Rhodri went to Anglesey to escape from the warring of his brothers, he was presumably of 'temper mild', and this is a plausible explanation by Stephens. But it is far from being the only interpretation. What was the 'trouble great and immeasureable' in which Rhodri was supposed to be? History suggests he lived in placid retirement. It is also somewhat stretching the imagination to suggest that 'in the bosom of the vast ocean' refers to the flat and most unbosomlike Isle of Anglesey, and much again depends on whether one interprets 'prowling' as finding or voyaging.

To complicate matters this ode was either 'borrowed', plagiarized or confirmed by Ieuan Brechfa, whose interpretation is composed in greater detail:

> *Two princes of base passions quarrelled fiercely;*
> *Their sire was loved by all and people mourned to*
> *see his sons at war;*
> *Their ambition was to wrestle for the land of their father;*
> *They brought disaster on a noble name.*
> *How nobler was Madoc, not yet a prince, yet noble*
> *as a prince,*
> *A dreamer, loved the seas more than the land*
> *which sired him,*
> *Determined to risk all for a dream,*
> *The dream of finding a fair land far across the*
> *oceans, unknown and unproved.*[11]

The theme is almost exactly the same in Ieuan Brechfa's ode as in Llywarch's: the only difference is that Brechfa is more precise and he introduces a third character, Madoc, perhaps an unpardonable liberty, but not historically incorrect. Note, too, the description of Madoc – 'not yet a prince, but noble as a prince'. For here lies a clue to the identity of Madoc as a son of Owain Gwynedd.

No honest scholar could admit this version of the ode as contemporary evidence, for Brechfa was writing three hundred years after the incidents described and developing his own theories of what had happened. This would obviously explain the preciseness of his phraseology. It is true that he does not identify Madoc as a son of Owain Gwynedd, but the two princes to whom he refers would appear to be not Dafydd and Rhodri but Dafydd and Howel, both sons of Owain Gwynedd, and the two who fought for the possessions he left. Rhodri was really quite out of the reckoning by then – a man who had exiled himself in Anglesey, or Mona, as it was then called. Brechfa clearly suggests that Madoc, though not a prince, was the son of one, therefore most probably an illegitimate son of Owain.

But even if one concedes that Brechfa's amended version is inadmissible as evidence there is evidence that Llywarch quite positively wrote about Madoc in another ode. Singing the praises of Llewelyn ab Iorwerth, grandson of Owain, he refers to him as

> Nephew of Madoc, whom we more and more
> Lament that he has gone.

Thus one can at least prove from contemporary records that there was a well-known and well-loved man named Madoc in the kingdom of Gwynedd who was referred to by two bards.

Various records make it plain that there was an illegitimate son of Owain named Madoc. In some ancient Welsh manuscripts in the Cottonian Collection in the British Museum there is a long account of the lineage of Gruffydd, the son of Conan, 'King' of Wales at the beginning of the twelfth century, and the manuscript clearly lists Griffin as the father of Owain Gwynedd and grandfather of 'Madawc'. In Latin, too, in this Collection there appears under the title heading of *Vita Griffini Regis* the following:

VITA GRIFFINI, FILII CONANI, REGIS VENODOTIAE
VEL NORTHWALLIAE, A THELWELLO JURISPERITO
MEREDITHI LATINE VERSA: FILIO OWENI GWYNEDD, ET
EIUS NAVIGATIONE TERRAS INCOGNITAS; WALLICE.

This reference to an explorer of unknown lands is dated 1477, and the sources of much of the information contained in the mss. are Maredudd ap Rhys, a well-known writer of the pre-Tudor era in Welsh literature, various genealogical documents and the findings of Llywarch and Gwalchmai, who were the two chief bards of Owain Gwynedd. In addition the *History of the Gwydir Family*, by Sir John Wynne, clearly lists Madoc as one of twelve 'natural sons by various women'. From the manuscript notes of the author of this work it appears that he had access to many ancient sources, including Robert Vaughan, of Hengwrt, the great antiquary, Sir Thomas Williams, of Trefriw; Dr. Percy, Dean of Carlisle; the Reverend Evan Evans, 'translator of some specimens of ancient Welsh poetry'; the records kept in Caernarvon Castle; and Nicholas Robinson, Bishop of Bangor.[12]

The detractors of the Madoc legend have always argued that it was not until after Columbus discovered America that Tudor historians and Welsh propagandists published the canard that Madoc was a son of Owain Gwynedd. Yet the manuscript just quoted and not previously introduced into documentation of the Madoc legend is dated fifteen years prior to Columbus's epic-making voyage. It is the first of several items of evidence which belie the claim of those who assert that the tale of Madoc was an invention of State-subsidized historians who sought any shred of evidence to counter the pretensions of Spain to have been the first nation to find the New World, at the same time choosing a Welshman to flatter the Welsh Henry Tudor VII who sat on the English throne.

The Welsh have often been charged with a certain gift for terminological inexactitude and for attaching to themselves things that belong to others – mainly, of course, by the English. Yet it is strange to find Welsh scholars taking up this theme and applying the same criticism to their own race, and it has been a lamentable trait among many Welsh scholars that they have so often denigrated the best of their race's work in all the arts and rarely given full credit for it. It is perfectly true that most of the *achyddwyr* and Welsh archivists and historians introduced much legendary matter into what they wrote, but in extenuation of this it must be admitted that often their only raw material was the stuff of legends, the odes of bards and scraps of gossip handed down from one generation to another. Not until the age of the Tudors and the introduction of printing were these things set to paper; until then Wales had suffered from a dearth of painstaking historians.

Flattery may have been a motive in the writing of some of these accounts, but even flattery is fraught with risks when there is no substance to it, and one may be sure that so shrewd a monarch as Henry VII would have wanted to see documentary proof of this claim. He was meticulous in checking records of all kinds. But to suggest that the Tudor historians invented the tale to counter the claims of Spain makes nonsense unless it can be proved that they followed up this thesis by demanding sovereignty over the New World. The answer is that no such demand on a diplomatic or official level was made by the Tudors on the basis of the Madoc legend: there is no official record of a claim to America on these grounds being put forward by the English, though foreigners of various countries made the plea at that time, most notably the Dutch.

The genealogy of Owain Gwynedd's family was set down by many authorities, though understandably some confine this to the legitimate line. However, Maredudd ap Rhys, Gutyn Owen, Humphrey Llwyd, Sir John Wynne, Robert Vaughan, Sir Thomas Williams of Trefriw, Sir Thomas Herbert and Meiron all testify to the existence of a Madoc in the family tree. In the archives of the Gwydir family there is an important note of a contemporary source, stating that 'famous actes' of the period were compiled by 'a most auncient frier or monk of Wales; this was found by the posterity of the said Gruffith ap Conan, in the house of Gwedir in North Wales, and at the request of Morice Wynne, Es., was translated into Latine by Nicholas Robinson, Bishop of Bangor'.[13] Having checked these various accounts one with another and combined the findings of all sources where three or more authorities agree on a single name, I find that the genealogy of the House of Gwynedd reads as shown on page 23.

This is not, nor can it be, a completely accurate genealogical table, though it is substantially confirmed by the *Dictionary of National Biography*. There is no certainty of the exact order in which Owain Gwynedd's children were born. The only dates included in the table are those where *all* the authorities and records concur; when dates are omitted this does not mean they have not been cited, but that the authorities disagree. The titles of the heads of the House of Gwynedd vary through the ages; sometimes they were known as 'Kings', sometimes simply as 'Princes'. But this is as near to accuracy as it is possible to get, including contemporary sources as well as those of later historians.

All sources name Iorwerth Drwyndwn as the eldest son of Owain, Dr. Powel saying that he was 'the eldest borne in matrimonie of Owain Gwynet . . . counted unmeete to governe because of the maime upon his face'.[14] Dr. Powel made particular reference

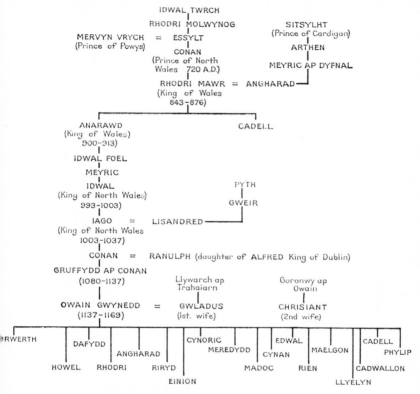

Genealogical tree of the House of Gwynedd

to Howel and Dafydd, two other sons, and added that though Owain had no legitimate son named Madoc, yet 'Madawc was one of his manie sonnes borne outside of matrimonie'.

Nineteen children of Owain are listed in the table given here, but records suggest he must have had others. Indeed, if all the names mentioned were recorded, they would total at least twenty-seven. Apart from one legitimate daughter, Angharad, who married Morgan ab Seissyl, some authorities refer to two other daughters, unnamed by most sources, but identified by others as Gwenllian and Goeral. Spellings vary considerably: Rien is spelt Rhun by some authorities, and Riryd becomes Eiryd in other versions. Various opinions have been expressed on the sons: 'Rhodri, Hywell [Howel], Dafydd and Madoc were the most distinguished,' wrote Meiron, and he acclaimed Howel as a poet of some distinction, eight of whose odes had been preserved, adding that Howel's mother was a native of Ireland, a statement which is also borne out by other sources, notably *Brut y Tywysogion*, which describes her as 'an Irish nobleman's daughter', whom the *Dictionary of National Biography* names as Pyvog. There was considerable disagreement as to which of Owain's children were legitimate, and the D.N.B. curtly states that 'few of his children are regarded as legitimate'. He lived licentiously and had many concubines as well as wives.

Owain's second wife, Chrisiant, is not included in some records on the grounds that this marriage was disallowed by the Church, but Professor Barbier and others who have delved deeply into the history of this period refer to her as Owain's second wife, and it is now generally accepted that she was the mother of Dafydd.

Not included in the genealogical table given here, though actually listed by some authorities as a wife, or concubine of Owain, is Brenda, daughter of Howel, Lord of Carno. There is no positive contemporary evidence of this – only a certain amount of bardic hearsay – but Arthur Rhys names Brenda as the mother of Madoc: 'Madoc was the son of Owain Gwynedd and Brenda, the daughter of the Lord of Carno . . . Cynan, Rhun, Maelgwyn, Rhodri, Rhiryd and Madoc were sons of Owain and Brenda.'[15]

It is certain, however, that Owain had only two wives, though doubtless a large number of mistresses. The fullest details are given in *Brut y Tywysogion*, but these are apt to be faulty, whereas the briefer information contained in *Latinae Annales Cambriae* are more accurate.

A later genealogical table, quoting contemporary sources such as the annals of Conway Abbey, shows Madoc as marrying Annesta, a maid of honour to Chrisiant, by whom he had a daughter, named Gwenllian. Gwenllian is credited with having married Meredydd, son of Llowarch ap Bran, Lord of Menai, by whom she had a son, Meredydd of Bodorgan, who in turn had a daughter Eva.[16] From Eva the descent is traced through Einion Sais, her husband, and Heylin of Bodorgan, their son, to Llewelyn ap Heylin, said to have fought at Bosworth on the side of Henry Tudor. This genealogical tree would appear to be mainly correct, but it is not confirmed by all sources and may well have been an attempt by later historians to prove the Tudors were descended from Madoc.

It is not surprising that the court bards – the only real historians of the age – failed to document every child, or mistress of Owain Gwynedd. They would be concerned in the first place with legitimate heirs, or with those who found favour at the court.

There are other pre-Columbus references to Madoc, and these should suffice to disprove the contention that he was solely an invention of historians after the discovery of America by Columbus. It is only when we come across some over-enthusiastic protagonists of Madoc that we find unnecessary and misleading data gratuitously and haphazardly tossed into the genealogical mixing-bowl, and such suspect ingredients were nearly always added after the Tudor age rather than during it.

Maredudd ap Rhys, who was a clergyman living at Ruabon (1430–60) and one of the chief bards of his time, wrote:

> *Helied Ifan, hael dyfiad*
> *Ar y tir teg, wedi'r tad;*
> *Mewn awr dda minnau ar ddwr,*
> *O fodd hael a fydd helwr –*
> *Madog wych, mwyedig wedd*
> *Iawn genau Owain Gwynedd*
> *Ni fynnai dir, f'enaid oedd,*
> *Na da mawr ond y moroedd.*
> *Madog wyf i'm oed, ei gais*
> *Ar foroedd hyn arferais'*
> *Rhodiaf hyd For ac Afon*
> *Ar hyd eu gro a'm rhwyd gron.*

It is important to consider both the Welsh text and the English translation to reply to criticisms of this source. Here is the translation:

> Let Evan of generous growth hunt
> Upon his fair land, his true patrimony;
> In an auspicious hour, I also on water,
> With the consent of the generous one,
>   will be a hunter.
> Madoc am I, who throughout my life will seek,
> Upon the water, that which I have been used to.
> Madoc the bold, of expanding form,
> True whelp of Owain Gwynedd,
> Would not have land (my kindred soul),
> Nor great wealth, but the seas.
> I am a Madoc to my age, and to his passion
> For the seas have I been accustomed.
> I will walk by sea and river,
> Along the strand with my circled net.

Those wishing to destroy any evidence that seems to support Madoc have developed sophistries to denigrate this poem. One argument is that the bard must have been referring to a brother of Madoc to whom he conceded his rights to any land by reason of his illegitimacy and that, as Owain Gwynedd had no son named Ifan, this shows how inaccurate were Maredudd ap Rhys's sources. But Maredudd was not referring to any other son of Owain. A careful examination of this ms. shows that this poem was dedicated by Maredudd to his patron, Ifan, for the gift of a fishing net. The patron – and all bards at this time still needed patrons – was a huntsman and devoted to the land, whereas the bard preferred to fish. He was comparing his own love of the rivers and the sea to that of Madoc centuries before. The phrase 'his true patrimony' refers not to the legitimacy of one of Owain's sons, but to the rights of Maredudd's patron to his lands.

In previous odes one has noted the argument about *mur* and *myr* – bulwark or seas: here there can be no room for doubt, as the translation of *mawr* is clearly 'seas'. If one accepts this indisputable translation in the ode of Maredudd, it is then probable that Cynddelw referred to seas and not a wall or bulwark.

There is no doubt that the more or less literal translation given here can be improved upon, and indeed Gutyn Owen interpreted it as follows in one important part:

> Madoc am I, the son of Owain Gwynedd,
> With stature large and comely grace adorned,
> No lands at home, nor store of wealth,
> My mind was whole to search the ocean.

Here cenau or genau is translated not as 'whelp', but as 'son'. One cannot, however, say positively that genau means 'son'. 'Whelp' is more accurate, and though a 'whelp of Owain Gwynedd' would imply a son, rather an illegitimate son than a son by marriage, the word admittedly was also used to describe faithful retainers. Critics of the Madoc legend have seized on this possibility to argue that here is further support of the theory that Owain Gwynedd had no son named Madoc and that Maredudd's Madoc is the same as the bodyguard of Owain described by Cynddelw.

Nevertheless, even if one concedes this possibility in the face of genealogical evidence to the contrary, it would be curious indeed if a mere retainer could become a legendary figure referred to by bards, who were undoubtedly as class conscious in the twelfth and thirteenth centuries as were the poets with aristocratic patrons in the eighteenth century, taking as their subjects those people who had fame, nobility and power. A mere retainer would be unlikely to acquire any of these qualities, and by the middle of the fifteenth century it is clear that a legend had grown up around a man named Madoc who was 'with comely grace adorned', 'with stature large' and 'bold', and this certainly fits the picture of the son of a prince, albeit a bastard son.

There is another ode about Madoc by Maredudd ap Rhys, which is either disregarded by the critics, or alleged by them to be a distortion of the previously quoted ode. Hakluyt, who quotes some of its stanzas, states that he was given the translation by William Camden, an authority on medieval Wales. Here Maredudd is more specific:

> *On a happy hour he is on the waters,*
> *Of manners mild the hunter will be,*
> *Madoc brave, of pleasing countenance,*
> *Of the true lineage of Owain Gwynedd,*
> *He coveted not the land,*
> *His ambition not great wealth*
> *But the sea.*

All this was unquestionably written more than thirty years before Columbus reached America.

But the detractors of Madoc will seize on any straw the bards may cast in their direction. Gwalchmai, the bard of Owain Gwynedd (1130–80), wrote:

> *Madog kindly apportioned gifts;*
> *He did more to please than offend me . . .*

From this the critics argue that if Madoc was an illegitimate son, or a retainer, he would not have had the power to apportion gifts; therefore the bard is guilty of further inaccuracy. But Gwalchmai, an Anglesey court poet, not only addressed odes to Owain Gwynedd and his sons, Dafydd and Rhodri, but also to Madog ap Meredydd, Prince of Powys, and this ode obviously refers to the Prince of Powys, and not to the son of Owain Gwynedd.

The Cardiganshire poet, Deio an Ieuan Du, writing in the same period more or less as Maredudd ap Rhys, possibly slightly earlier, also makes it clear that Madoc was by the fifteenth century a legendary figure, almost a patron saint of fishermen, and renowned as a sailor. His references to Madoc make this much clear, though they still give only a vague portrait of the man:

> *fal Madog, marchog y medd,*
> *baun gwyn, fab Owain Gwynedd.*
> *Y gr siwrneio a gai*
> *ar foroedd yr arferai.*
> *Lle ing y bu mewn llong bell*
> *ban golles, uwch ben, gyllell,*

a'r mab hynaf a'i cafas
ar y bwrdd, nid cyfwrdd cas,
a'r mab hwn a'i adnabu,
a'r ail arwydd f'arglwydd fu.

Here Madoc is clearly defined as the son of Owain Gwynedd – 'knight of the mead, fair peacock, son of Owain of Gwynedd'. The ode is a lament for Jenkin, the son of Meredith of Tywyn of Cardigan, who had been captured at sea by French pirates. The poet expressed the wish that if only he possessed the ship owned by Meredith of Tywyn, he would have sailed away in quest of Jenkin in the same adventurous spirit as the noble Madoc who was accustomed to voyaging far and wide.

This evidence to date confirms that there was an adventurous, sea-loving, handsome (all the odes pay tribute to his looks, his stature and bearing) man named Madoc who lived in the period 1160–70 and who was the son of Owain Gwynedd, illegitimate or otherwise. It could also be that, as an illegitimate son, his father used him in his bodyguard, but that nevertheless the legend of his patrimony awed the bards who sang his praises.

Not until printing was introduced do we find any detailed accounts of Madoc. In 1584 Dr. David Powel published *The Historie of Cambria,* which bore on its title page the following description:

THE HISTORIE OF CAMBRIA, NOW CALLED WALES by Caradoc of Llancarfan (translated Humphrey Llwyd) 1584, corrected, augmented and continued out of 'Records and best approved authors' by David Powel, D. D. Dedicated to Sir Philip Sydney.

Scholars have argued over the centuries as to how reliable this work is, and the phrase 'augmented' has been severely criticized as implying undocumented amplification. It could, of course, equally be argued that David Powel used the word 'augment' in the sense of checking the records. The difficulty is that Caradoc's book is known only through Powel's version: the original is not available. Dr. Powel undoubtedly used this work as the basis of his *Historie,* but he also interpolated into the text some of the writings of Gutyn Owen.

Powel described Owain Gwynedd as the son of Gruffyth ap Conan, Prince of North Wales, saying that he died in 1169 'after he had governed his countrie well and worthilie thirty-two yeares. This prince was fortunate and victorious in all his affaires, he never took any enterprise in hand but he achieved it. He left behind him manie children gotten by diverse women which were not esteemed by their mothers and birth, but by their prowes and valiantnesse'.

Dr. Powel lists all Owain's sons and adds that Madoc was one of those 'by diverse women'. Then comes the picture of Madoc, the illegitimate son, loved by many, but caring nothing for power, who 'left the land in contention between his brethren and prepared certain ships with men and munition,[17] and sought adventures by seas, sailing west'.

Finally, there is the fact that the *Dictionary of National Biography* sees fit to include Madoc ab Owain Gwynedd in its lives of distinguished people. True, it expresses doubts, only claiming that he was the 'reputed' son of Owain Gwynedd who had discovered America. Somewhat curiously, and without citing any authority, it gives as the period of his life '1150–80?', admitting that Madoc was not mentioned in *Annales Cambriae*, or in *Brut y Tywysogion*. The D.N.B. cites Powel, James Howel, Sir Thomas Herbert, Dr. William Owen-Pughe and Iolo Morganwg as sources, but makes scant reference to any other authority and no mention at all of American, Spanish, French and Dutch sources, surely a serious omission.

The foregoing evidence is suffice to establish beyond doubt that Madoc, the son of Owain Gwynedd, lived in the first half of the twelfth century and that his association with the sea had made him a legendary figure, not only in his own time but as a symbol of the sea-faring life as late as the fifteenth, sixteenth and seventeenth centuries.

So powerful was the legend that the name of Madoc was evoked in all parts of Wales. When Edward Morus was killed at Llanfyllin Fair in 1689, he was described as:

> *A good man – of the race of Madoc,*
> *of celebrated residence, son*
> *of the brilliant Owain Gwynedd.*

The 'celebrated residence' may well have been Gallt Vadog, near Barmouth, which was reputed to have been a medieval home of splendour, and in the same parish (Llanaber today) there are places named Gae Madog and Hafod Vadog.

3

THE AGE OF OWAIN GWYNEDD

No OTHER NATION in the British Isles has such a shadowy, elusive historical past as Wales. It is almost impossible to say where legend ends and fact begins. The influences of Wales date back into the misted limbo of Celtic folk-lore; even its origins are uncertain. Traces of Palaeolithic man in Wales are extremely vague, but there are numerous remains of the Neolithic period, especially the *dolmens*, or *cromlechs*, now regarded by archaeologists as the stony frameworks of ancient tombs from which the soil has been washed away.

The earliest Welshmen were probably dark, of short stature and dolichocephalic. Sometime during the Bronze Age these people were probably conquered by a tall, fair and brachycephalic race from the continent of what is now Europe, possibly around 1200 B.C. The Welsh were more deeply rooted in pre-Christian Celtic legend than any other part of the British Isles, and this has even conditioned their Christianity because neither the Roman nor the Norman conquests made the same impression in Wales as in England and the cult of paganism not only lasted but rooted itself in the Welsh Christian tradition.

The Romans conquered Wales under Ostorius Scapula, Suetonius and Agricola. The last-named sent Roman legions to guard the Welsh frontier at Deva (Chester), Uriconium (Wroxeter) and Isca Silurum (Caerleon-on-Usk). Julius Caesar, incidentally, stated that the West Britons, presumably including the Welsh, of his day used Greek letters. Some ancient Welsh manuscripts still reveal traces of this lettering.

In the fifth century after Christ the Welsh were engaged in constant warfare against Irish pirates and later they suffered from the marauding Danes. Not until the advent of Rhodri Mawr (A.D. 844) was Welsh prestige restored. Then, under Hywel Dda (Howel the Good), a system of laws and customs was established, named the Code of Hywel after its founder. After 1066 Wales went through a lengthy period of fighting the Norman barons, who were sometimes aided by the English sovereign. The family which ruled in Gwynedd at this time was Gruffydd ap Cynan, the 'Son of Conan' already mentioned.

All this time the real historians of Wales were the court bards of the various chieftains. The Welsh had then, as now, a deep love of music and especially of the music of words. Giraldus Cambrensis (1146–1223) has said of this passion for music: 'In their musical concerts they do not sing in unison like the inhabitants of other countries, but in many different parts. They have the gift of making the human voice a musical instrument.' The bards gave meaning and nobility to life; they sang of the battles of their chieftains, praised their victories, lamented their defeats and their passing.

The death of Henry I of England in 1135 was a signal for a Welsh rebellion against the Normans. Howel ap Maredudd ravaged from Llwchr to Tawe, while Gruffydd ap Rhys, Grufydd ap Cynan (his father-in-law) and Owain and Cadwaldr, the sons of Cynan, allied themselves together and won battle after battle against the leaderless Normans of Wales, getting back the Vale of Clwyd and the lands on the Welsh side of the Dee.

Wales at that time had three main dialects which corresponded roughly to her three domains, ruled by rival princes – Gwynedd, which covered Anglesey and Caernarvonshire and other parts of North Wales and the west coast, Powys (mid-Wales) and Dimetian, spoken in Deheubarth, the southern part of Wales. Almost without exception the chief original works of Welsh literature in this early period were comprised entirely of poetry, or the odes of the bards, and the two zones where this poetry flourished were Gwynedd and Powys.

Very little is extant in the literature of this period; much of what was composed in the eleventh and twelfth centuries did not appear in manuscript form until the end of the twelfth century, or even much later. In the *Book of Taliesin* and the *Black Book of Carmarthen* there appears a great deal of poetry which reflects the monastic studies of the time, but from 1100–1300 Welsh poetry is mainly represented by the works of such court bards as Benfras, Cynddelw, Gwalchmai, Llywarch, Meilir and Gruffyd ap yr Ynad Coch. In translation these odes lose their native vigour and terseness of expression, their vivid imagery and technical skill; anglicization robs the bard of the fire in his belly and the music in his heart. Neither Welshman nor Englishman can translate these effectively in a poetic sense, as so often this means substituting three English words for one Welsh word and losing the esoteric magic of the Cymry.

Yet from those songs of the bards, amplified by documentation from the English side, it is possible to reconstruct a picture of life in the age of Owain Gwynedd. The wars between the Welsh chieftains and the Norman overlords had revealed the Welsh need for a defensive system of fortifications throughout the country. This had begun during the reign of Gruffydd ap Cynan and was carried on by Owain Gwynedd when he succeeded his father in 1138. Such building as there was started a revival of civilization in Wales and nowhere was the development of the arts and literature more marked than in Gwynedd.

Ecclesiastical disputes between Wales and England occurred on numerous occasions between 1135 and 1170. Bishop Bernard of St. David's appealed to Rome to be freed from the yoke of the Norman Archbishop of Canterbury, then, receiving no response, appealed to Owain Gwynedd and his brother Cadwaladr. The two princes ruled that there must be no ecclesiastical submission to England – 'no law can subject the King of Gwynedd to subjection to a Canterbury'[1] – and their indignation was aroused when Uchtryd and Meurig on their respective appointments as Bishops of Llandaff and Bangor were consecrated by Theobald, Arch-

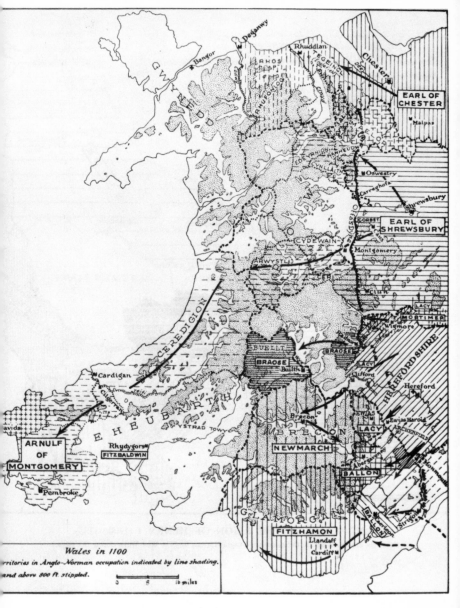

Wales in 1100

Above left, a fifteenth-century impression of a twelfth-century British vessel (From the *Chroniques de Normandie* MS depicting Richard I's crusade of 1199); *below*, Dolwyddelan Castle, reputed birthplace of Madoc

THE EAST VIEW OF DOLWYDDELAN CASTLE, IN THE COUNTY OF CAERNARVO

bishop of Canterbury. Owain is believed to have summoned all the Welsh bishops to a conference, but there is no record of whether this was ever held. All that is known is that Owain wished to keep the Bangor bishopric free from the intrusion of Norman nominees of the English king, and that the Norman Bishop of St. Asaph, Gilbert, dared not visit his diocese because of his fear of Owain Gwynedd.[2]

Even before he came to rule Owain had had considerable experience of warfare. In 1135-6, with his two brothers, he had led the invasion of Ceredigion and defeated the French and Flemings, who had been settled in Pembrokeshire, at Aberteifi. Owain's armies, together with those of his allies, totalled 6,000 foot soldiers and 3,000 on horseback, all well armed. In the campaign the ranks of Gwynedd killed 3,000 Flemings, Normans and English, and the dead were left on the battlefield until the wolves collected and devoured them.

The year he succeeded his father Owain once again invaded Ceredigion, and his forces reached the shores of the Bristol Channel, burnt Ystradmeurig, Llanstephan and Carmarthen. Meanwhile, dissension grew between Gwynedd and Powys after the death of Howel ap Maredudd, when his two sons, Madog and Howel, took charge. In 1140 Owain's son, Cynoric, was killed in battle against Howel of Powys, and the following year Howel himself was slain. Owain, in an effort to strengthen his system of alliances, proposed to marry his daughter to his nephew, Anarawd. This move, far from strengthening Owain's hand, however, revealed a deep rift within his own family. His brother Cadwaladr bitterly opposed the suggested marriage, incited his soldiers to kill Anarawd and carried off Owain's daughter. Owain retaliated by ordering his son Howel to take action against Cadwaladr, who responded by trying to seek an alliance with the Irish against his brother. In 1144 Cadwaladr, who had fled to Ireland, appeared off the Menai Straits with a fleet of 'Irish Danes'.

There was a reconciliation between Owain and Cadwaladr almost immediately after this attack, whereupon the Irish, furious with Cadwaladr, blinded their treacherous ally before Owain's army and small sea force drove them back to Dublin. The reconciliation proved to be only of temporary duration as in the next ten years Owain was more or less permanently at war with his brother. Owain's sons again attacked Cadwaladr in 1145 until he was forced to take refuge with the English.

The princedom, or kingdom, as it was designated, of Gwynedd had had close connection with the Irish over a lengthy period. Gisle Brynjulfsson, of the Royal Society of Northern Antiquities of Copenhagen, communicated with the Cambrian Archaeological Association in 1862 to say that Gruffydd ap Cynan was, through his maternal lineage, descended from the Scandinavian Kings of Dublin and this is borne out in the Cottonian mss.[3]

There was undoubtedly a close association between Ireland and the House of Gwynedd during the reign of Owain, sometimes marked by hostilities, but earlier on by cordiality and an exchange of envoys.

The Normans took advantage of the dissension in the ranks of Gwynedd and recovered some of their lands in Wales in the resultant confusion from Cadwaladr's opposition to Owain. But in 1145, when an attack was launched on South Wales, Owain sent his sons, Howel and Cynan, to the south, and the intervention of the troops of Gwynedd ended in a complete victory for the Welsh. Owain set up his camp near Corwen, and though the lightly-armed Welsh troops were no match for the well-armed mercenaries of Henry II, the respect of the English for Owain's tactics was such that they would not attack the Welsh in the woods, or mountain passes, where they feared ambushes. By the following year the southern part of Wales was liberated. Only Ranulph remained to threaten the Welsh from Chester in the north, and an intensive drive by the armies of Gwynedd, tactically brilliantly led, ravaged Cheshire; Ranulph was captured and imprisoned and all that then remained in Norman hands was a narrow strip of coast. Henry II was so enraged at his losses that he ordered that the eyes of all his Welsh hostages should be gouged out.

The year 1147 was a sad one for Owain. He lost his favourite son, Rien – 'the noblest of them all', as the bards described him. Then came the final breach between Owain and Cadwaladr, and

Howel and Cynan marched on Cynfale Castle, which belonged to Cadwaladr, and took it by storm. Two years later Cadwaladr built Llanrhustud Castle, which he handed over to his son, Caedfan. The following year Howel took Caedfan prisoner, and then in 1152 Owain drove Cadwaladr into Monmouthshire at the same time as he was warring with Powys.

Little is known of Owain's first wife, Gwladys, daughter of Llywarch ap Trahaiarn, except that she died in 1162, and is generally accepted as the mother of Iorwerth. It was Owain's second spouse who was the cause of much disunity in the ranks of Gwynedd as well as the disapproval of the Church. Chrisiant, daughter of Goronwy ab Owain ab Edwina, was Owain's first cousin, so the marriage was in fact illegal and regarded by the Church in those days as incestuous. Owain's defiance of the Church's ban on such a union resulted in his excommunication by Thomas à Beckett, Archbishop of Canterbury.

The King of Gwynedd was a mighty warrior, but he demanded fierce and brutal penalties for disloyalty. Gwalchmai, his bard, described Owain in an ode as a prince who will 'neither cringe, nor hoard up wealth'. Yet, if he was generous, he was more bloodthirsty than most of his age, and contemporary chroniclers record many murders, mutilations and tortures, especially of his kinsfolk, carried out at his command. In 1150 he imprisoned his son, Cynan, and in 1152, in order to remove one he suspected of intriguing for his succession, he sentenced his nephew, Canedda, to be blinded and castrated. According to Ieuan Brechfa, 'Madoc was the outcast son of Owain, and commanded by his father to be slain at birth.' It is not clear from the narrative whether Owain's reason for this was to remove another contender for the succession, or because the child was conceived out of wedlock. Whatever the reasons, the order was not carried out; if we accept Brechfa's version, he was smuggled away from the court by the connivance of his mother and the appointed executioner.[4]

Madoc seems to have had a charmed existence during the early part of his life, and no doubt reports of his death were bruited around each time he was forced into exile. But these reports, of which the critics of the Madoc legend always made so much, when analysed usually reveal an element of doubt. One comes across such phrases as 'disappeared', 'put away by order of Owain', and 'commanded to be killed and not seen again'. Yet in all cases there are explanations for the disappearance and repudiation of his alleged death. Brechfa probably came nearest to explaining the air of mystery which the court cast over his very existence in the lines:

> *Madoc, alive in truth, but slain in name,*
> *A name that could be whispered on the waves,*
> *But never uttered on the land.*

One must, admittedly, treat Brechfa with reserve. He was not a contemporary of Madoc; he was merely reviving a legend that was in his lifetime already more than three hundred years old. On the other hand he was not merely a bard, but an historian and a genealogist. Little is known about Brechfa except that he was a native of Brechfa, Carmarthenshire, that a number of his poems are in manuscript (many others are copies, or works reputed to belong to him, and in several cases the originals are lost), and that an historical work or *Brut* is attributed to him. There are many references to his Pedigree Manuscript and there seems no doubt that he traced the lineage of many ancient families of Wales.

Doubtless Owain was so ringed by enemies both outside his realm and within his own ranks that he adopted methods which were often harsh even by the standards of his age. Yet he was, in the assessment of most historians, brave, capable and a great leader. Professor Barbier says he was 'a brilliant soldier, with no record of ever being defeated . . . a sagacious diplomat and a prudent governor'.[5]

In 1157 Henry II attacked Gwynedd, but was repulsed, an event which encouraged the South Walians to rise once more against the Normans. The Prince of Powys treacherously sided with Henry against Gwynedd, but found himself outnumbered when Henry withdrew from the country. By 1164 Powys was forced to make a treaty with Owain against Henry. Such was Owain's prowess that outside his own lands and in England he was known as the 'King of Wales'. Indeed, even much farther afield, he was called by this title, and Barbier's description of him as 'a sagacious diplomat' is not overdrawn when one considers that this Welsh chieftain, remote in his mountainous domains from the seats of power in Europe, was nevertheless able to negotiate an alliance with the French King Louis VII against King Henry. Louis le Jaune had in 1152 repudiated his marriage to Eleanor of Aquitaine, who had not only since married Henry II of England, but brought with her as dowry some of the richest possessions in the south-west of France, not to mention a less important but equally delightful attribute, her personal patronage of the code of courtly love. Not unnaturally Louis was bitter towards England and welcomed any ally who would be in a position to cause his English adversary embarrassment.

From his castle in Aberffraw in Anglesey, the seat of all rulers of Gwynedd since the Danes sacked Deganwy, Owain ruled with two aims – the prosperity of his people and the unity of all Welsh kingdoms against the English. That he failed to achieve this was due not to any fault of his own but to disloyalty among his adherents and lack of foresight among his opponents. But his power of command was such that King Henry II wrote to the Emperor of Constantinople that 'there is a people called Welsh, so bold and ferocious that, when unarmed, they do not fear to encounter an armed force; being ready to shed their blood for their country and to sacrifice their lives for renown'.

Joan Dane, in a book published in 1909,[6] created a fictional romance out of the legend. This was not so much an historical romance as an imaginative recreation of the Madoc story. Miss Dane trod the primrose path of Bob Southey, if not to the sound of lutes, at least with an eager eye for colourful imagery. Yet Miss Dane claimed that her story was based on research into the works of Gutyn Owen, Maredudd ap Rhys and extracts from the *Abbeys of Strata Florida and Conway*. The annals of Strata Florida, or Caron Uwch Cluwdd, an abbey founded in 1091 in Cardiganshire, were supposed to have formed the basis of the writings of Caradoc of Llancarfan. Very few records of this abbey remain today; what there are have been fully documented by Stephen W.

Williams in *The Cistercian Abbey of Strata Florida*.[7] There is nothing there about Madoc.

The Abbey of Strata Florida would be much less likely to contain information about Madoc than that of Conway. Alas, when Edward I moved Conway Abbey to Maenan, when he built a castle at Conway, many records were destroyed. There were said to be relics of Madoc in the abbey but they no longer exist, and only the site of Conway Abbey remains today.

Miss Dane also subscribed to the Brechfa theme that Madoc was ordered to be killed at birth, but, while acknowledging her sources, she does not always indicate clearly or precisely which account is attributable to which source. Her novel tells how Madoc returned to the court of his father at the age of sixteen, disguised as a wandering minstrel, in order to see his mother again. While he was at court Owain surprised Madoc being embraced by his mother, and, not knowing the identity of the youth, assumed the pair to be lovers. So once more Madoc was forced to escape the wrath of his father and go into exile.

Meiron quotes Llywarch as saying that 'Owain Gwynedd was wrathful with his son and jealous of Madoc's love for the boy; he wrongfully suspected them of an incestuous relationship. Not for many years was Owain's suspicion of this completely allayed and then only on his mother's death-bed'.[8] This is, however, second-hand evidence, and one cannot rely on it. At the best one must assume that it was a prose paraphrase of an ode by Llywarch which does not appear to have survived.

Joan Dane also describes Madoc's return to the court only to find his mother had died. According to her, Madoc fell in love with a handmaiden of Chrisiant, named Annesta. This tallies with the genealogical sources already quoted.

In a letter to a friend Miss Dane referred to her own investigations of the Madoc legend: 'I have often since regretted,' she wrote, 'that I did not attempt a serious history of the story, but I found the theme so tempting to a novelist that I couldn't resist making it a work of fiction. I worked up my material from translations of the Ystrad Flur (*Strata Florida*) Abbey records and from these it seemed clear that Madoc was born some time between

1134 and 1142 and that he was skilled in the making and handling of boats.

'There was an ode by Llywarch, telling of "Madoc, the lonely one, robbed of his love; forced to find consolation on the great ocean". This I used as an excuse for developing a love story, telling how Annesta was murdered by Madoc's brother, David. There is some support for this idea, but not as much as I made of it. Long after I finished the book I heard mention of Madoc having an island retreat not far from the coast of Wales, from which he planned his expedition to America.'[9]

That single phrase, 'an island retreat not far from the coast of Wales' provides a vital clue in the Madoc story. It is one which is of immense importance in tracing the narrative of this early part of the book. Could it be Skomer, or Skokholm, or Bardsey or Anglesey? Skokholm had frequently been seized by the English kings during its earlier history on account of the treason of the Earls of Pembroke, but there was no trace of any civilized occupation of this island, nor of Skomer in the twelfth century. Bardsey seemed a possibility, and indeed later it will be shown to have a link with the Madoc story, but Miss Dane's slender clue led to an unexpected island rather closer to the English than the Welsh coast – Lundy Island in the Bristol Channel.

In 1163, when Henry II's forces again moved against Gwynedd, the archives of Lundy Island recorded that 'an emissarie of the Prince of Gwynet landed at Lund to seek aide against Henrie of Englande'.[10] This, supported by the existence of Welsh manuscripts in the archives of Lundy, was the first hint that Miss Dane's island might be the tiny 'kingdom' some fifteen miles off the coast of Devon which for more than a thousand years has retained its complete independence from the mainland.

The year after this envoy of the House of Gwynedd had landed at Lundy (it takes its name from the Norse, *Lund*, meaning a penguin) Owain and Rhys ab Gruffydd allied against the English king and a wave of national fervour swept Wales. Henry was defeated at Oswestry in 1165 and his troops were once again forced to withdraw. The prestige of Owain Gwynedd had reached its zenith: this mighty warrior, turbulent of temperament, but firm of purpose, relentless yet sagacious, had done more to fight for real Welsh unity than any man since Rhodri Mawr.

More than this, however, Owain in particular and the House of Gwynedd in general had contributed much to the creation of a distinct Welsh culture, mainly, of course, in the sphere of poetry. Two chief zones existed for this poetry, Gwynedd and Powys, and in the former greater encouragement was given to the bards. Owain's links with Ireland and France also played a part in stimulating culture; he encouraged minstrels at his court and there is some evidence of itinerant minstrels from France and Ireland visiting his territory. Owain was frequently on the move and held court in various parts of Gwynedd, in this manner extending his influence over a wide area of north and mid-Wales.

Owain reigned for thirty-two years. He died in December, 1169, and was buried at Bangor. As he had been excommunicated by Beckett because of his illegal marriage to his cousin, controversy over his burial in consecrated ground raged for some time. Owain had continued to live with Chrisiant until her death and the ban on him was not lifted by the Church even then, as Owain had been openly defiant of the ecclesiastical authorities. When Baldwyn, Archbishop of Canterbury, came to preach at Bangor in support of the Crusades against the Saracens, he saw the tomb and charged the Bishop of Bangor to remove the body from the cathedral. The Bishop, who had his own ideas as to how a Welsh hero should be treated, made formal signs of obedience, withdrew the body from the tomb but made a passage from the vault through the south wall of the cathedral and secretly deposited Owain's remains outside, but still in consecrated ground.[11]

4

CURRAGHS, CORACLES AND SQUARE-MASTERS

ETAILED ARGUMENTS HAVE been put forward to discount the possibility of anyone from the British Isles being able to discover America in 1170, and these have been set out at length by the critics of the Madoc legend. As these critics have gone to great pains in assembling their arguments, it is essential to reply to them in equal detail, especially as in recent years research has shown that the ancients had navigational techniques not appreciated by previous historians.

The main argument has been that in the twelfth century there did not exist the type of craft able to venture on such a voyage. In the first place this view completely ignores the fact that long-distance exploration of the Atlantic Ocean had already been carried out centuries before by such authenticated figures as Erik the Red and St. Brandon. The Vinland Map, recently discovered, also supports the view that adventurous expeditions certainly as far afield as Greenland, possibly even to Labrador and Newfoundland, had been made long before the age of Columbus. But, to refute completely the suggestion that the type of craft for such a voyage did not then exist, one has only to examine the records of recent years. These provide the most factual and positive refutation of this charge.

Thor Heyerdahl crossed the Pacific Ocean on a raft simply to prove that centuries before the Indians crossed this same ocean in rafts exactly the same as his *Kon-Tiki*, making use of the ocean currents. In 1952 Alain Bombard, a French doctor, carried out an endurance experiment by crossing the Atlantic Ocean alone in a small metal raft constructed of two metal cylinders joined at the prow with an in-built wooden stern and a 6-ft. mast with a leg-of-mutton sail. Dr. Bombard's experiment proved that the Atlantic could be crossed in a small craft, relying solely on what he was able to catch for food and drink. He lived mainly on fish caught on a line and plankton scooped up in a trailing sieve, occasionally adding passing birds to his fare. He had no stored water for fourteen days and extracted sufficient from plankton in a press. The raft, which was only 14 ft. by 6 ft., carried a pair of paddles, one of which was used as a rudder.

Heyerdahl set out to explain, following a later expedition to the Galapagos Islands, how the Peruvian Indians quickly learned about ocean currents and made use of them for voyages of discovery. 'I had been puzzled,' he wrote, 'by the fact that . . . when we drifted in the Humboldt Current with the raft *Kon-Tiki*, also from Peru, we almost ended up in the Galapagos ourselves. It would therefore seem logical to me that the Peruvian Indians in the course of centuries of off-shore navigation would also have found the islands, although they might not have found them fit for settlement because of the almost complete lack of sweetwater and the volcanoes which occasionally were very active at that time.'[1]

Dr. Hannes Lindeman, a German doctor, achieved in 1957 what the *New York Times* described as 'a remarkable voyage across the Atlantic at its stormiest time, in a craft so frail in appearance that one would have thought it unlikely to outlive even in moderate storm'. Setting out from Las Palmas in the Canary Isles in a kayak, Dr. Lindeman arrived at St. Martin in the Lesser Antilles after a trip lasting seventy-two days. His boat was 17 ft. long, made of rubberized canvas stretched over a wooden frame, and contained air tubes for buoyancy. With no room to lie down, the doctor had to snatch what sleep he could sitting up. He made the trip primarily to learn about 'survival at sea', embarking with 176 lbs. of concentrated food and liquid but carrying no fresh water. 'The milk and beer took some salt out of the body so I was able to drink more brackish water than would otherwise be possible. It rained about fifty days and I was able to catch rain-water on a plastic cloth, although it was contaminated with salt spray.'

Thus, from the endurance test, a transatlantic voyage, even with scanty provisions, would seem perfectly feasible in the twelfth century, especially to a warrior race, trained to live on what they caught during their campaigns.

There have been many Atlantic crossings in tiny craft during the last few years in the light of utilizing experience gained by the Norsemen and others centuries ago, and in one way or another they have all proved that voyages of discovery in the twelfth century and even before that were in the realms of possibility. Heyerdahl demonstrated conclusively that the Peruvian Indians, using balsa-wood rafts, which withstood the violent storms that sometimes ravage the Pacific, used the Humboldt Current to discover Polynesia. Bombard not only proved that one can live on rain-water and fresh water from fish and plankton, but that he could use the ocean currents of the Atlantic as an effective aid to navigation.

The smallest boat to cross the Atlantic was the 12-ft. *Nonoalca*, which made the trip in 65 days in 1966. But even more interesting, and possibly more significant when assessing a twelfth-century voyage, is the fact that in 1897 two men rowed across the Atlantic from New York to the Scilly Islands in 55 days.

One might also point to the twentieth-century counterpart of Madoc's alleged exploit by mentioning Welshman Val Howell's lone voyage from Pembrokeshire to Long Island Sound in an equally small craft.

Modern research has shown that the Old World knew a good deal about the New even in the Dark Ages of Europe. If any navigator took full advantage of the Atlantic currents and winds, even a small sailing craft could achieve a crossing in a surprisingly short time. With favourable winds such currents could take a tiny craft with the minimum of sail at a speed of fourteen knots. There is ample evidence in the annals of Norse sea-faring that the early sailors, having few navigational aids, depended greatly on the currents and developed their own navigational systems from their knowledge of these. In later centuries, when other aids were available, much of the ancient lore on currents was either discarded or forgotten. Thus it was that people living within sight of the north-eastern reaches of the Gulf Stream did not suspect the role it played in their lives until long after Ponce de Leon made it part of the known New World, or that 'Ocean River' as Benjamin Franklin described it.

In 1513 Ponce de Leon went looking for the Fountain of Youth; he discovered Florida instead and sailed away a disappointed man. It was as he turned back that he ran into the Gulf Stream. He found its force so great that his ships would not stem it, despite a strong northerly wind. Long after Columbus's day seamen had inadequate knowledge of the benefits of the Gulf Stream. Then one or two New England traders found out why it sometimes took them three or four weeks to sail from Boston to Charleston, while they could often make the return journey within a week.

In 1770 the maritime authorities in London received a report from America which stated that 'for reasons unknown' English packets sailing from Falmouth to New York regularly took two weeks longer crossing the ocean than the Rhode Island merchant ships sailing from London to Providence. Benjamin Franklin was consulted, and he was as baffled as the other experts until he called on a Nantucket whaling captain who claimed that the Gulf Stream was the cause of this. So Franklin persuaded the captain to mark the Gulf Stream on a map.[2]

Dr. John Williams, of Sydenham, who carried out his own inquiry into the truth of the Madoc legend in the latter part of the eighteenth century, suggested that Madoc might have sailed north until he found the sun to be in the same position as in Wales for the season, and then followed the Pole Star, making use of the currents which would help to ensure his arrival back in Wales.[3] This is a somewhat obscurely, amateurish theory, but it can more scientifically be argued that Madoc made use of the Canaries current, which would bring him from the direction of Madeira to the coasts of Florida and Alabama, and that on his return trip he was aided by the Gulf Stream. Obviously his navigation would be partly by instinct and partly by the stars and sun, encouraged by the advent of birds when he approached land and without doubt luck played a role in giving him both favourable winds and currents. The more one considers some of the arguments used against Madoc's having discovered America the more it appears that the facts they are based on can just as feasibly be used in support of the theory. The critics make great play of the fact that there is no unanimity among the sources who support Madoc's claim as to where he actually landed. Yet if one accepts that Madoc made two trips to America, one must equally assume that it is highly improbable that he would land at the same place, or even in the same region, on each occasion. In the twelfth century that would have been almost navigationally impossible except for a miraculous coincidence. Therefore it is probable that his two landing places, though in the same region of America, were at least some hundreds of miles apart.

Dr. Bradford K. MacGaw, of the Department of Geology and Geography at the University of Chattanooga, has admirably summed up the possibilities of a Madoc voyage in this statement: 'Between Europe and America there are two great currents in the ocean, one bearing from Europe to America, and one powerful stream flowing towards Europe. By means of these forces and the trade winds early voyagers reached the American continent and later returned to Europe. It is a well-established fact that Europeans visited America centuries before Columbus and these visitors had to depend upon winds, ocean currents and ocean drifts for propulsion. For short distances they certainly used man power, but that would not suffice for an ocean trip. The voyagers were aided by the trade winds which prevail throughout the year. The return voyages were routed to take advantage of the Gulf Stream and the prevailing winds would land the visitors on the shores of Europe.'[4]

Stephens, no seaman himself, suggested in his refutation of the Madoc legend that any transatlantic voyage would have been 'too arduous without a compass'. The short answer to this is that neither the early Norse explorers nor St. Brandon had compasses. But, primitive as navigation may have been in the twelfth century, seamen then did not completely lack navigational aids. The invention of the mariner's magnetic compass was formerly attributed to Flavio Gioja, a native of Amalfi in the fourteenth century, but it is now almost certain that he merely improved on and adapted an earlier and cruder form of compass. Without doubt the compass was used in some European ships in the twelfth century, including a few of the Crusaders' fleet. It consisted of a primitive kind of needle, magnetized by a lodestone, floating on a chip in a bowl of water. It is equally certain that, because of the nature of the gently sloping coastline around the British Isles and north-west France, pilotage was developed through use of the lead-line for soundings much earlier than in the Mediterranean where the coast sloped steeply to considerable depths.

This is, of course, not intended to suggest that Madoc possessed a compass, though as will be seen he would have known all about the lodestone. The Phoenicians, Syrians, Carthaginians, Greeks and Romans conducted their voyages solely by keeping observation of the heavens and by not venturing too far from the coast. There was no semblance of modern navigation techniques before the expeditions carried out by Prince Henry of Portugal ended in 1514. But the knowledge of the stars and currents was carefully assessed and re-assessed by the ancients and long before the twelfth century seamen were sailing by both the sun and the Polar Star. If any proof is needed that the Welsh knew about these things, one only has to study the history of the Druids and the Welsh vocabulary of that era. The Druids were diligent astronomers as distinct from astrologers, claiming that Star Temples (or observatories in modern jargon) existed as far back as 3000 B.C. In the language of twelfth-century Wales one comes across such words as *seron, seronydd* and *seronddiaeth*, meaning star, astronomer and astronomy respectively.[5]

Thomas Stephens belittled the Welsh capacity for seamanship and for ship-building in developing his case against Madoc, even going so far as to suggest that with one or two exceptions Wales had never produced any notable seamen. He cited Lord Lyttelton as expressing the view that the natives of Wales were less expert as mariners than any other in Europe. Stephens even made the assertion that the British ships mentioned by Caesar were not Welsh, but those of Veneti of Gaul, and said that foreign trade from Wales was carried on in Phoenician vessels. This is quite inaccurate, as we owe to Julius Caesar the earliest record of British skin-covered craft such as were used in Wales: 'Caesar ordered his soldiers to make boats of the kind that his knowledge of Britain a few years earlier (55–54 B.C.) had taught him. First, the keels and ribs were made of light timber, then the rest of the hull of the boats was wrought with wickerwork, and covered over with hides.'[6]

From the wording of the account it seems clear that Caesar had encountered skin-covered craft during his raids to Wales and South-west England and that this type of boat, as far as Caesar was aware, was to be found only in Britain. That these craft were also used on the sea, as well as on the rivers, is clear from Lucan's account a century later of the 'white willow, its twigs in water, is woven into small boats and covered over . . . adapted for passengers, it floats along the swelling stream. Thus does the Venetian on the flowing Padus [Poa] and on the expanded ocean the Briton sail'.[7]

The Irish curragh was, of course, always used for sea voyages, being larger than the Welsh coracle, but it is evident from many contemporary reports that the coracle was also employed around the coast of South-west Britain. Pliny, quoting the authority of the historian Timaeus, who died about 256 B.C., said that 'an island called Mictis[8] is within six days' sail of Britannia, in which white lead is found, and that the Britons sail over to it in boats of osier, covered with sewed hides'.[9]

Evidence that there were sea-going coracles as distinct from the Irish curraghs operating from the Welsh coasts is considerable in these early years. Caius Julius Solinus referred to the 'pear-shaped boats of plaited willow propelled by the nimble Welsh even across the seas'. And in yet another of his accounts of life in Britannia he writes that 'they voyage in small boats formed of pliant twigs, covered with the skins of oxen. During the time they are at sea the voyagers abstain from food'.[10]

Festus Avienus (A.D. 370) wrote verses about the inhabitants of the Scillies (Oestrymnides, as he calls them) which are particularly illuminating:

> *Lying far off and rich in metals*
> *Of tin and lead. Great the strength of this nation,*
> *Proud their mind, powerful their skill,*
> *Trading the constant care of all.*
> *They know not to fit with pine*
> *Their keels, nor with fir, as use is,*
> *They shape their boats; but strange to say*
> *They fit their vessels with united skins,*
> *And often traverse the deep in a hide.*[11]

Yet with the coming of the Roman artificers, combined with the rise of a thriving iron industry in the Weald of Sussex and elsewhere, the sea-going curragh and coracle began to disappear from the seas around Britain and was superseded by the Welsh with craft made out of wooden planks. Only in a few remote parts of Wales, in Lundy Island and in Cornwall, did the sea-going coracle still exist after A.D. 700. The curragh, which was sturdier, still flourished in Ireland and there was for some centuries traffic between Wales and Ireland with these craft, while St. Brandon certainly made his long voyages of discovery in a curragh. But despite the decline of the sea-going coracle and its use being gradually confined to the fishermen on the Rivers Teifi, Severn and Towy, J. Hornell, the historian of the coracle and the curragh, writes: 'By long practice these people (the coracle men) have acquired amazing dexterity in the handling of their curraghs and even consider them to be safer craft in which to wrest their living from the tempestuous Atlantic than those built of planks. That their cost is not one-tenth of that of planked boats is probably the main reason of their survival (today), for these people find life a hard and difficult struggle.'[12]

Stephens, in seeking to prove that the Welsh had no aptitude for the sea in the twelfth century, quoted Giraldus as saying that

Williams (Iolo Mor-
), the bard who inspired
n Evans Expedition in
.est of the 'Welsh
Indians'

Governor John Sevier of
Tennessee, whose letters
claimed to establish Madoc's
landing-place in Alabama

Above, remains of the old stone pier said to be the departing point of Madoc's first expedition, now a garden rockery at Rhos-on-Sea; *below*, Marisco Castle on Lundy Island, departure point of Madoc's second expedition

the Cambrians 'pay no attention to commerce, shipping or manufactures'.[13] This was a sweeping and unfair statement by Giraldus, who was often a prejudiced writer, for in effect he is comparing a tiny and poor nation such as Wales with a maritime power such as England. But to assert that the Welsh neglected overseas commerce is not to say that they were not good seamen. There are, in fact, countless references to Welsh seamanship, and especially in the kingdom of Gwynedd. Even in Maelgwyn's reign, long before A.D. 1000, he ruled from his court on the Rock of Deganwy 'with the backing of his army and a fleet of ships', while Gruffydd ap Conan, when he claimed the throne of Gwynedd usurped by Trahaiarn of Powys in 1075, sailed across from Ireland with a fleet of ships. It would be truer to say that the men of the sea were often belittled by the earlier bards as being of lesser breeds. Cynddilig, in the seventh century, wrote of one who, 'having led a sea-faring life, he bore no shield'. There is a slightly derogatory touch here, but equally Cynddilig orated about 'the blue flag against naval foes'. Stephens, however, expressed the opinion that it did not appear the Welsh had a navy in the twelfth century, yet Professor Barbier in the *Age of Owain Gwynedd* made special reference to a Welsh fleet. The Triads also bear witness both to some form of a Welsh navy and to Welsh shipping. Geraint of Devonshire, a Welshman who sailed from Lundy, is listed as one of 'the three naval commanders of the Isle of Britain, having six score ships and six score men in each'.[14] It is interesting to note that this tallies exactly with some of the estimates of the men carried in one of Madoc's craft.

Whether Wales had a fleet or not at this period is largely irrelevant; it is undisputed that they had ships and that Welshmen voyaged between Wales and Ireland regularly, and still carried on a trade, albeit desultory, with Cornwall, Brittany and the Scillies. The sailors of Brittany were the most knowledgeable of any outside the Mediterranean in this age and the Welsh probably learned much from their contacts with them. There was some boat-building in various parts of North Wales and at a few ports in the south. Though the Welsh learned little of ship-building from the

Romans, the latter adopted from the Welsh both the structure and name of a strange kind of fast-sailing boat which they called *pictae*. These craft were longer than a modern pinnace and smeared with wax, probably to quicken their passage through water. 'As their principal use was to gain intelligence, or to dart suddenly upon an enemy, it was desirable that they should remain unseen for as long as possible, for which reason their sails and rigging were dyed of a light-blue colour, to resemble the sea, and their crews wore clothing of the same hue.'[15] Here was a medieval pointer to camouflage later adapted to the battleship-grey paint of World War I and the Mountbatten-pink of World War II, designed to harmonize with the pink dawn of a Mediterranean morning.

Long before the twelfth century it was recorded that Corvenor, 'the bard of Ceri, first made a ship with sail and rudder for the people of the Cymry'.[16]

By the latter half of the twelfth century British shipping, both naval and otherwise, had developed to such a high pitch of perfection that Matthew of Westminster was able to enthuse: 'Oh, England! Thou who most lately equal the ancient Chaldeans in power, prosperity and glory. The ships of Tarshish could not be compared to thy ships, which brought thee spices and every precious thing from the four corners of the World.'

Matthew also referred to the 'great traffique of ships in the sea which separates Cambria and England (*the Bristol Channel*)', mentioning English, Cambrian and Flemish vessels of all kinds and sizes. The history of the Crusades mentions Richard I's Crusade Fleet of 1190 having 'one hundred and sixty three-masted ships'.

There are no contemporary sketches of Welsh ships of the period, but from seals of the country's ancient ports it is apparent that some of them had square-masted sails – interesting when one recalls the Aztec legend that Quetzalcoatl came from the east in a vessel with a square sail.

Stephens posed the question 'why should Madoc go west with no apparent prospect of finding land, and sail for nine weeks (*why nine weeks?*) on an open sea?'[17]

The same question might be asked of any explorer. To this Stephens would doubtless reply that most other explorers would only attempt such a voyage if they had reasonable prospects of finding land, or had heard rumours of land far to the west. Yet, if we apply this test, it soon becomes apparent that Madoc probably had a good deal of information to work on, quite apart from the legends that then existed in Wales of a 'magic Country beyond the looking glass of the sea' mentioned by Taliesin.

The Welsh had learned much from both the Irish and the Danes about boat-building and seamanship. One need not go so far as did Sir Thomas Herbert in asserting that 'without doubt Madoc had heard of Seneca, Plato and other soothsayers',[18] but he had every means of knowing of the Irish discovery of Iceland, of St. Brandon's voyage and even of the Norsemen's exploration of the Far West.

The House of Gwynedd had close associations with Ireland both by maintaining their links with the Irish and by marriage. The Welsh manuscripts in the Cottonian Collection testify that Gruffydd ap Conan (died 1137) was, through his maternal lineage, descended from the Scandinavian Kings of Dublin. Mr. Gisle Brynjulfsson, of the Royal Society of Northern Antiquities in Copenhagen, who did much research into the Gwynedd ancestry, wrote, 'It also deserves mention that Madoc, supposed to have visited America at the close of the twelfth century, was a grandson of this same King Griffin (Gruffydd) and that he is likely to be acquainted with the Scandinavian accounts of Vinland and the other western countries, this being well known to the Scandinavians in Ireland.'[19]

Ievan Brechfa is cited by J. Morgan Lewis as referring to 'Winetland' in an ode which he translates as follows:

Hail to thee, Winetland, fabled country of the Norsemen,
Green and glorious in song and verse,
Honoured by Cambria for our marital ties,
A realm of joys for poets to play with.[20]

Recent investigations by the Norwegian archaeologist Helge Ingstad, who has examined much more closely the sagas of the

Edda, in which Leif Eriksen's exploits were related, proved that the authors of the sagas were not just romanticists but had a penchant for verifying references and producing authentic-sounding descriptions of the coastline discovered by Leif as well as giving convincing sailing directions. According to these early scribes the Vikings had to row and sail through some fairly rough weather on their Atlantic voyage. Close study of these texts persuaded Mr. Ingstad that the Vikings landed in Labrador. Every summer for a decade he made excavations in Canada and finally proved his point: he found sufficient remains to show that the ancient Norsemen had been there.

Indeed Mr. Ingstad's quest suggests many parallels in our own quest for Madoc. He, too, was frustrated at first by the almost unanimous scepticism of historians and experts, for the Vinland Map had not then been found. Ridicule was poured on his efforts by geographers and archaeologist. To make his task even more difficult he was obstructed by hoaxes, false reports and even by the spurious remains of Viking ships before he finally came across the genuine remains of a Viking settlement at L'Anse aux Meadows in Newfoundland. So, too, is the part of the researcher into Madoc's story beset by false reports and manufactured evidence. Then again historians stressed the point that the fate of Leif Eriksen was obscure and this, like the critics' insistence that there was no trace of Madoc's ultimate end, was used to reject the story.

Yet Mr. Ingstad's findings go a long way towards answering Thomas Stephens's criticisms of nearly a hundred years earlier. Stephens, referring to the statements that Madoc made two voyages to America and one back to Wales, referred to this as the fatal flaw in the arguments of the pro-Madoc school. To have found his way to America, argued Stephens, would have been well-nigh unbelieveable, but to have found his way back as well utterly impossible, as accurate navigation would not have been feasible in an age when the compass was unknown. But, if Madoc had only made one voyage, then it is fairly certain that nothing would have been heard of it on the Welsh side of the Atlantic: there would have been no iota of proof from that quarter. But

Mr. Ingstad's findings show that the Vikings, without compasses or navigational aids of a mechanical nature, were able to make such voyages and find their way back. Their craft had open hulls, they could sail only before the wind, and they depended as much upon oars as on sail. No Viking craft in Leif Eriksen's time was more than 50 ft. long. For navigation they relied on steering by the sun, the stars and the birds.

5

VOYAGE WITH 'TEN SAILES'

FORGERY AND FANTASY, careless research, sailors' tales and unscrupulous romancing have so distorted the story of Madoc's discovery of America that they have played into the hands of the traducers of the legend.

At first it seems strange and even positive proof of the unreliability of the legend that the chief traducers are themselves Welsh scholars. One does not, however, have far to look for the reason for their disbelief. For in the controversy over Madoc we have a classic case of a critics' argument, mainly a series of duels between Welsh scholars, and in the academic hierarchy the anti-Madoc school triumphed belatedly in an overwhelming victory.

Yet it was a Pyrrhic victory, not a refutation of Madoc's story so much as a rejection and disavowal of the forgeries, sophistries and fantasies woven around it. In short it was an argument almost solely about literature, in which each side quoted what best suited their purposes.

The prime cause of this controversy was Edward Williams, better known as the bard Iolo Morganwg (1740 – 1826), an Eisteddfod oracle of his era whose enthusiasm, rather like that of Dylan Thomas's Reverend Eli Jenkins, outran his veracity. Williams developed an obsessive interest in the stories of Madoc and, with his friend, Dr. W. Owen-Pughe, wrote a series of notes in defence of the legend in the *Gentleman's Magazine*, the *Cam-*

brian Biography and the *Cambro-Briton*.[1] This pair worked up a cult for Madoc, Iolo Morganwg chiefly by popularizing ancient bardic odes, Own-Pughe, who was the author of the *Dictionary of the Welsh Language*, by collecting ten different accounts of Madoc, all affirming that he sailed west and discovered land. It is perhaps unfair to bracket Owen-Pughe with Edward Williams, even though each was working for the same end, for the former was a diligent and conscientious researcher, highly respected in London literary circles, and, though his translations have been criticized on the grounds of inaccuracy, he never allowed his imagination to take charge of him as did Iolo Morganwg. Dr. Owen-Pughe was responsible for popularizing Madoc as a subject for discussion in literary London; through him Robert Southey heard the story, resulting in his poem, *Madoc*, in 1805:

> *Not with a heart unmoved I left thy shores*
> *Dear native isle! Not without a pang,*
> *As the fair uplands lessen'd on the view,*
> *Cast back the long involuntary looks!*
> *The morning cheered our outset; gentle airs*
> *Curl'd the blue deep, and bright the summer sun*
> *Played o'er the summer ocean, when our barques*
> *Began their way.*

Southey, of course, needed little prompting to burst into verse on the flimsiest theme, which he would proceed to endow with his own blend of pompous, bogus authority, plunging from cliché to cliché and gilding each hackneyed, overworked noun with equally trite adjectives as he went along, conjuring up what history there was out of a febrile rather than a fertile imagination. 'Multi-scribbling Southey' was Byron's description of the Poet Laureate; at any rate it cannot be argued on aesthetic standards, as some Madoc enthusiasts claim, that he 'did for Madoc what Tennyson did for King Arthur'.

Southey in a preface to his poem stated that when he decided to write it he leased a house in Wales and lived there for months to absorb the atmosphere and scenery. He did not, however, go so far as to venture out on the Atlantic in a medieval-style craft.

Some of his material he obtained from Iolo Morganwg, to whom
he paid tribute in his poem:

> *Iolo, old Iolo, he who knows*
> *The virtue of all herbs of mount or vale,*
> *Or greenwood shade, or quiet brooklet's bed:*
> *Whatever lore of science, or of song*
> *Sages and bards of old have handed down.*

Poor Southey, he would have fallen for any story, whether in a
tap-room, or Nonconformist Wales.

How much material he obtained from Iolo and Dr. Owen-
Pughe and how much came from his ruminations in the Welsh
mountains is far from clear; much would seem to have come
from Aztec legend and the writings of Francisco Lopez de Gomara.
He works himself into a melodramatic menopause as, with a
middle-aged woman's delight, he tells of Madoc returning from
America and visiting his brother's court at 'Aberffraw in Gwynedd', how he went back again to the country of the Aztecs, being
captured by them and chained to the stone of human sacrifice.
Then, to make a happy ending, Cadwallon rescues Madoc and the
Aztecs are driven out of Aztlan.

Southey's description of the landing is full of rhetorical verbiage:

> *. . . I looked*
> *And saw a bird slow sailing overhead;*
> *His long white pinions by the sunbeam edged*
> *As though with burnished silver . . . Never yet*
> *Heard I so sweet a music as his cry.*
> *Three days more and at last*
> *A long shadowy line . . .*
> *Skirted the sea; how fast the night closed in!*
> *I stood upon the deck and watched till dawn,*
> *But who can tell what feelings filled my heart,*
> *When like a cloud, the distant land arose*
> *Gray from the ocean; . . . when we left the ship,*
> *And cleft with rapid oars, the shallow wave,*
> *And stood triumphant on another world.*

But if Bob Southey, a notorious distorter of fact, as his *Vision of Judgement* bears such deplorable witness, paid heed to the Madoc legend, so also did a man of very different and far less credulous turn of mind, the questioning, doubting Dr. Samuel Johnson himself. He turned one of the ancient Welsh odes on Madoc into a Latin poem:

> *Inclytus hic haeres magni requiescit cenii,*
> *Concessus tantum menti Modoque patrem.*
> *Serviem talis cultum contempsit agelli*
> *Et petiit terras per freta longa novas.*[2]

Iolo Morganwg's enthusiasm for the Madoc legend was such that at one time he seriously considered visiting America to search for the 'Madogwys' who, he claimed, were the descendants of Madoc and his followers. This pilgrimage never materialized, but Iolo's obsessive interest in the subject led him to employ his natural gift for inventiveness and embellishment by interpolating his own version of the Madoc story into what he claimed were genuine Welsh medieval texts. These appeared in the third series of Triads in the *Myvyrian Archaiology* and at first sight seemed to be a sensational historical revelation. The triads were a cunningly contrived hotch-potch of some genuine medieval material supplemented by Williams's own imagination. His contemporaries, including some leading Welsh scholars, were deluded into accepting them as authentic.

A casual examination of the Triads certainly gives an impression of authenticity, because so much of the material is above suspicion, and in an era when Welsh manuscripts were either uncatalogued, or in many instances lost, deception was relatively easy. The tenth of these Triads claims to be a record of three great mysteries of the sea; the first, that of Gafran ab Aeddan and his followers who set out in search of the Isles of Llion and were never heard again: the second, that of Merlin, the bard of Aurelius Ambrosius, and his nine *Cylfeirdd*, who sailed off in the Glass House into oblivion; the third, that of Madoc ab Owain Gwynedd who 'went to sea with three hundred men in ten ships and nobody knows where they went to'.[3]

There was much that was genuine in all this: the first story was based on the Triad of the Faithful Retinues, the second was about the Thirteen Treasures which Merlin was supposed to have taken to sea in his 'Glass House', but the nine bards, or *Cylfeirdd*, were an addition by Williams, and the Madoc story, such as it was, came solely from his fertile brain, borrowing some of the detail from Gutyn Owen.

When scholars are deceived, and it was eventually established beyond doubt that the Triads were a forgery, they are slow to forgive. Poor Iolo Morganwg was never forgiven; his literary tragedy was that his own efforts to establish the story of Madoc only resulted in its being firmly repudiated by later scholars. Iolo was condemned as a fraud.

The first published work in Tudor times to affirm the discovery of America by Madoc was a pamphlet entitled *A True Reporte*, written by Sir George Peckham and dedicated to Sir Francis Walsingham, published in 1583. This pamphlet set out briefly 'to prove Queen Elizabeth's lawful title to the New Worlde, based on not onlie upon Sir Humphrey Gilbert's discoveries, but also those of Madoc'. It referred to David Ingram, of Barking, who had sailed with Sir John Hawkins, as one source of its information and to 'an ancient Welch chronicle' as the other.

Ingram confirmed the story, claiming to be the first of many travellers to hear Welsh words spoken in America. The pamphlet was followed a year later by a much more detailed account of the feats in the *Historie of Cambria*. Here it is in full:

'Madoc . . . left the land in contention betwixt his brethren and prepared certain shipps with men and munition, and sought adventures by seas, sailing west, leaving the coast of Ireland so farre north, that he came to a land unknown where he saw manie strange things. This land must needs be some part of that countrie of which the Spaniardes affirme themselves to be the first founders since Haunoe's time; for, by reason and order of cosmogrophie, this land to which Madoc came, must needs be some part of Nova Hispania, or Florida. Whereupon it is manifest that that country was long before by Brytaines discovered, afore either Columbus or Americus Vesputius led any Spaniarde thither.'

Here two points are worth making. First of all it should be clearly stated that at this time all North America was known by the name of Florida, so this account cannot be taken as indicating that Madoc actually landed in what is now known as Florida. Secondly, the phrase 'leaving the coast of Ireland so farre north' is somewhat ambiguous. But, judging by the usage of English in Tudor days, it would seem that the writer meant he gave Ireland a wide berth to the north and sailed south-west.

'Of the viage and returne of this Madoc,' continued Dr. Powel, 'there be manie fables faimed, as the common people do use in distance of place and length of time, rather to augment than diminish; but sure it is that there he was. And after he had returned home, and declared the pleasant and fruitfulle countries that he had seen without inhabitants, and upon the contrarie part, for what barren and wilde ground his brethren and nepheues did murther one another, he prepared a number of shipps, and got with him such men and women as were desirous to live in quiet-nesse, and taking leave of his freends tooke his journie thitherward againe. Therefore it was to be presupposed that he and his people inhabited part of those countries; for it appeareth by Francis Lopez de Gomara, that in Acuzamil, and other places, the people honoreth the crosse: Whereby it may be gathered, that christians had beene there before the comming of the Spaniardes. But because this people were not manie, they followed the manners of the land and used the language found there. This Madoc arriving in the countrie, into the which he came in the yeare 1170, left most of his people there, and returning back for more of his own nation, acquaintance, and freends to inhabit that fayre and large countrie, went thither againe.'

Objection has been made to the accuracy of Dr. Powel's account by drawing attention to the fact that he first referred to a country discovered by Madoc said to be 'without inhabitants', and yet later spoke of the people whom he carried there 'followed the manners of the land, and used the language found there'. It is highly probable that on the first voyage Madoc found no traces of habitation in what was a sparsely-populated territory. On his second voyage of discovery nobody could say what he found as he never returned. But it was surely reasonable in 1584 for any historian to deduce that there were other native tribes in America and the probability was that in the course of time their languages and customs were adopted.

There is no doubt that Dr. Powel's edited version of the *Historie of Cambria* was mainly based on the chronicles of Caradoc of Llancarfan, which covered a period of Welsh history up to the end of the first half of the twelfth century. Stephens stressed that as Caradoc died in 1156 he could not have written about the discovery of America by Madoc in 1170. But, as has already been noted, Dr. Powel quite frankly admitted that his revised version of the *Historie* was 'augmented and continued out of records and best approved authors'. Therefore, in assessing the reliability of this evidence, it is necessary to look more closely at his other sources, as it is from these that the Madoc story came. As Humphrey Llwyd, of Denbigh (1527–68) did not finish his translation of Caradoc (it was not continued after 1559, as far as can be ascertained), Dr. Powel had to rely almost entirely for the latter part of the book on Gutyn Owen, the *Brut y Tywysogion* and possibly *Latinae Annales Cambriae*, supplementing and presumably checking his information with his friend, Sir Philip Sydney, Sir Humphrey Gilbert and other Elizabethan explorers.

Humphrey Llwyd, apart from his work as translator of Caradoc, could have assisted Dr. Powel with much information of his own. He was not only a widely-read man, but something of an authority on cartography. His *Cambriae Typus* is one of the earliest known maps of Wales. A Member of Parliament first for East Grinstead and then for Denbigh Boroughs, he carried on a lengthy correspondence with Ortelius, who, in his *Theatrum Orbis Terrarum*, described Llwyd as 'a noble and erudite man'. Many of Llwyd's friends were in Holland, especially in Antwerp, and it is interesting to note that the first edition of Francisco Lopez de Gomara's *Cronica de la Nueva España*, which appeared at Medina in 1553, was published in Antwerp in 1554.

Humphrey Llwyd was also a friend of that strange, learned alchemist-scientist, John Dee, who made a hobby of collecting evidence of ancient voyages of exploration, and another probable source of his information was the bard, Cynfric ap Gronow, who also testified to Madoc having discovered 'a wondrous new lande of strange and delectable fruites, surrounded by a warm sea in which plantes do grow'.[4] Cynfric might, without knowing it, have been describing the Sargasso Sea, about which early discoverers romanticized to the extent of calling it 'an impenetrable equatic jungle which trapped anie shippe that entered it'. It is perhaps a tribute to the Elizabethan writers that they were sufficiently knowledgeable to doubt Cynfric's account: none of them quoted it.

Gutyn Owen was a versatile writer; his career is well documented in the *Dictionary of National Biography*, yet unfortunately the dates of his birth and death are unknown.[5] An avid collector of scraps of information from explorers and travellers from all parts of the world, a bard and herald, a genealogist and compiler of pedigrees, he lived near Oswestry and left for posterity some memorable poems, the *Cywyddau*. He was a historian and historiographer at Basingwerk Monastery in Flintshire, writing *Llyfr du Basing* [*The Book of Basingwerk*]. Without doubt Gutyn Owen was a vital source of the Madoc story in *Historie of Cambria*, even though Dr. Powel specifically cites him on only two points, stating that 1170 was the year Madoc 'went thither . . . with ten sailes, as I find noted by my friend, Gutyn Owen.' So this disposes of the criticism that Dr. Powel was relying on the evidence of a man who died before 1170 (Caradoc). The doctor, again quoting Owen, stated that Madoc left most of his followers in America after his first trip.

No man was better situated to delve into this legend and to provide facts to support it than Gutyn Owen. He had access to the annals of Basingwerk Monastery, to the Abbey of Strata Florida and what scanty records then existed of the history of the House of Gwynedd. But the argument which has ranged between scholars has hinged on the question of whether he wrote his history of Madoc with pre-knowledge of Columbus's discovery of America. Stephens posed this question and the Reverend Thomas Price thought the issue of the authenticity of the story depended entirely upon whether Gutyn Owen's account was written before or after 1492.

Sir Thomas Herbert, who was made a baronet by Charles II as a reward for his faithful service to his father, did some research of his own into the subject. He doubted whether, because of his age, Owen survived the beginning of the sixtenth century. Certain it was that most of his writings were done before Columbus discovered America. Owen is cited as having attended the 'Great Carmarthen Eisteddfod of 1451'.[6] This would make him probably at least sixty-five in 1492, an exceptional age to reach in those days. On the other hand he is named as one of the heralds consulted by the Royal Commission appointed to trace King Henry VII's descent from the 'ancient Brytish Kings'; the date of this Commission is unknown, but it is said to have been shortly after the King's accession to the throne. Owen may indeed have died before this, as there is a hint that his 'evidence' was taken from his earlier writings. He is named as a 'source consulted', not as a member of the Commission.

Dr. Powel then introduced other sources in support of the Madoc theory. It should be noted that he was frank in that the story depended on 'manie fables faimed', and that such fables tended to be augmented rather than diminished with the passage of time, but he made it abundantly clear that he accepted the accounts and had checked them with other reports. Had he wished to embellish them he could easily have done so. But his report is singularly free from embellishment and keeps strictly to the facts as he had been given them. He makes no dogmatic attempt to name the probable landing place of Madoc, but allows that it might have been Mexico because of 'A common report of the inhabitants of that countrie, which affirme that theyr rulers descended from a strange nation that came thither from a farre countrie: which thing is confessed by Montezuma, king of that countrie, in an oration made for quieting his people, as his submission to the king of Castille, Hernando Curteis [Cortes] being present, which is laid downe in the Spanish chronicles of the conquest of the West Indies.'[7]

Dr. Powel referred to 'Brytish words and names used in that

territory, mentioning *gwrando* (hearken or listen); . . . the island of *Corroceo*, the river *Gwyndor*, and the white rock of *Pengwyn*, which be all Brytish (or Welsh) words, do manifestly show, that it was that countrie Madoc and his people inhabited'.

Cortes supported the accounts of Mexico having been peopled by a strange race from far across the ocean. The actual speech by Montezuma, referred to by Powel, was not only mentioned by Cortes, but was contained in an ancient Spanish manuscript found in Mexico in 1748. The speech was as follows:

'Kinsmen, friends and fellow-countrymen, you must know that I have reigned as a King over you for eighteen years, as a lawful descendant of my ancestors, who reigned before me. We came from a generation very far, in a little island in the north; the language and religion continue here to this day. I have been an affectionate Father and Prince, and you have been my faithful subjects and willing servants. Let it be remembered that you have a claim to illustrious blood and that you are worthy of your kindred, because you are a free, manly race.'[8]

There is a version of another part of the speech, which is said to be found in *Spanish records*, though the exact authority for it is uncertain. Stephens quoted it, needless to say with intent to confound. While it is not without interest, it cannot be said to be entirely authentic or particularly relevant. Montezuma, according to this, went on to say that they were all 'well acquainted with the ancient tradition that the Great Being, who had once ruled over the land, had declared, on his departure, that he should return some day to resume his sway. That time had now arrived. The White Men had come from the quarter where the sun rose beyond the ocean, to which the Good Deity had withdrawn. They were sent by their master to reclaim the obedience of his ancient subjects. For himself, he was ready to acknowledge their authority.'

This speech, said Stephens, without dealing with the earlier version, was in the old traditions of an Aztec god who, like King Arthur, had promised to return in time of need. He dismissed it as the evoking of a legend without meaning. Yet, whatever the motives of Montezuma, it is surely evident that he was finding an excuse for obeying the Spaniards, while at the same time seeking to gain their favour by claiming kinship with them on the grounds that he, like them, came from the east.

Richard Hakluyt, Samuel Purchas and Pagitt took up the narrative of Madoc, and later John Marriott, Sir Walter Raleigh and Dr. Campbell, in his *Naval History of Great Britain*, repeated it, but these, with the exception of Raleigh and Hakluyt, added little to Dr. Powel's account.

In Raleigh's *History of the World* Sir Walter referred to the use of Welsh words in the Americas. Stephens rightly points out that the language of the Mexicans differed completely from that of the Welsh, but this proves nothing. Madoc's expedition was a solitary one and what Welsh words he might have implanted in the country could only have been adopted by relatively few tribes; three hundred years later there could have been only isolated cases of Welsh having been spoken and the influx of Spaniards in large numbers would have gradually changed the native tongues. Stephens had a curious theory about Raleigh. He says that Sir Walter left 108 colonists behind him on one voyage, but, when he returned, there was no trace of them. 'It was presumed later that they amalgamated with a friendly tribe, the Hatteras, which would account for the Welsh tradition among them. Welshmen were among the colonists.'[9]

This is an attempt by Stephens to prove that if there were traces of Welsh ancestry or Welsh words in America (something which, in his essay, he tries also to disprove), they came from Elizabethan colonists and not from Madoc. But there is no absolute proof – indeed practically no proof at all worth mentioning – that Raleigh landed Welshmen. Mass emigration to America only came when Welsh religious liberty was threatened, nearly a century later. The first major emigration of Welshmen came at the time of William Penn.

All the Tudor authorities who vouched for the Madoc legend have been criticized or derided in one way or another. One criticism was that they were merely copying Dr. Powel and that none had anything vitally new to offer in support of the theory. But the recurring scholastic arguments against them were based on the claim that the accounts of Madoc were blatant propaganda for the House of Tudor at a time when scholars were re-examining Tudor historians and finding them biased to the point of distortion. The distortions that have now been revealed, such as the false portrait of Richard III, apply in fact only to the enemies of Henry VII and Henry VIII. Some critics have even pointed to the dedication of Sir George Peckham's pamphlet to Sir Francis Walsingham as being evidence of a conspiracy, insinuating that because Walsingham was supposed to have been the first head of the British Secret Service, such as it was in Tudor times, he had inspired the pamphlet to further England's claims to America. True, the pamphlet made such a claim in a mild kind of way, but it was never followed up by any further actions. Peckham's source is believed to have been mainly the unpublished notes of Humphrey Llwyd, apart from the information given him by David Ingram.

De Voto thought that reports of Columbus's landing in America might have 'reached the hills of Wales and made them recall Madoc'.[10] This could well be, but the fact that there was a legend to recall is something in Madoc's favour.

By far the most impressive arguments and evidence in Tudor times supporting the Madoc story came from Richard Hakluyt. It must be admitted that, as far as is known, Hakluyt himself never ventured farther afield than Paris, and that, after leaving Oxford, where he was a graduate of Christ Church, he spent much of his time in country vicarages before becoming Archdeacon of Westminster. But he was, as he described himself, 'a dedicated person', dedicated to becoming the historian of 'great traffiques and discoveries' of his countrymen over a period of 1,500 years. A man of very great integrity, easily the ablest expounder of Britain's expansion overseas and explorations, he was a geographer as well as an historian. Indeed, if he had no first-hand experience of far-off lands, he remedied this by his diligent study of the travel literature of other nations when he spent five years in Paris, and in making copious notes of the experiences of travellers. It was his realization that the English had made such little effort to develop such a literature of their own that made him determined to set the matter right.

Out of this determination came his great work *Principall*

Navigations. An absolute perfectionist, Hakluyt concentrated on what he called the 'burden and huge toil' of bringing up to date the history of discoveries, adding in new material derived as a result of the Anglo-Spanish war. He did more than work on Dr. Powel's *Historie*; he consulted the mss. of Gutyn Owen, satisfying himself at least that Owen's material on Madoc was written before Columbus discovered America. He delved into ancient Welsh bardic odes, quoting some stanzas from Maredudd ap Rhys. There is also evidence that Hakluyt checked his British sources with statements made by foreigners, not only the Spanish Chronicles and Cortes, but Dutch records as well. It was this supporting evidence from foreign sources, which we shall examine later, which formed the basis of Hakluyt's belief in Madoc's voyages.

'I am of the opinion,' wrote Hakluyt, 'that the land whereabouts he came was some part of the West Indies.'[11]

In 1620 *A Brief Description of the Whole World* was published in London. The writer made several remarks on the supposed voyages and discoveries of King Arthur and justified Queen Elizabeth in not having made them a basis for claiming land in the New World because they were only 'grounded on fabulous foundations'. But, added the writer, 'there was a knight of Wales, who, with shipping, and some petty company, did go to discover these parts [America] whereof, as there is some record of reasonable credit amongst the monuments of Wales, so there is nothing which giveth more frequent shew thereunto than that, in the late navigations of some of our *monta Norumbega* and some other parts of America, they found some tokens of civility and Christian religion'.

Monta Norumbega was the name given by the first discoverers of the New England coast to the Bay of Penobscot.

Thereafter the development of this fascinating story was, unfortunately, increasingly in the pattern of sheer romanticism, and, marred by invention, imagination and false reports, it was distorted into a geographical whodunit.

James Howel supported the theory, claiming that Madoc died in the West Indies and quoting the lines found on his tomb in one of those islands where they had been 'nere upon 600 yeares since'.

The epitaph he quoted was:

> *Madoc wismio ydic wedd*
> *Jawn yenan Owen Gwynedd*
> *Ni sannum dvisig enridiloedd*
> *Ni dv mawr ondy mervedd.*[12]

Needless to say no such tomb has ever been discovered. The epitaph, apart from doubtful spellings (Owen Gwynedd would have been spelt *Ouain Gwynet* at the time of Madoc's death), is merely a paraphrase of a bardic ode about Madoc and quite unoriginal.

Yet the tomb story was accepted and repeated by Theophilus Evans [Drych y Prif Oesoedd] in the eighteenth century.

Prescott in his *History of Mexico* quoted the speeches of Montezuma and described how the Mexican king told the Spaniards of his 'Great God Ancestor who came from beyond the rising sun'. He has often been quoted as an authority in favour of the Madoc claim, but he added little to what we already know.

Even the supporters of the Madoc legend showed great carelessness in gathering evidence; sometimes they relied on inaccurate sources, often they failed to check their sources or were too lazy to follow them up; more often they quoted only what they had been told at third hand. Yet there was much evidence available to them, if they had taken the trouble to check it.

6

DID COLUMBUS KNOW OF MADOC?

IT IS WHEN one comes to examine Dutch, French, Norse and Spanish authorities – ignored by Madoc's critics and little quoted by his supporters – that the evidence which must have impressed Hakluyt becomes apparent. Yet Hakluyt heard only a small part of this evidence. Thomas Stephens, though undoubtedly an expert on Welsh medieval literature and the works of the bards, did not examine the evidence of many foreigners who could have thrown further light on the story. The same applies to other nineteenth-century critics of Madoc's feats, for the Vinland Map had not then been found, and much untapped material in Europe touching on the legend had not been discovered. Only since 1945 has much of this material come to light.

Dr. John Williams, in his eighteenth-century examination of the case for Madoc, mentioned that Hornius, the Dutch writer, thought that the Americans were descended from Jews, Canaanites, Phoenicians, Carthaginians, Greeks and Scythians, to which colonies had been added by the Chinese, Swedes, Norwegians, Welsh and Spaniards – in that order.

But why did he not check Hornius's works, which were then available for research? In *De Originibus Americanis*, published at the Hague in 1652, more positive statements are made, certainly not based on any Welsh works but from sources in America, or from travellers who had been there. In this work Hornius observed that 'Madoc, a Prince of Cambria, with some of his nation, discovered and inhabited some lands in the west, and that his name and memory are still retained among the people living there scarcely any doubt remains'.[1]

Hornius referred his readers to Peter Martyr's *Decades*. Martyr was a celebrated scholar of Anghiera, and was invited to the Spanish Court by Ferdinand V. His first *Decade* was issued *Ex-Hispana Curia* on November 6, 1493. This date is important, as Columbus returned from his first voyage of discovery in March of that same year, so it would appear that Peter Martyr was at the Court of Spain when the great explorer came back, and it is reasonable to conclude he obtained his evidence at first hand. Martyr testified that 'some of the inhabitants of the land' (he obviously referred to the Americas, though he may have included the West Indies in this category) 'honoreth the memory of one Matec (or Mateo) when Columbus arrived on the coast' and that 'the nations of Virginia and Gautimale (*Guatemala*) celebrate the memory of one of their ancient heroes whom they call Matec'.

Such testimony from Holland and Spain, traditional enemies of Britain in those days, is surely of some value in assessing the purely British records of the Madoc legend. It is unlikely the Spaniards would have mentioned Madoc unless they had proof of his feats; indeed, the surprising fact is that they mentioned him at all, for his very existence would tend to take away some of the credit from Columbus. This discovery posed the question of whether the Spaniards knew more of the Madoc story than they cared to admit. Did Columbus know of Madoc either before or after he discovered America? Did the Spaniards conceal vital evidence?

Hornius, while accepting Peter Martyr's account, had done some research on his own. He based his later conclusions on reports from eight travellers and thought that Madoc probably made two landings, once in 'Chicimeccas Indian territory and again in Mexico'. Sir John Hawkins, the Elizabethan explorer, when trading with Mexican chieftains, claimed they told him that they believed they were descended from 'ancient Brytons'.[2] Hornius also opined – and here events have since justified his supposition – that there was in existence a map showing the New

World, or 'parts thereof', based on knowledge of the Norsemen's exploits and probably known to Madoc on account of his Danish ancestry. Hornius thought this map had at some time been copied by the Belgian, Cnoyen, and that Nicholas of Lynne, a Carmelite monk from Oxford, had also known about the map when he made a voyage to lands near the North Pole in 1360. Nicholas, however, remains a shadowy figure, whose birth and death dates are unknown, but who was chiefly noted for his astronomical work and arranging, in the medieval sense of the word, the latitude and longitude of Oxford. But of his alleged explorations there is very little evidence, and most of this is unconfirmed.

Whatever else may still be in doubt, two certainties now emerge: that the story of Madoc was supported by various authorities on the continent of Europe in the sixteenth century and that Columbus had heard of land having been previously discovered in the west. In 1490, when the Spanish Commission rejected Columbus's plan for exploration of the Atlantic Ocean, his brother Bartolomé went to London to seek financial aid from King Henry VII. The English King was more eagerly interested in these proposals than were the Spaniards and requested Bartolomé to get his brother to bring his plans and charts to London. As Bartolomé returned to Spain, his ship was seized by pirates and he was held prisoner for a long period. When eventually he reached Spain his brother had already sailed on his quest for the New World.

A useful clue to whether the Spaniards had detailed knowledge of Madoc was provided in Catalogue No. 713 (1947) of Bernard Quaritch, the London booksellers. Among the manuscripts to be auctioned the following was listed:

'222 HARO (Biud de). *Anatomie of Spayne*. Composed in the Castilian tonge bu Don Biud de Haro. An⁰ 1598. Translated into Englishe by Harye Bedwood gent. 1599 ... The work consists of an historical account of spain and the Spanish Monarchy, the wickedness, tyranny and cruelty of which the author is at great pains to stress. On page 33 is a long paragraph . . . under the heading "Presumcions to proue ye Spaniardes not to be ye first discouerers of the Yndes".'

This manuscript was purchased by Mr. James Osborn, of Yale University, and, with his permission and that of Mr. Edwin B. Knowles, of the Renaissance Society of America, I quote the salient passage on page 33 of this work:

'. . . Francisco Lopez de Gomara, in his recorde booke, wrighteth that the inhabitants of Acuzamil and other places, longe before the Spaniardes ever arrived, honored the crosse, which is a sure token that there had been Christians before, who padventure not beyinge of force sufficient to conquer, wer fayne to folowe the customs of the countrie, usynge the same tonge. And for the better confyrmation hereof, some wright that a sonne of the Prince of Wales (of wch the eldest sonns of the Kings of Englande doe ever take their names) called Madoc in the year 1170, sayled into the West Yndies, and inhabited the countrie of Mexico, wch Fernando Cortes afterwardes conquered by meanes of the Queene of the Tlaxcallabs, who with one hundred thousand men assisted him against Montezuma the emperor; which may wel be warranted by Montezuma his oration made unto his people, perswadinge them to yealde unto the Spaniardes, in which he let them to understand how they wer descended from a white nacion, come from far off: & that their profetts had often tolde them, how they were to be agayne subjects to another nacion of the same qualities & besydes al this, manie wordes of the language of that countrie are at this daye the verie same which are used in Wales. Some likewise reporte, that when Christonal Colon made his first projecte for the discoverie of the Yndies, he offred yt first to Henrie the Seventh K. of Englande, and after such time as the King had accepted thereof, Don Fernando coveted ye vyadge and delt so with Christonal Colon, as he returned not backe agayne unto Englande. Which K Henrie wel perceavinge, he sent and set on worke Sebastian Gabota, who as histories set downe, discouered in the K. of Englande's right, a great parte of the West Yndies.'

No doubt the purpose of the English translation was to further British claims to having discovered America first, though there is no evidence that the manuscript was ever published. There can be no denying its authenticity: it is written in a neat Elizabethan, cursive hand on English manuscript paper of that age, partly stained in the upper part of most leaves, but generally in excellent condition, bound in contemporary calf, gilt line frame on sides containing gilt centre-pieces and corner ornaments, and on the verso of the title the armorial bookplate of Francis Gwyn. There is no trace of the translator, or of the Spanish original, but Biud de Haro is known to have been a forceful critic of tyranny in his own country, and the ms. includes accounts of Spanish cruelties in the West Indies and a long report of the Spanish Armada and its destruction. Englishmen are described as 'the onlie offensiue enemies and inuaders of the Spanishe Monarchie', but there is a reference to 'wronges and greauances don to Englonde'.

'Christonal Colon' in this text is, of course, a misspelling of the Spanish version of Columbus's name – Cristoval Colon. His original name in Genoese was Cristoforo Colombo, which became Latinized into Christopher Columbus.

Biud de Haro thus confirms Francisco Lopez de Gomara's statement. It is unfortunate that the original text in Spanish cannot be found, though this is not surprising, as so hostile a document would almost certainly have been destroyed if discovered, and may indeed have been smuggled out of Spain. What is most significant is that de Haro was a bibliographer of the works of Peter Martyr.[3]

Peter Martyr, who was a voracious student of the discoveries of his age and a great chronicler of contemporary events, was in Valladolid at the time of Columbus's death, yet never recorded it. A number of Columbus's biographers have commented on this omission, but the truth was that Martyr had come to regard Columbus as somewhat of a fraud and a twister of facts, an adventurer whose discoveries, as a result of diligent public relations

work on his behalf, had been represented as rather more glorious
and original than in fact they were. In recent years Peter Martyr's
doubts have been echoed by further revelations, which also justify
de Haro's allegations. A Russian historian, Professor Isypernik, of
the Uzbec Academy, discovered in 1959 a secret letter written by
Columbus, completely quashing the theory that he arrived in
America by accident. This letter revealed that Columbus was well
aware of the existence of the West Indies when he set off on his
first expedition and that he even had a map of the islands provided
by earlier navigators.[4]

This letter was written to Queen Isabella of Spain, and was
obviously intended to seek her support in obtaining financial aid
for his expeditions. It showed that Columbus not only knew of the
existence of the West Indies, but also what was to be found there
and how the islands could be used by Spain. Columbus, claimed
Professor Isypernik, distorted his diaries and reports to the
Spanish Court and other official documents to encourage
Spaniards to emigrate to a barren land which he painted as a
paradise. 'The new land he discovered did not make a favourable
impression upon members of the expedition . . . Then the Spanish
authorities decided to whitewash reality. A version was circulated
saying that Columbus had discovered countries of fabulous
wealth, rich in gold mines, pearls, precious stones, spices and
perfumes. As the countries of Asia were fabulous for such wealth,
it was declared that the new lands were in fact the blessed lands of
Asia. Later research workers decided on the basis of these reports
that Columbus had discovered America by accident and that Asia
had been the real goal of his voyage.'[5]

This Russian claim was immediately supported by Mr. G. R.
Crone, Librarian and Map Curator of the Royal Geographical
Society. He stated that there was a secret letter written by
Columbus to Queen Isabella of Spain, and that it showed the
new location of the West Indies and that the United States
Library of Congress had charts which bore out this theory. One
of these maps was discovered in the 'thirties by B. Malil Eten
Elden, then director of the National Museum of Turkey, while
converting the Palace of Tophapu in Istanbul into a museum. It

proved to be a map prepared by the Turkish Admiral Piri Reis in 1513.[6]

This fascinating discovery threw new light on the whole question of pre-Columbian voyages. The admiral had apparently gone to immense pains to produce one of the most detailed maps of his time, a veritable mine of information, not so much in the actual drawings but in the copious notes he made around the chart. In one of these notes describing the sources used in compiling his chart Reis wrote in Turkish on the face of the map: 'From about twenty charts and *mappae mundi* – these are charts drawn in the days of Alexander, Lord of Two Horns, which show the inhabited quarter of the world; the Arabs name these charts Jafferiye – from eight Jafferiye of that kind and one Arabic map of Hind, and from maps just drawn by four Portuguese which show the countries of Hind, Sind and China geometrically drawn, and also from a map drawn by Colombo in the western region I have extracted it.' On the Piri Reis chart there is a cartographic picture of the entire Antilles as conceived by Columbus.[7]

Samuel Morison argued that most of the New World portion of this map 'is so fantastically incorrect that it cannot possibly have been copied from a chart of Columbus'. But the evidence is that the chart was partly based on a map in Columbus's possession before he discovered America – one group of eight islands off the American coast is in fact remarkably accurate – and the map in question was one prepared by Columbus's official chart-maker and pilot, Juan de la Cosa, who later became one of the slaves of Piri Reis's uncle, Kemal Reis. This much is made clear in the marginal notes.

Another map, believed to have been prepared under the direction of Columbus himself, was found in the *Bibliothèque Nationale* in Paris in 1924; this did not show America, but it marked clearly the islands of the Antilles (West Indies), said to have been the secret goal of Columbus's expedition.

A descendant of Columbus, the Duke of Veragua, of Madrid, made a further claim in 1964: that his famous ancestor discovered America in 1467 and not in 1492, that is to say that he kept his original voyage of discovery a secret. The Duke is curator of the Columbus Building in Madrid, which houses the archives of the explorer; his theories have been developed by Jose Fernandez Martinez, a Spanish scholar, who has also expressed the belief that Columbus knew all about the existence of the New World when he sought a sponsor for his project. Columbus, he states, 'was keeping this knowledge a secret for fear that, if it became known, the riches of this undiscovered land would be taken by interlopers'.[8]

There could, however, have been other reasons for Columbus hiding the fact that he had heard of the existence of lands in the west. These may well have been inspired by the hostility of the Roman Catholic hierarchy to the idea of a New World. Columbus met with considerable opposition from the Church even when he propounded the theory that the world was round and not flat, and that an Atlantic voyage would lead him to new lands in Asia. The objections to his project were mainly based on theological and dogmatic grounds, not on geographical theory. A mathematical thesis was disallowed if it appeared to go contrary to the Scriptures and previous pronouncements of the Church. Lactanius was cited as having said: 'Is there anyone so foolish as to believe that there are men in the antipodes with their feet opposite to ours, people who walk with their heels upwards and their heads hanging down?'

Yet the Council of Priests who examined his project included some who were prepared to accept the globular theory of the earth's construction. But to any suggestion that there were new lands in the west there would have been unanimous objection. This, in the view of the Church, would have meant there were nations on the other side of the world who were not descended from Adam, and this struck at the roots of Biblical teaching. Columbus would have made no progress in pursuing this theory, not even if he had alleged his expedition would lead to the Promised Land itself!

The geographer Malte-Brun stated categorically in his *Histoire de la Geographie* that when in Italy Columbus had heard of the Norse and other discoveries of land beyond Iceland. Probably he had heard a great deal more from Martin Behaim, the Jewish cartographer. Behaim was the most knowledgeable cartographer of his day. A number of the marginal notes on Piri Reis's map are not easy to decipher, but Bay Hasan Fehmi transcribed a great many of them. One in particular makes enlightening reading:

'These coasts are named the shores of Antilia. They were discovered in the year 896 of the Arab calendar (A.D. 1492). But it is reported thus, that a Genoese infidel, his name was Colombo, he it was who discovered these places. For instance, a book fell into the hands of the said Colombo, and he found it said in his book that at the end of the Western Sea (Atlantic) that is, on its western side, there were coasts and islands of all kinds of metals and also precious stones. The above-mentioned, having studied this book thoroughly, explained these matters one by one to the great of Genoa and said: "Come, give me two ships, let me go and find these places." They said, "O unprofitable man, can an end or a limit be found to the Western Sea? Its vapour is full of darkness".'[9]

But we are not told the title of the book. The story might be dismissed as apochryphal, but the marginal notes also refer to the voyage of Saint Brandon, claiming that reference to it was made in 'the ancient *Mappae Mundi*'.[10]

Peter Martyr asserted that Columbus had marked on one of his charts somewhere in the direction of the West Indies the words '*Questo he mar de Cambrio*' ['These are Welsh waters'].[11] It was the custom in those days to indicate on maps what discoverers had been in a given area previously, often, unfortunately, without adding the date of the amendment. A French map of the seventeenth century showed the Azores with two names written beside these islands: 'Saint Brendan? Matec?' A handwritten memoir in one corner of the map made references to various voyages of discovery and after the word 'Metec' added '*voyez Guillaume, P – B et Jacob van Maerlant.*'

Such obscure and puzzling clues to the Madoc enigma might easily remain unsolved mysteries for centuries. 'Guillaume, P – B' told one nothing: it might as well have been a cipher. Jacob van Maerlant, however, provided some evidence of the probable source of the memoir-writer's statements. About the year 1260 he had written in Dutch several romantic epics on the subject of Merlin and the Holy Grail. The Arthurian legends had been introduced into Flemish literature by Flemish colonists from Wales on their return to Holland. These had so fascinated Lodewijk van Velthem, a Dutch patron of poets, that he commanded a few of the Flemish settlers in Wales to translate such Celtic legends into Flemish from the original version in Latin compiled by their priests. Jacob van Maerlant in his *Spiegel Historiaal* referred somewhat vaguely to 'Madoc's dream', without, however, giving much information about the form this took.[12]

Undoubtedly one of the poets who retold the Welsh legends was 'Guillaume, P – B', or Willem the Minstrel, to whom this reference seemingly is made. Willem was a friend of Walter Map, the twelfth-century English poet and historian, best known as a writer of erotic tales but a diligent collector of legends, contemporary stories of adventure and ancedotes of all kinds. In a section of the *Encyclopaedia Britannica* dealing with the history of Holland there appears this passage: 'The sagas of Charlemagne and Arthur appear . . . These were evidently introduced by wandering minstrels and translated to gratify the curiosity of the noble women . . . The earliest existing fragments of the epic of Reynard the Fox were written in Latin by Flemish priests and about 1250 a very important version in Dutch was made by Willem the Minstrel, of whom it is unfortunate that we know no more than that he was the translator of the romance of Madoc.'[13]

There is the possibility that the letters 'P – B' may stand for *Pays Bas*, meaning 'Willem of Holland', or they could indicate *Père Brandon*. At any rate here was a Frenchman of the seventeenth century, obviously widely read, to judge from the notes he made on his map, compiling what purported to be a record of previous discoveries, drawn up almost entirely from a perusal of the literature of France, Holland, Spain, Portugal, Turkey and England. In this instance the chart-maker had drawn on what must be the nearest to a contemporary account of the Madoc story written by a foreigner. Although the Flemings were originally brought over to Britain by Henry I and settled on the borders of England and Wales and in Pembrokeshire, with a view to being used as mercenaries against the Welsh, some of them moved over to the other side. Records show that Flemings were attached to the armies of Owain Gwynedd. They would therefore have had every opportunity of hearing the odes of the bards and they lived in Wales both before and after Madoc's voyages. But the story of Willem properly belongs to another chapter, when it can be examined against the background of Madoc's life.

There is a good deal of evidence to suggest that the Spaniards were perturbed at suggestions that America had been discovered by somebody from the continent of Europe before Columbus, and the persistence of such reports from returning travellers turned perturbation into a desire to eliminate any trace of previous occupation. Spanish archives show that a number of such expeditions were dispatched, not only to search for the *Gente Blanco*, or white people, but for any traces of the landings of Madoc and St. Brandon.

In 1526 the Spaniards sent out three expeditions, one in the West Indies in quest of Madoc's trail, the other two to the Canaries in search of St. Brandon's legendary Isles of the Blest. Letters exchanged between the King of Spain and Luis de Rojas, Governor of Florida, between 1624 and 1627 testify that expeditions were made in quest of the *Gente Blanco*, that the people they were searching for were reputedly of British origin and, more significantly, that the searches were carried out in those areas from which reports of Madoc's landings had already come – Mexico, Florida, Alabama and Georgia.

No doubt the earliest expeditions were prompted by Hernando de Soto's reports after his voyages to Mexico and Alabama. He had landed at Mobile Bay in Alabama and was intrigued by the remains of ancient fortifications which he found in the vicinity and which he doubted could be the work of Indians. His chronicles of his journey in the Chattanooga area in 1540 reveal that he passed many of the places where pre-Columbian forts had been erected.[14]

In a letter from Luis de Rojas to the King of Spain, dated January 20, 1625, he stated that soldiers and sailors had been dispatched by Governor Salinas the previous year to scour the Georgia–Carolina interior for a hundred and fifty leagues, but 'they found no trace of the rumoured *gente blanco y cabella*'.[15] A year or two later Pedro de Torres, ten sailors and sixty Indians searched the territory around Chattanooga without success. The next Governor of Florida, d'Alonzo de Aranquiz y Votes, on September 8, 1662, informed the Spanish King that, following a report of the *Gente Blanco* having been seen in the Appalachians, a Spanish expedition had been dispatched across Georgia to search this area.

That the Spaniards failed to find the *Gente Blanco* is not surprising, for, with the coming of Spaniards in large numbers, many of the native tribes had retreated up the rivers or deep into the interior of the continent. Every traveller confirmed the gradual migration of the Indians away from the coast. But the fact that such expeditions were made suggests that the Spaniards took serious notice of reports of previous landings and that, as long as Spain administered these territories, they were anxious to prevent claims by England or anyone else of having made discoveries before them. In 1670 Spain made a treaty with England which recognized that 'possession and settlement' were proof of title. There were no further quests for the *Gente Blanco* after that. The treaty legalized Spain's claims as far north as St. Elena and British claims as far south as South Carolina.

Not until more than a hundred years later did the Spaniards allow themselves to give the Madoc story another thought. Then, as will be seen later, a young Welshman caused them more than passing anxiety.

7

MADOC THE SAILOR

SO FAR THE picture which has emerged of Madoc is of a man who was rather vaguely, almost allegorically, associated with the sea. There is the bardic image of one who loved the sea passionately, who dreamed of exploration and unknown lands rather than a skilled seaman.

Among a mass of parchments, receipts and manuscripts found by the Heaven family, former owners of Lundy Island, was a faded manuscript poem in Welsh which read:

> Y tlws lle caed Madwg
> Bola croen ar waith bual crwn
> Blwch byrflu (byrflew) tondew tindwn . . .
> Nofiwr o groen anifail
> Noe serchog foliog o fail . . .
> Llestr rhwth fal crwth fola croen . . .
> Coflaid o Ledryn cyflo . . .
> Myn Pedr, mae yn lledryn
> Rywiogaeth wyll a dwyll dyn.[1]

The unknown author of this ode must have lived not later than the fifteenth century. He gives to Madoc a mysterious origin, which must be part poetic licence, part allegory based no doubt on the story of Moses, or that of Taliesin, and to some extent a polite camouflage of Madoc's illegitimacy. He refers to the 'jewel' in which Madoc was found – a skin bag shaped into a tiny vessel with a broken bottom, which 'by St. Peter, is a craft with the nature of a devil which bewitches man'. Later in the poem the author employs the word *corwc*,[2] which positively identifies the nature of the vessel as a coracle. The suggestion is that Madoc as a tiny baby was cast adrift in a coracle, that his affinity with water enabled him to survive to manhood. It could be that a coracle fisherman was paid to ferry Madoc away from the castle of Owain Gwynedd when his mother saved him from execution. Yet this poem would seem to be in romantic rather than factual vein, for Welsh bards were fond of utilizing the story of Moses in the bulrushes and creating a Cymric version of it around the coracle. The Llanstephan Ms. 11 and the Peniarth Ms. 240 show an almost identical story told in verse about Taliesin.

The poet, however, despite his romantic opening, does give us some facts. He describes Madoc as 'a skilled handler of the coracle, both on river and sea, learning much from his experience among the Irish curraghs in his long exile'. In another place he refers to him as 'the sailor magician of Bardsey, the creator of a magic ship that could not sink, wise in his knowledge of the seas, their tempers and deceits'.

There is confirmation of this account in a prose work by Roger Morris, of Coed y Talwrn on March 13, 1582, in which he seeks to give an explanation of the Welsh name of *Ffrydiau Caswennan* for that seaman's nightmare, the deceptive race of Bardsey Sound off the Caernarvonshire coast. Morris stated that the story explaining this name was handed down by word of mouth through the ages, according to his informant, Edward ap John Wynn.[3]

Morris asserted that 'the son of Owain Gwynedd was a great sailor, much given to voyaging far afield', but that, despite considerable experience of the sea, he had always been baffled by the hazards of the 'vortex' of Bardsey Race. To remedy this he constructed 'a ship without nails, but fastened with stag horns so that the sea would not swallow it'. This novel ship Madoc named *Gwennan Gorn* [Horn Gwennan], and, in Morris's words, he 'traversed the seas in it and visited many foreign lands without fear or misadventure'.

Yet Madoc's inventiveness does not seem to have enabled him

to conquer the treacherous Race, however much it may have served him well far out on the open ocean. For, on returning home near Bardsey Island, the current there savaged the ship and severely damaged her. Such was the fame of Madoc's craft that this part of the sea was called from that day *Ffrydiau Caswennan*, the Currents of Gwennan's Bane.

This legend, though recorded in 1582, makes no reference to America, though it clearly depicts Madoc as a sailor who made voyages to foreign lands. Certainly nobody could assert that Roger Morris subscribed to the Tudorian history of Madoc, though, as the *Historie of Cambria* was published two years later, it is just possible that Dr. Powel may have heard this story, though very doubtful, as he makes no reference to it, despite the fact that he cited sources in his book. What this prose item clearly establishes is that the legend of Madoc as a sailor had existed for centuries.

Gwennan Gorn is mentioned as a ship of legendary fame by various Welsh writers, and Dr. E. D. Jones makes the point that Morris's version does not 'imply that *Gwennan Gorn* was entirely lost as some traditions indicate'.[4]

Both in Wales and Ireland it was customary in the Middle Ages to associate whirlpools, races and treacherous currents with some maritime disaster and to name them accordingly. When Breccan, son of Niall, King of Ireland, lost his fleet of fifty curraghs in the great tidal whirlpool off Rathlin Island, that whirlpool was named thereafter Coire-Breccain, or Breccan's Cauldron.

G. D. Burtchaell, the Irish antiquarian, in his researches into the Kavanagh family of County Carlow, referred to 'Madoc, a Welsh-Irish sailor-prince, a friend of Caomhinach [Kavanagh], son of Dermot McMorrough, King of Leinster, descended from the Scandinavian Kings of Ireland'.[5] Burtchaell cites an old Irish song, which, he says, tells how Madoc was learned in 'ways of the sea, creator of a ship hardier than the curragh, and how he praised the beauties of the sea as he sang to the music of his harp':

> *Caine amre lasin Madawc Ouain*
> *Ina nailong tar muri glan.*

A rough translation would be:

> Madoc (son of) Owain regards
> His ship as a thing of beauty,
> Sailing on the clear sea.

Note the phrase *nailong*, which is especially interesting from a geographical point of view. Whereas the Gaelic equivalent for curragh is *curach* in Donegal and Western Ireland, it is known as *naomhog* in County Clare, the area of Ireland which Madoc is reputed to have visited. *Nailong* is unusual, but explicable; it could be used for describing an unusual type of ship and one larger than a curragh. The Old Irish word for a curragh was sometimes *nai*, possibly derived from the Latin *navis*, and *long* was applied to a ship.

The Irish bards were particularly devoted to songs about ships and the sea, and the story-tellers of the age were fond of narrating the adventures of the early explorers like Saint Brandon. Even in pagan times in Ireland the legend grew up of an 'Otherworld' (*Ui Breasil* in folk-lore) situated somewhere in the Western Ocean, peopled by a fair race and noted for its glamorous females. T. Gwynn Jones has stated that Madoc was so wretched at the strife in his native land that he sought counsel of a priest named Mabon, who spoke to him of a fair land in the west where all was peace and suggested that the two of them should set sail together to find it. It is much more likely that Madoc heard such talk of a 'fair land in the West' in Ireland from an Irish priest, for by the twelfth century the legendary exploits of St. Brandon were widely circulated in that country.

He may, too, have heard much about the exploits of his Norse ancestors and of his own grandfather, Gruffydd ap Conan, for that redoubtable ruler had made full use of the seamanship he had learned from the Scandinavian Kings of Dublin. He was a skilled navigator, and it is recorded in the *Gwentian Brut* that on July 3, 1088 – a rare preciseness in dates in such an age – he entered the River Conway with three ships, landing under the castle at high tide and beaching the craft on shore at the recess of the tide.

Riryd, Madoc's brother, who was Lord of Clochran, in Ireland, was also reputed to be a skilful ship-handler. He, like Madoc, must have heard the stories of Brandon and the Norsemen's explorations in the Far West. By the twelfth century, except in the remoter parts of Ireland, the *curragh* had long since been ousted by the planked ship of wood, introduced by the Norsemen.

The earliest days of Madoc must remain largely a matter of conjecture. Of his reputed birthplace we know little, except that from the records of the House of Gwydir it seems more likely to have been Dolwyddelan Castle in the Lledr Valley than Aberffraw Castle in Anglesey. Both of these were residences of Owain Gwynedd. There are no traces of either castle today. Pennant in his *Tours of Wales* described Dolwyddelan as 'placed on a high rock, precipitous on one side' and consisting of 'two square towers'. But what Pennant saw was probably an adaptation of the original fortress of Gwynedd. Even in Southey's time the Poet Laureate records that all that remained at Aberffraw and Dolwyddelan were 'stones and slabs'. Brechfa believed that after years of hostility Madoc was 'forgiven by his sire'. The Reverend Benjamin F. Bowen took this story somewhat further by naming Madoc as 'commander of his father's fleet' and suggesting that in 1144 when Cadwaladr appeared with his fleet of 'Irish Danes' in the Menai Straits, Madoc's naval forces defeated them.[6] This is nonsense: there was no naval battle in the Straits. The battle took place on land, where the forces of Owain drove Cadwaladr's men back to sea.

On the other hand it could well be that the 'emissarie of the Prince of Gwynet' who landed at Lundy Island to seek aid against Henry II in 1163 was none other than Madoc himself. Not only is there the ode by the unknown Welsh poet found at Lundy, but other suggestions that Madoc was closely associated with Lundy. In a ship-load of granite which arrived from Lundy at Barnstaple in 1865 a stone tablet was found. On it, carved in old style Welsh lettering, was the legend:

> *Mae yn ffai–(th) gened–(leith)–ol*
> *I Madoc o Lund fudo'n ormodol,*
> *Ir mor-gor–(lle)-winol,*
> *Ond ni ddaith byth y-(nol).*[7]

Thus on a remote island in the Bristol Channel, a long way from his native Gwynedd, Madoc the sailor was commemorated by the bald statement that, 'It is an established fact, known far and wide, that Madoc ventured far out on the Western Ocean never to return.'

There was no date on the tablet, which is unfortunate in assessing this evidence, but experts expressed the belief that it was probably carved at least as far back as the fourteenth century, possibly earlier. Some of the letters were barely decipherable, others were missing and the gaps that had to be filled in are shown in brackets, notably the words *genedleithol* and *gorllewinol*. But there seems no doubt that this version of the inscription is an accurate one.

The phrase 'Madoc of Lund' suggests that he must have had close and extensive associations with the island; the fact that this inscription was carved in Welsh means that it was probably done before 1242, the year in which William de Marisco, Lord of the Manor of Lundy, was taken prisoner to London, thus marking the end of a long era of defiance of the Kings of England by the lords of Lundy and the disappearance of their Welsh allies.

On the death of Owain Gwynedd there was immediate strife within the House of Gwynedd. The sons of Owain fought among themselves as to who should rule the land. Iorwerth was already out of favour because of his disability and misshapen appearance, and he appears to have had no stomach for a battle with his brothers, retiring to Dolwyddelan and abstaining from the fray. Howel, 'a base sonne begotten of an Irishwoman',[8] was the first to seize power. It was inevitable that he should provoke civil strife and a stern challenge to his authority, for in 1146 he had joined forces with the Normans temporarily against the sons of Gruffydd ap Rhys. Howel was an opportunist and prepared to change his loyalties for an offer of property or loot.

For two stormy years after Owain's death Howel precariously held the reins of power. Then he went to Ireland to claim his mother's property, and on his return found his brother Dafydd asserting his right to rule by force of arms. There are conflicting versions as to what happened to Howel after this. According to the *Myvyrian Archaiology*, he was wounded in battle, and taken to

Ireland where he is said to have died. But *Annales Cambriae*, a more reliable source, states that Howel was killed by Dafydd's forces in armed conflict in 1171.

Dafydd certainly succeeded Howel as ruler of Gwynedd, but this by no means brought peace to the strife-torn nation. Opinions about Howel and Dafydd are conflicting. From contemporary accounts it would seem that each brother was an opportunist, warped by greed and hatred. Sir Thomas Herbert, however, paints a somewhat different picture. He claims that Iorwerth was 'thought unworthy of the Crowne and dignitie both in respect of his deformity and simpleness'.[9] He refers in somewhat odd terms for an undemocratic age that 'Howel was excluded by vote of the common sort in that his mother was an Irishwoman', and seems to imply that Dafydd, though younger, was 'by marriage to Emma Plantagenet, a sister to King Henry the Second, by generall applause judged worthiest'.

Nevertheless it would seem that Dafydd was just as treacherous as Howel. He had not only married a sister of the hated English King, but gave his brother-in-law money and men and even attended the English Parliament at Oxford. Disgust at Dafydd's treachery turned many of his supporters against him and uprisings became so frequent in Gwynedd that, to check the trend which had grown in favour of the previously spurned Iorwerth, Dafydd slew his brother's supporters and took away their lands, carrying out a systematic campaign of terror. He also imprisoned Rhodri, who had been one of the claimants, though not a very willing one, and forced the other brothers into exile.

Rhodri escaped from prison in 1175 and before the end of that year had driven his brother Dafydd out of Anglesey and made that island his own retreat from the civil strife in Gwynedd. Few now remained to challenge Dafydd's power: Riryd, Edwall, Einion and Madoc had long since gone into exile. Indeed such was the disaffection in North Wales during this period that there was constant emigration from that country to Ireland. This tendency was noted even before Owain's death in the *Annales Cambriae* of 1167, but it became more marked later and the *Book of Aberpergwm*, 1169, 1172 and 1173 makes mention of it. About this time Henry II turned his attention to Ireland, collecting a flotilla at Milford Haven in 1170 to send an expedition to that country.

In the period immediately prior to 1170 there was no mention of Madoc by the bards other than Llywarch's *Ode to the Hot Iron*. The bards were all silent on the subject until their laments of later date. They must indeed have been terrified at the turn of events, wondering whether the swiftly changing fortunes of the various claimants to the throne of Gwynedd would affect their own status. Llywarch's odes frequently struck a note of foreboding. He wrote many poems on Dafydd and Rhodri and, reading between the lines, one can discern a certain wistfulness and the mournful note of one who sighed for happier days and feared to tell all. Gwalchmai, somewhat disillusioned, sought relief in love lyrics, composing some exquisite odes to his wife, Eve, rather than enter into the quarrels of the warring brothers of Gwynedd, and he, too, seems to have been torn between duty and his innermost feelings. Love was a safer subject than family vendettas.

'During which turmoiles and unnatural strife,' wrote Sir Thomas Herbert, 'the said Madoc, loath to be an Agent of Discord to either party, and feeling propositions of peace ineffectual, studies by all good meanes to avoid the knowledge of it, and aymes at some forren place of ease and profit, neither discouraged by improbabilities nor likely disasters . . . Madoc ingeniously perusing the older illustrations and seeing in some things the prophecie of this authentique Bardh accomplished . . . employing his patrimonial estate upon me, ships and provisions.'[10]

In Portmadoc in North Wales there has been in existence for many years a verse entitled *Llangan Madoc*:

> *Thirteen little ships sailed*
> *On a bright morning.*
> *Hail, Madoc, brave his soul,*
> *Captain of the fleet,*
> *In search of lands unknown.*
> *A good army*
> *And a strong fleet*
> *That was his desire.*'[11]

This follows the old, romantic pattern of Madoc-worship. The verse is undated and the author is unknown, but this is immaterial for Madoc possessed neither an army nor a fleet. Port Madoc has been cited by some non-British writers as the place from which Madoc set out to discover the New World and it has been erroneously stated that the little town was named after him. Portmadoc and neighbouring Tremadoc were both named after William Alexander Madocks (1773–1828), a North Welsh industrialist and Radical Member of Parliament, who reclaimed seven thousand acres from the sea in this region between 1808–11 and later established a port there. No maps prior to 1800 make any mention of either Port Madoc or Tremadoc.

It may be that the story about Port Madoc originated with the Reverend Isaac Taylor who, in a book entitled *Words and Places*, wrote that 'from Ynys Hir, now some way inland (*from Port Madoc*), Madoc is said to have sailed in quest of unknown lands'.

There would, however, appear to be no historical foundation for this and the number of places from which one could sail even with a very small craft in the North Wales area in those days would be limited to the estuary of the Dee, the River Clwyd, Abergele, what is now known as Rhos-on-Sea, Conway, Bangor, the Menai Straits, Caernarvon, Nevin, Pwllheli and Abersoch.

There were varying versions of where Madoc's original sailing place was situated. James Howel suggests it was Milford Haven.[12] This would not have been in Gwynedd territory and it is most unlikely that Madoc would have been able to set out from there in 1170, when it was being used as an assembly port for Henry II's Irish expedition. Mr. John O. Morgans, of Detroit, has put forward the view that 'the ships were made at Abergwili and sailed to the open sea along the Towy by crewmen from Carmarthenshire and Cardigan'.[13] Both the Towy and the Teifi are rivers where the coracle-men flourish; even today they are the last strongholds of the coracle, and it seems improbable that Madoc would employ coracle crews in a sailing ship. Inquiries in Carmarthenshire and Cardiganshire reveal no trace of Madoc in this area, not even a legend to substantiate this claim.

The theory that Madoc sailed from Abergwili and that his ship was built in that tiny Carmarthenshire village comes from a statement to the effect in Sir Thomas Herbert's book.[14] But to satisfy oneself absolutely on this point it would be necessary to see Sir Thomas's original script, for it is not at all certain that the printers did not misread his handwriting. There were several editions of this book. It was first published in London in 1626, but most editions, while referring to *anno 1626* in the sub-title heading, give 1634 as the year of publication. There were various later and enlarged editions and it is essential to read each one to gain a thorough appreciation of the author's evaluation of the Madoc story. In one edition the sailing place is given as *Abeyville*, which is obviously a misprint; in another it is *Abergwilley* and in two others *Abergwili* and *Abergili*.

Thomas Stephens thought that Herbert may have confused Abergwili near Carmarthen with Abergele in North Wales. This certainly seems possible and the *Abergili* of a later edition of the book could have been intended for Abergele. There is no record of ship-building at Abergwili in the twelfth century, but this is not, of course, conclusive proof. There is, however, one good reason why Abergwili was an unlikely point of departure. The old Roman bridge there was certainly in existence in Madoc's day and it would have been difficult, if not impossible to have sailed a ship underneath it.

Sir Thomas Herbert (1597–1682) was descended from Sir Richard Herbert of Monmouthshire, but he himself was a Yorkshireman. A scholar, widely travelled in most parts of the world and a man of great integrity, he served as Groom to the Royal Bedchamber of Charles I and was with him constantly during that unhappy monarch's last days, even attending him on the scaffold. He cited as sources for his account of Madoc such names as Cynfric ap Gronow, Gutyn Owen, Humphrey Llwyd, David Powel, Sir John Price, Richard Hakluyt, and Samuel Purchas. It would seem that he relied on Cynfric ap Gronow for the additional details, especially those of Madoc's departure.

If one examines carefully the last source the picture becomes somewhat clearer. Cynfric claimed that:

Horn Gwennan, brought to the Gele
To be given a square mast,
Was turned back to Afon Ganol's quay
For Madoc's famous voyage.[15]

The Gele is a very small stream flowing into the sea at Abergele in Denbighshire. Probably it was larger in Madoc's day, as was the Clwyd, not far away. If Madoc's ship had been repaired, or partially fitted out there, Sir Thomas Herbert could have believed it to be built in that place. He was not closely associated with Wales and he may easily have confused Abergele with Abergwili, or, alternatively, his printer may have done so. The latter seems to be the likeliest explanation.

Certainly if *Gwennan Gorn* was the ship Madoc used on the voyage it would have been from North Wales he sailed. All legends of *Gwennan Gorn* centre around Anglesey, Bardsey, Caernarvonshire and Denbighshire.

One of the complaints against Sir Thomas Herbert's account is that it is not borne out by other writers, but when one examines these alleged discrepancies closely they do not seem to be as irreconcilable as the critics assert. One can discount the theories of those who suggest Milford Haven and Port Madoc, just as one can treat with the gravest suspicion the poem about the thirteen ships. The Reverend John H. Parry cites that other garrulous and inventive parson, the Reverend Theophilus Evans, as the source of the thirteen ships theory.[16]

What is important is to compare the narratives of Herbert with those of 'Meiron'.[17] Herbert stated that Madoc sailed with Edwall and Einion, his brothers, and that the point of departure was Abergwili, or Abergele, whereas 'Meiron' asserts that he went with Riryd, another brother, and set off from Lundy. These two apparently contradictory accounts are, however, quite consistent if one compares the two writers in detail. To arrive at a more accurate assessment it is important to make this comparison, because the two reports are complementary rather than contradictory.

Herbert stated: 'Anno 1170 he left his countrie, and after long saile and no less patience, blest with some happy winds, at last descried land in the Gulph of Mexico not farre from Florida.' This obviously refers to the first voyage made from Abergwili, or Abergele. As to what happened after the landing, he added: 'Madoc was overjoyed and had reason to account his happy estate superiour to that his brothers strive for, so eagerly emulating with ambitious hate and bloud each other for a little Territory, incomparable to that good destiny allotted him, being a vast and weal Kingdome, obtained in some part without opposition, and able to satiate the most covetous. There he planted, fortified some advantagious places, left a hundred and twenty men to finish what he had begun and returned home after some bad windes, guided by supremme providence and the benefit the Pole-Starre gave him in the night.

'When he had landed and had accounted his happy and miraculous voyage, told the hopes of succeeding Conquests, and other motives of persuasion and admiration, these and the words of Madoc himselfe drew so many willing minds and purses to a returne, that he attempted it with ten good Barques, loaded with all necessary provisions, a matter that confidence required.

'At his arrivall he found many of his Britaines dead, caused by the Natives' Villany, or alternation of the clime, which notwithstanding he digested patiently, and with Edwoll and Eneon, his brothers, bettered the first intention, living with content, and dying in no less distance from Heaven, than when at home, unhappiest in this that their own Nation forgot them quite, either judging them lost, because never after hearing from them, or because their own Beings were turned topsie turvy by the fatall end of the last unhappy Prince Lluellyn ap Griffith . . .'

There is no reference to the sailing place of the second expedition in Herbert's narrative.

'Meiron' and Herbert both seem to agree that Madoc was a man of mild disposition, loathing strife. 'Meiron', unlike Herbert, made no reference to the first sailing point. His version was as follows:

'The country became embroiled in civil war. Influenced by disgust, Madoc, who is represented as of a very mild disposition, resolved upon the matchless enterprise of exploring the ocean westwards, in search of more tranquil scenes. The event was, according to various old documents, the discovering of a new world, from which he effected his return to inform his country of his good fortune. The consequence of which was the fitting out of a second expedition, and Madoc, with his brother Riryd, Lord of Clochran in Ireland, prevailed upon so many to accompany them as to fill seven ships and, sailing from the Isle of Lundy, they took an eternal leave of Wales.'

Thus, in effect, 'Meiron' fills in some of the gaps in Herbert's narrative. True, there are minor discrepancies; 'Meiron' mentions Riryd as accompanying his brother, whereas Herbert speaks of Edwal and Einion. Possibly Enion accompanied his brother, but Herbert must have been misinformed on Edwal, who, according to Pennant, was murdered at Llyn Idwal by Dunawt, son of Nefydd Hardd, to whom Owain had entrusted Edwal as a youth.[18] Riryd seems to be the likeliest, from contemporary accounts, to have taken part in the expeditions. According to Irish sources. 'the Lord of Clochran sailed away from Ireland and was never seen again'.[19]

If one read Herbert carefully, it is also quite feasible that Einion went with Madoc on the first trip and that Riryd joined him on the second.

The estimates of the number of ships for the second expedition differ; one says ten, the other seven. Similarly the number of men taken to the New World is variously assessed by different writers as ranging from one hundred and twenty to three hundred men. One must assume that the expeditions included some women if the intention was to populate a new land.

'Meiron' makes an interesting allusion to the *Ode to the Hot Iron* in his narrative. 'Llywarch, the son of Llewellyn, seems to have composed two of his poems in the time between the first and second voyages of Madoc. One of these pieces must be considered of great importance and curiosity; it is an invocation, as if he were undergoing the fiery ordeal to exonerate himself from having any knowledge of the fate of Madoc.'

Could it be that Llywarch was questioned by the enemies of

Madoc as to his intentions and whereabouts? Did he know something of Madoc's mission and had he sworn to keep silent on the matter?

On one point Cynfric ap Gronow and Ieuan Brechfa are agreed: they both stated that Madoc's ship was built from wood produced in the forests of Nant Gwynant in Caernarvonshire. Both bards refer to 'ship' rather than ships, but this may have been because the most famous of all the ships was *Gwennan Gorn* and the only one to have been written about. We must assume it was a Welsh-built boat, as there was some ship-building along the coast of Gwynedd in that era, though very little from all accounts. If there were more than three ships on either of the expeditions, the probability is that they were built elsewhere. It is uncertain from contemporary records whether the Welsh then acquired ships from other nations. Lord Lyttelton in his life of Henry II observed that King Gruffydd ap Llewellyn ap Seisyllt, who lived a century before Madoc, had paid some attention to his naval concerns by procuring from a foreign country a few ships for protecting the coast. But he gave no source for this statement. The Reverend John H. Parry affirmed that Owain Gwynedd 'also realized the necessity of a navy for a sea-borne nation'.[20]

It is unfortunate that Ieuan Brechfa is nearly always cited at second- or third-hand, and that often neither the original words, nor specific references to the work from which they are taken, are given. The *Brut Ieuan Brechfa* would appear to be reasonably reliable, but the *Book of Pedigrees* is no longer available. It comes to us second-hand through a variety of sources, and not all Welsh versions of it tally. Two of them are different in one or two vital words that could make translations at variance with one another.

The first in Welsh reads: '*Madoc a Riryd a gawsant dir yn mpell yn y Merwcryz, as yno y cyvannezasant.*'[21]

The second version reads: '*Madoc a Rhiryd a aethant draw i'r Morwerydd, i diroedd a gawsant yno, lle trigfanasant.*'[22]

The gist of both these versions is that Madoc and Riryd went across the sea to land they found there and where they remained. There can be no quarrel with this interpretation. It is when one tries to seek a more precise definition that the difficulties arise. As

Riryd was Lord of Clochran and had inherited lands in Ireland, some translators suggest the meaning is that the first version indicates the brothers 'acquired' land in Ireland and that they went there and 'prospered', while the second version implies that they 'received' lands in Ireland. Now Riryd certainly inherited lands in Ireland from his mother, but there is no evidence that Madoc had any such inheritance. Thus the translation really hinges on the question of what sea and what land was indicated by the bard. The passage has been interpreted in a variety of ways. Dr. John Williams, of Sydenham, thought it clearly indicated that Madoc and Riryd found land far across the Western Ocean. The vital words that need reconciling are *Merwcryz* and *Morwerydd*. They can also be spelt *Mor Werydh* and *Mor y Werddon*. In modern Welsh this could be accurately interpreted as meaning the Atlantic Ocean, but Stephens pointed out that this meaning for *Morwerydd* was not to be found in any Welsh dictionary prior to 1821, and that in Brechfa's time it could have meant merely a trip across the Irish Sea *(Mor Iwerydd)*, or even across the Menai Straits to Anglesey.

This was carrying a quibble too far. If Brechfa was referring to a voyage to Ireland, or to Anglesey, he would surely have said so and not used the phrase 'to a land they had found there'. Stephens argued that the word was sometimes used to describe the St. George's Channel between Wales and Ireland. But it was also used to describe the Bristol Channel, where the Isle of Lundy is situated, and if one takes the more ancient *Merwcryz,* or *Merwcryd*, which is most probably the spelling Brechfa would have used, this in the Middle Ages referred specifically to 'British seas', or seas around Britain, the word *Merwcryd,* or *Mor Werydh* being extended in the fourteenth century to cover all seas to the west. *Werydh* was derived from the *Oceanus Vergivius* of Ptolemy. The whole sense of the Brechfa narrative is that Madoc had *already* found unnamed and seemingly unknown land out in the ocean and that he returned there with Riryd. Brechfa was a Carmarthenshire man and it is almost certain that if Madoc had sailed from Abergwili he would have heard about it. On the other hand he is undoubtedly one of the sources who named Lundy as the sailing point for the second expedition.

8

THE FIRST EXPEDITION

FROM THE EVIDENCE of the previous chapter it is now possible to deduce that Madoc's departure point for his first voyage was somewhere on the North Wales coast.

From the odes and contemporary records everything suggests that this was somewhere between Abergele and Conway, an area in which between 1169 and 1175 the rule of Dafydd was most disputed. His main sphere of influence was in the district around Rhuddlan Castle in Flintshire. In the *Welsh Port Books* of 1550–1603[1] there is listed in the names of landing places in Caernarvon and Denbighshire during the reign of Henry VII 'Aber Kerrik Gwynyon'. Unfortunately no place of this name appears on any map of the period. But a clue to the exact situation was brought to light by perusal of the details of a lawsuit which was fought in 1687 between the Pughs of Penrhyn (Old Hall) and Robert Davies of Llannerch, who had acquired the lands at Bryn Euryn, formerly belonging to the Conway family. In a rare booklet entitled *The Archaeological History of Llandrillo-yn-Rhos*, the Reverend W. Venables Williams quoted details of this lawsuit, mentioning that Robert Dudley, Earl of Leicester, favourite of Queen Elizabeth who gave him the lordship of Denbigh, rented to Robert Conway some thirty-four acres of marshland known as Morfa Dinerth.

'It is presumed that this marsh was then in the nature of a common and the sea overflowed it at most spring tides in the yeare and soe Mr. Conway little minded it,' the preamble of the lawsuit states. What follows in the preamble is much more interesting and reveals an entirely different picture of the earlier coastline of this stretch of the North Wales coast between Abergele on the east and what is now Great Orme's Head on the west:

'There is a channell on the West side of the marsh that divides the Counties of Denbigh and Caernarvonshire: at the lower end of which channell of water adjoining to the sea was as is reputed a creak wherein Boats and Shipps of 20 or 30 tun might at a certain time of flowing water gett in there and soe lye safe from storms, and soe it hath never continued from beyond memory to 1687. A Mr. Pugh was owner of another marsh that runs along southerly from the sea on the west side of the channell lying in Caernarvonshire (*and*) had under some pretence got some small rent of the marsh in Dinerth in Denbighshire, for many years (perhaps beyond memory) and in 1687 built a bridge upon the creake and stopped the sea from overflowing and also all boates and small vessells from getting in there for shelter in stormy weather.'

In the report of a trial for conspiracy of Yorke and Young in Elizabethan times reference was made to a rising in North Wales and to a 'Mr. Pew', who kept a pinnace in this district – possibly belonging to a member of the family whose name was spelt 'Pugh' and in the very same creek.[2]

The late Rector of Iden, in Kent, the Reverend E. F. Synnott, made a remarkable discovery in a sale-room at Rye in Sussex several years ago. Together with a collection of old books he purchased an assortment of ancient and mould-infected manuscripts which had obviously been rescued from destruction. Many of them were torn in pieces and some charred as though they had been consigned to a bonfire before their previous owner thought better of it. The manuscripts, such as they were, appeared to be some form of port records for the twelfth and thirteenth centuries, compiled partly in Latin and partly in broken English. Mr. Synnott was of the opinion that, though not every manuscript was part of a whole, some of the pieces when placed together added up to what was a list of ships lost, or unaccounted for in various ports of England and Wales.

Map of the world, 1482, from the Nicolai Doni edition of *Ptolemaei Cosmographia*. The Fortunatae Insulae (Fortune Islands) are shown at the extreme Western edge of the map. With each succeeding map they were moved further and further West

In memory of Prince Madoc, a Welsh explorer, who landed on the shores of Mobile Bay in 1170 and left behind, with the Indians, the Welsh language.

Authority is - Encyclopedia Americana copyright 1918 - Webster's Encyclopedia - Richard Hakluyt, 1552 to 1616, a Welsh Historian and Geographer - Ridpath's History of the World - ancient Roman coins found in Forts in Tenn. These Forts resemble the Forts of Wales of the 9th and 10th centuries and of the white Indians of the Tennessee and Missouri rivers.

ERECTED BY THE VIRGINIA CAVALIER CHAPTER OF THE D.A.R.

Above, the commemoration marker of Madoc's landing erected by the Daughters of the American Revolution at Mobile Bay, Alabama; *below*, Mobile Bay from the air, showing the Spanish-built Fort Morgan. The Madoc marker is on the left of the picture, close to the shore

Among the entries was one which particularly interested the Iden rector because he knew something of the Madoc legend. It read:

ABER-KERRIK-GUIGNON:
non sunt
Guignon Gorn, Madauc.
Pedr Sant, Riryd, *filius*
Oueni Gueneti
an. 1171.[3]

In most cases the names of the ship and those presumably of her owner, or master, were given. The purpose of the compiling of the list itself was not clear, but it seemed to be an inventory of missing ships; such ports as Rye, Winchelsea, Bristol and Milford Haven were mentioned and the dates ranged from about 1166 to 1183. It was only partially complete and often indecipherable owing to mould and burns. There was no indication as to whose property it had been, but Mr. Synnott thought it might have formed part of the archives known as *The Black Book of Admiralty*, long since lost. This seems a debatable theory, but it may well have been that from material such as this the mysterious and secret *Black Book* was compiled. Here at any rate was a clear association of Madoc not only with the legendary *Gwennan Gorn*, but also with his brother Riryd, the latter being clearly indicated as a son of Owain Gwynedd.

Why, it may well be asked, was not Riryd named as the discoverer of America instead of Madoc? Madoc was described as just 'Madoc', a mere name to the authorities of the day, but Riryd was positively identified as a son of Owain Gwynedd. The answer here may be that Riryd was known as Lord of Clochran and a possessor of estates in his own right, whereas Madoc was more or less a nomad without estates. Could it be that Riryd's ship was sunk at sea? On the document there were no marks against the name of Madoc's ship, but against that of *Pedr Sant* there was the sign of the Cross and a small indecipherable word. The sign of the Cross may have indicated that this ship was sunk. If, of course, Riryd did reach the New World with his brother, and stayed there, it would be Madoc, the one who returned to Wales, who would take the credit for the discovery.

At least this seems further contemporary proof that Madoc had a ship named *Gwennan Gorn* (which is given a French-corrupted spelling in the ms.) and that in 1171 this ship was missing, or her whereabouts unknown.

An explanation of the purpose of the information assembled here may be found in an ordinance issued in 1181 by King Henry II. This ordinance not only regulated the quantity of arms which persons of various ranks were to furnish for the defence of the realm, but also contained a remarkable clause respecting the Navy. The justices itinerant were commanded to declare in each county that no one under the heaviest penalties should buy or sell any ship to be taken from England or Wales, nor induce any seaman to leave the country.[4]

By this time Henry II's need for shipping was great. Not only did he require to encourage commerce, but he needed ships to mount his expeditions to Ireland and elsewhere. No doubt, too, he had been alarmed at the number of craft which had disappeared from Wales to take dissatisfied Welshmen to Ireland. The ordinance could have led to the compiling of a census of ships, with a careful note of any that appeared to be missing. If he sought such information from Dafydd ap Owain Gwynedd, no doubt the latter would be only too glad to inform him of the defection of his brothers. If scapegoats were needed, then Madoc and Riryd could usefully fill the roles.

The quest for the actual site of Aber Kerrik Gwynyon was a laborious one. There was nothing to help in the way of maps, documentation or records other than the *Welsh Port Books* and Mr. Synnott's find. Mr. Synnott's own theory was that this ancient port may have been known by the abbreviated title of Aber Kerrik, or shortened to 'Aberkerry', and that in this way Herbert had confounded it with Abergwili. But the evidence seems to point to the fact that Abergele – some few miles away from the Caernarvonshire–Denbighshire border – was the place Herbert intended to name.

It was necessary therefore to examine closely the whole history

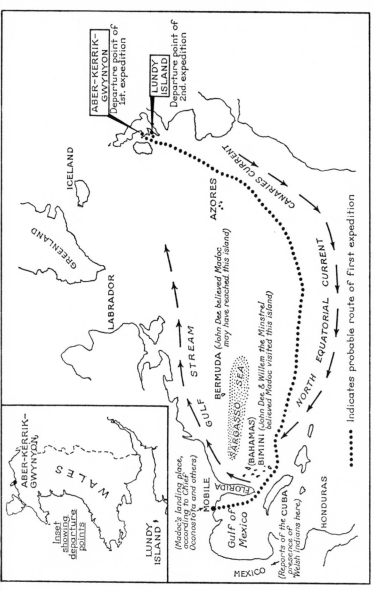

The probable course of Madoc's first expedition

of that region of North Wales on the borders of these two counties, between Conway and what is now known as Rhos-on-Sea, close to Colwyn Bay. Conway itself was obviously ruled out by the fact that Aber Kerrik Gwynyon was not situated there.

Quite fortuitously two clues came into the author's possession almost simultaneously. The first was a letter from Mrs. Victor Wilde, wife of a Justice of the Peace at Rhos-on-Sea, dated October 19, 1965, which stated:

'I have lived here (at Odstone, Rhos-on-Sea) for fifty years, and my father always told me that Prince Madoc set sail for America and left from an old stone pier which is part of my garden, now a rockery, full of flowers. Years ago it was difficult to make a garden here, as the soil was all sea-stone gravel. In my father's time we had antiquarians examining the remains of the old pier and they declared the concrete was as old as that of Conway Castle, the secret of which has been lost.'[5]

Mrs. Wilde enclosed photographs of her rockery, which clearly revealed that the structure was that of a very ancient wall.

Mr. Norman Tucker, of the Caernarvonshire Historical Association, who is a leading authority on this history of the area, confirmed that there is a local legend that Madoc sailed from these parts, but that there appeared to be no evidence how this arose. It merely seemed to be a case of a story handed down the ages solely by word of mouth. The first sentence of Mr. Tucker's letter to me provided a further clue: 'It is correct that Mrs. Wilde's home stands at the old mouth of the Afon Ganol, and there is a rockery in the grounds with masonry of some ancient structure. I have seen documents concerning an old lawsuit (National Library of Wales, Gwysaney Papers), which show that at certain tides vessels of 20 to 30 tons could take shelter in this "creek" in Stuart times. The draining of the marsh and the building of the sea wall has altered the complexion greatly.'[6]

Afon Ganol! That was the missing piece in the jig-saw puzzle. There was that phrase in Cynfric ap Gronow's lines:

> '. . . *Was turned back to Afon Ganol's quay*
> *For Madoc's famous voyage.*'

A *Souvenir of Llandrillo-yn Rhos* was written by the local curate, the Reverend T. E. Timothy, in 1910. He stated that 'when the sewerage pipes in connection with the drainage scheme carried out by the Colwyn Bay Urban District Council in 1907 were being laid, the Contractor, at a spot near the lowest watermark, had to cut through a wall about six feet in width – evidently an old stone dyke erected to withstand the sea'.

Mr. Tucker, however, thinks that the 'dyke' inference was wrong, and that the wall more probably had some association with the old stone pier.

Leland wrote: 'There is northwards in Credine a bay or rode very goode for shippis, and that greate, caullid Carrig Gonnyon Anglice White Stonys.'[7]

Carrig Gonnyon is obviously a corruption of Aber Kerrik Gwynyon, and a farm which stood here until about half a century ago was known as Rhyd y Cerrig Gwynion.

There are other witnesses to the site being used by shipping. Old Price mentioned Robert Foulkes, of the Rising Sun Inn, which stood beside the old highway in Pwllycrochan Woods, Colwyn Bay, recalling 'men who should say they had seen vessels in the aforesaid River Afon Ganol, under Llandrillo Church'.[8]

From the slopes south of Mochdre the small river, known in ancient times as Afon Ganol, and then almost certainly larger and certainly much more important, wound its way across the swamps to the sea, actually forming the boundary of Denbighshire and Caernarvonshire. An artificial cut now takes the water to the sea, but the river's original bank before it reaches the shore crosses the ornamental gardens of Odstone, the home of Mr. and Mrs. Wilde.

'Their drive,' writes Mr. Tucker, 'passes over the crest of an ancient wall of masonry now disguised as a rockery. This is reputed to be a fragment of an old quay.'[9]

It is important to note that there is an ancient wall, probably the remains of sea defences, which is quite distinct from the stonework in the gardens of Odstone. The masonry of this is lost to sight when it nears the rails of the Llandudno and Colwyn Bay Electric Railway, beyond which stretches a rough coastal road protected by a now derelict sea wall. This wall is undoubtedly old, but not as old as the remains of the quay.

In September, 1955, when a new sea wall was being erected between Penrhyn Bay and Rhos-on-Sea, excavations made it possible for the remains of the Odstone stonework to be inspected. From this inspection it was possible to reconstruct a fairly accurate picture of the original. The rockery wall, after being lost to sight by the construction of the road, extended to the west, fanning out into two walls which widened from 7 to 9 ft. apart before they disappeared. It seems probable that the walls originally made an even wider gap farther on, but that a section of this stonework was demolished when the other sea wall was built. In Mr. Tucker's opinion the walls formed a channel by which the Afon Ganol River was directed seawards.

Everything, whether from an historical, documentary, archaeological, geographical or nautical viewpoint, suggests that the flower-filled rockery of Odstone marks all that is left today of Madoc's most probable port of departure.

As to the type of ship in which he sailed, this can only be a matter of conjecture. Again one can only guess how many ships went with him on this first expedition, or whether he went alone, whether there were one hundred and twenty persons accompanying him, as Herbert asserted, or possibly a mere twenty. All one knows is that the number of ships seems to have grown with the legend – from three to thirteen – and so do the personnel – from thirty to more than three hundred.

By the fifteenth century at least the legend had been developed from one, or possibly two, missing ships to the story of a large expedition. It is almost impossible to accept that there was a large expedition. The departure of ten or more ships would have been very difficult to have gone unnoticed. It would almost certainly have attracted the attention of the bards and found its way more positively into history. Apart from that there is the question of the financing of a large expedition. It is highly unlikely that one man, let alone a man who was in no position of power, could have obtained possession of as many as ten ships and been able to man and provision them. It is even less likely that he would have been able to persuade as many men to undertake such a voyage into the unknown.

It is much more likely that the voyage was more or less a lone expedition, with probably no more than two ships. The cost of building a modest-sized, sturdy ship would not be great, provided there was access to ample timber, such as there would be in the near-by woods of Nant Gwynant. One cannot accurately gauge the cost, as no comparable figures are available. But what was within the means of Saint Brandon and a few poor Irish peasants centuries before should not have been beyond the scope of Madoc's purse. Ship repairs and masters' fees in those days should be multiplied by a hundred to give a comparison with modern costs. In the same period it was recorded that Henry II paid £12 15s. for repair of the 'Bishop of Durham's Great Shippe', while a mere 13s. 4d. was paid to Robert de Stockton for his services as master for a voyage from Stockton to London.[10]

There are no contemporary sketches of ships of the period by which to reconstruct a picture of *Gwennan Gorn*. The nearest one can get to accuracy is to recreate one of the ancient ships depicted on the seals of the old ports. Most of these seals are, however, of English ports, and there is every reason to believe that Madoc's craft would owe more to Irish and Danish influences in ship-building. His grandfather, who was a seaman, had closer associations with Ireland and the Scandinavian Irish than did Owain Gwynedd. During the preceding century, if not earlier, there had been a fundamental change in the design of all Irish trading vessels, and planked vessels certainly plied between Ireland and Wales. Not all these ships required great technical skill in their construction; some of them were really scooped-out canoes of a very large size (large enough to transport timber and produce from one country to another). For this type of ship the rate for the job in that particular age would not even apply, according to the Brehon laws, and they were tackled by unskilled labour.

Some planked vessels of this period are believed to have combined as a safety measure some of the technique of *curragh* and coracle building with that of the more orthodox design. Quite often the finished craft would be covered with cow-hide, tanned in oak bark, with the joints tarred. If, as is probable for one who had been to Ireland and Lundy Island, where Icelandic and Danish influences were marked, Madoc put into the design of his ship ideas he had acquired on his travels, he possibly aimed to combine the best of several plans from various types of craft. From what little we know of ship-building in the British Isles in the twelfth century, one can assume his ship would have a single mast with a large square sail, that was buoyant and tubby, with a straight keel to take the beach without strain at an ebb tide, and possibly had a stern rudder, hung on the stern-post by means of pintles. She would have been slow and clumsy to handle, but with the advantage of requiring a much smaller crew than a lateen-rigged Mediterranean craft, possibly as few as twenty with half a dozen unskilled apprentices.

One need not pay much attention to the romantic descriptions of Madoc's ship by some of the early poets – 'a magic ship that could not sink' – but one can accept the use of stag horns in the place of nails as being a seamanlike if unorthodox innovation. When nails were of poor quality, the early Norse ship-builders did likewise; they also used stag's horns as fairleads and bollards. What is perhaps more important is that the use of stag's horns in place of nails is a further pointer to a planked ship and not a curragh.

To what other countries Madoc had sailed before making his Atlantic voyage is uncertain. As we have seen, contemporary writers all suggest he had visited 'foreign lands' and was widely travelled. The fact that the story of Madoc was known on the Continent suggests that he almost certainly touched some parts of Europe. The Madoc legend has circulated in Brittany and Provence, though there he has become *Saint* Matteau, which could show that his voyage has been confused with that of St. Brandon. The Bretonese legend is pure folk-lore, without any documentation of any kind, as far as one is able to ascertain, but the picture one has of him is of a kind of medieval ambassador–sailor–minstrel. Perhaps it was from Brittany that Joan Dane obtained her imaginative portraits of the minstrel-Prince. Madoc's grandfather, Gruffydd ap Conan, was a patron of minstrels and one of his chief legislative achievements was the revision of the minstrelsy laws which refused to recognize any minstrels who were not admitted to the triennial Eisteddfod. If Madoc was an emissary of Gwynedd on the Isle of Lundy, it is equally possible that he may have been sent to the court of the French King.

Motives for Madoc's urge to sail west have to some extent already been established. One knows that many in Gwynedd were so unhappy, so disillusioned and terrorized by the régime of Dafydd that they emigrated to Ireland. It is clear that Dafydd outlawed and exiled some of his brothers; he may have threatened Madoc's life and made it essential he should escape from his native land. It is possible, too, that Madoc paid rather more attention to the legends of land in the west than did most of his contemporaries. The combination of these factors would probably suffice for a motive.

Yet there is one other theoretical motive, and the sole reason for mentioning it is that it was attributed to Madoc by Willem the Minstrel and it could partly explain Llywarch's *Ode to the Hot Iron*.

According to Willem, Madoc undertook his voyage as a penance inflicted on him by a bard.[11] Such penances were on occasions imposed by priests in the early ages. Quite a few such penances are recorded in Spanish history and perhaps a classic case of its kind was that related in the Life of St. Patrick. One Mac-Cuill, a sinner who sincerely wished for repentance, was ordered by St. Patrick to place himself at the mercy of God in a curragh without a paddle.

But there is no instance of this type of penance being imposed by a bard, though without doubt some bards were so powerful that their commands, however strange and outrageous, were obeyed. Could it be that Llywarch knew that Dafydd wished Madoc out of the way, and that he imposed on Madoc the penance of sailing away as an exile in search of other lands? This would explain his remorse and his plea that his was not the hand that had slain Madoc, if and when, with the lapse of time, it was presumed that Madoc and his ship were lost.

9

THE ORIGINS OF THE WELSH INDIANS LEGEND

MR. JOCK WHITNEY, a former United States Ambassador to the United Kingdom, has declared that while the population of Wales is only 2,500,000, there are six million persons of Welsh descent in the U.S.A.

Ninety-nine per cent of the American Welsh came to America after Elizabethan times, and most of the odd one per cent must have been the relative shipful who may have landed with the Tudor explorers. There was no substantial migration of Welsh people across the Atlantic until the seventeenth century, when religious persecution drove them from their homelands. Religion was always the driving force of the Welsh whether in politics or home-making customs. One of the earliest to go was Roger Williams, founder of the state of Rhode Island, and the apostle of civil and religious liberty in America. He became a Nonconformist minister and sought asylum in the New World in 1631, settling at Salem, that centre of witch-hunting, where he was driven from his pastorate because of his 'new and dangerous opinions against the authority of magistrates'. Founding the city of Providence, Rhode Island, he procured for it a charter and became first president of the colony.

An especially interesting link with the Madoc story was the arrival in Charleston, Massachusetts, in 1636, of the Merrick brothers, who sailed from Bristol in the *James*. The Merricks were descended from Meyrick ap Llewellyn, whose father, Llewellyn ap Heylin, fought at Bosworth on the side of Henry Tudor and was, through the Heylins of Bodorgan, a reputed descendant of Madoc. The Merrick crest is still to be found on colonial silver in the U.S.A. One of the brothers, William, married a daughter of a Great Yarmouth family and they settled at Cape Cod.

The Quakers were among the first Welshmen to emigrate, and they were soon followed by the Baptists and other Nonconformists. Many Welsh Quakers sailed with William Penn to establish the colony of Pennsylvania, and their influence is felt today in the settlement of Brynmawr, Penn., and the famous women's college there where the hostels bear familiar Welsh names. Welshmen were also among the Pilgrim Fathers, and in Pennsylvania many towns bear Welsh names such as Gwynedd and St. David's.

It was perhaps in the realm of political thought and action which led to the Declaration of Independence that Welsh influence was most remarkable. The quest of the early colonists for a coherent expression of their philosophy of liberalism was eventually crystallized by Dr. Richard Price, who wrote a pamphlet entitled *The Nature of Civic Liberty*, which gave these early gropings for the truth purpose and a code of life.

Among the generals of Revolution were such Welshmen as Daniel Morgan, John Cadwaladr, Andrew Lewis, Morgan Lewis, John Thomas, Joseph Williams and James Reese.

Thomas Jefferson's ancestors came from Snowdonia and some of his co-signatories to the Declaration of Independence were of Welsh origin. Among them were William Williams, Lewis Morris and Francis Lewis. The last-named was a native of Llandaff and sat as a member of the Committee of One Hundred; his son, Morgan Lewis, became Governor of New York in 1804.

The vast majority of these migrant Welshmen were from the villages and remote country places of Wales, and they naturally sought similar territories in America, settling prolifically in Indiana, Illinois, Wisconsin and Minnesota. A few centuries later they joined the great trek of the Mormons to Utah, and it is interesting to note that incidents of the Madoc legend and of the supposed migrations of his colony are paralleled in *The Book of Mormon*, published by Joseph Smith at Palmyra in 1830. The Brigham Young University at Provo, forty miles distant from Salt Lake City, has a collection of Welsh Americans and intends ultimately to set up a Department of Welsh American Studies. Yale, too, is another American university with links with Wales, and one of its towers is a replica of Wrexham Church.

The first report from America of any confirmation of the Madoc story is said to be that of Captain John Smith, of Jamestown, in 1621. This, however, can be discounted as corroboration because a close examination of Captain Smith's opinions reveals that he must have copied almost word for word from Dr. Powel's book.[1]

First narratives of the presence of 'Welsh' Indians in America came from Spanish and English explorers, but it was not until the Welsh emigrants themselves arrived in large numbers that detailed accounts of such a tribe, or tribes, became available. The early European reports were, naturally enough, scanty and lacking in reasoned comparisons with the Welsh, as the earliest explorers either had no knowledge of Welsh customs and language, or at best only the most superficial acquaintance with them.

One of the earliest accounts by a Welshman about the existence of Welsh Indians was contained in a remarkable letter written on March 10, 1686, by the Reverend Morgan Jones, the minister of a church in the neighbourhood of New York, to Dr. Thomas Lloyd, of New York. This letter was eventually presented by Dr. Lloyd to Edward Llwyd, Keeper of the Ashmolean Museum at Oxford.

In the letter Morgan Jones described how in the year 1666, when he was chaplain to Major-General Bennett, the Governor of Virginia, he was sent by ship to Carolina. Having landed at a place named Oyster Point, he and his party suffered great hardships until lack of provisions induced them to travel back to Virginia overland. 'I and five more travelled through the wilderness till we came to Tuscarora Country. There the Tuscora [*sic*] Indians took us prisoners ... That night they took us to their town and shut us close to our no small dread.

'The next day they entered into consultation about us, which after it was over the interpreter told us that we must prepare to die the next morning. Thereupon, being much dejected, and speaking to this effect in British [Welsh] tongue: "Have I escaped so many dangers and must I now be knocked on the head like a dog?" Presently an Indian came to me which afterwards appeared to be a War Captain belonging to the Sachem of the Doegs, whose origin I find is from the old British, and took me and told me in the British tongue that I should not die, and thereupon went to the Emperor and agreed for my ransom.

'They then welcomed me to their town where they had entertained us for four months during which time I had the opportunity of conversing with them familiarly, and did preach to them three times a week in the same language and they would confer with me about anything that was difficult therein; and at our departure they supplied us with what was necessary to our support and well being.

'This is a brief recital of my travels among the Doeg Indians. They are settled on the Pontiago River, not far from Camp Atros. I am ready to conduct any Welshman, or others, to the country'.

It is, indeed, a brief recital, and there is no evidence that his information was followed up, or that any expedition was made to the Tuscarora country. Possibly attempts were made to check the report, but no confirmation was forthcoming: twenty-six years after the event it would not be easy to trace this same tribe of Indians. One cannot help wondering why Morgan Jones waited so long before he set his experiences on paper and why even then he gave such a meagre account of the whole affair, with no corroboration by his companions, whose names were not even mentioned. The offer to conduct other Welshmen to Tuscarora country to confirm his story may well have been bluff. One cannot regard this as serious evidence of the existence of the Welsh Indians, even though Morgan Jones was a graduate of Oxford. Professor David Williams, who has made some study of the story, writes that 'what we know of Morgan Jones shows that he was a person of rather doubtful character'.[2] On the other hand he offers no evidence of what might have been 'doubtful' about this clergyman.

Professor Williams gives as the most damning indictment of Morgan Jones's story the fact that nobody, either at that time or since, had heard of a tribe or sect of Indians called the Doegs. But this is not quite accurate. Paul Marana, a native of Italy, who had led an adventurous life in espionage, living for forty-five years in Paris without being discovered, published in 1673 his *Letters writ by a Turkish Spy*, in which he refers not merely to the Doegs as being an Indian tribe reputedly descended from the Welsh, but mentions the Sachem as well. This was written seven years after the incident described by Morgan Jones is said to have occurred, but thirteen years before the clergyman wrote his account of the affair. It would not seem likely, therefore, that Marana had heard of Morgan Jones's adventure. This is perhaps the sole reason for giving the clergyman the benefit of the doubt.

As so often happens with the story of Madoc, the account of Morgan Jones finding the Welsh Indians has been distorted by other writers to such an extent that truth is often buried beneath a mound of lies. Alexander von Rumboldt, who examined some of these reports, was sceptical about the whole affair and described them as 'periodically rehearsed fables'.[3]

One example of how Morgan Jones's story was twisted out of all recognition is provided by such an authority on American Indians as Samuel Drake. Referring to the Morgan Jones account, he wrote: 'The clergyman, in preparation for another world, prayed in the Welsh language. One or more of the Indians was surprised to hear him pray in their own language. Upon this they spoke to him, and, finding he could understand them, got the sentence of death reversed, and his life was saved. They took him with them into their own country, where he found a tribe whose native language was Welsh ... They showed him a book which he found to be the Bible, but which they could not read; and on his reading and explaining it, their regard for him was much heightened.'[4]

One must assume that Drake had not read the Morgan Jones letter, for this is a highly coloured and exaggerated version of the same story and the Virginian Governor's chaplain never mentioned anything about a Bible. Drake's source for this statement was

Charles Beatty, a missionary from New York, in whose journal this incident is mentioned as having been told to him.

Dr. John Williams also mentioned a clergyman taken prisoner by the Indians in Virginia who had a language almost identical with Welsh. 'They produced a book which he found to be the Bible, but which they could not read,' declared Dr. Williams.[5] As this clergyman is not named we must assume that this, like Drake's story, is simply another version of the Morgan Jones narrative.

A keen sense of the ridiculous is an essential qualification for anybody probing some of these accounts of the Welsh Indians and it would seem that this was often lacking among those who so soberly, but without a touch of humour, recorded the stories. The idea of the Indians being impressed by a reading from the Bible is somewhat far-fetched, however heartening this might be as propaganda for would-be missionaries.

At some date between 1660 and 1665 a Welsh sailor named Stedman from Brecon was shipwrecked in the Atlantic and washed ashore somewhere between Florida and Virginia, which, geographically speaking, makes his story somewhat hard to assess. He was found by Indians and claimed to recognize the language they spoke as being similar to Welsh. When he replied to them in that language they expressed astonishment, were extremely friendly and 'supplied him with the best things they had. They told Stedman that their ancestors came from a country named *Gwynedd* in *Prydain Fawr* (Great Britain)'.[6]

Unfortunately, like the Morgan Jones episode, this story was not put on record until 1777, when the Reverend N. Owen published his account of it as told to him in a letter from one Charles Lloyd.

There is no confirmation of Stedman's adventure, though Charles Lloyd also related in corroboration of it that one Oliver Humphreys, a merchant of Surinam, had told him that the master of an English ship, while repairing his vessel at a remote part of the Florida coast, became acquainted with the Indian tongue spoken there and afterwards found it to be similar to Welsh.

What is possible is that in some instances travellers meeting the

Indians mistook some of their phrases for Welsh words and out of this was built a legend of Welsh-speaking Indians. Sir Walter Raleigh produced some evidence of Indian words that were identical with Welsh words of the same meaning, and he claimed that some colonists were greeted by Indians shouting 'Hao, houi, iach' and 'Yachi Tha', which, though grossly misspelt, might phonetically be interpreted as Welsh.

Nevertheless, sceptical though one may be of these early accounts of Welsh Indians, the fact is that as the years passed by there was abundant evidence, much of it more factual and authenticated than that already given, that travellers and administrators had met Indians who not only claimed ancestry with the Welsh, but spoke a language remarkably like it and were able to understand Welsh when it was spoken. It must also be borne in mind that though the number of Welsh-speaking emigrants was growing towards the end of the seventeenth century they still formed a small minority of the total population. For this reason alone the probability is that the Welsh-speaking Indians would almost have died out before they were discovered. Other Europeans coming into contact with them would not have the knowledge to identify them.

In fact some Europeans were baffled by the 'white Indians' whom they came across. Father Charlevoix, a Catholic priest, travelled from Canada to the Mississippi in 1721 and made a study of the history, religion, language and customs of various Indian tribes. Some Indians, whom he called the Aiouaz (probably the Iowas), told him 'that the Omans, three days journey from them, had white skins and fair hair, especially the women'.[7]

In 1735 the Sieur de la Verendrye, a French explorer, set out on a lengthy expedition into the interior of America in quest of a strange tribe who were reputed to live in earth-covered lodges. Verendrye was a cultured man and a competent and painstaking observer and in his travels he met a large number of Indian tribes and made copious notes of comparisons between their modes of living. But the mysterious tribe he sought were said to be the Mandans, who lived close to the Missouri River. After a trek lasting some months Verendrye eventually came across the

A section of John Evans's map showing the Mandan Villages

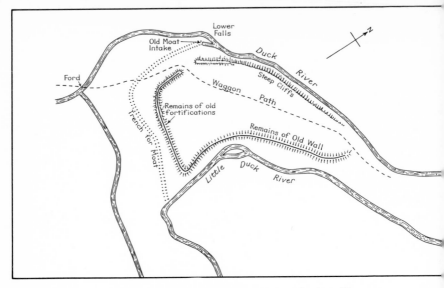

A map of the ancient fortifications at Duck River, Tennessee

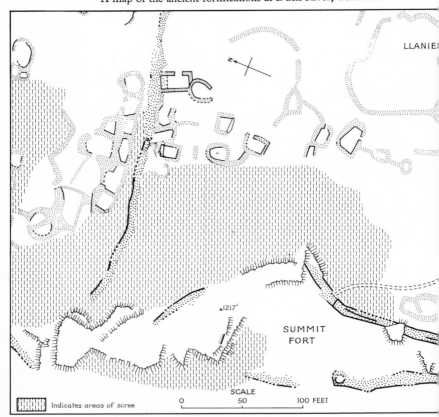

Plan of the remains of the 'Castle of the Sons of Owain'. Mentioned in Giraldi Cambrensis in 1188 as being 'newly built', it bears a striking resemblance to some of the features of the ancient fortifications in Tennessee

Mandans and received an invitation from one of their chiefs to stay among his tribe as a guest. Thus in 1738 we get the first authentic account of this then almost unknown tribe.

Verendrye found that in their customs and mode of living the Mandans differed from every other Indian tribe he had met. They had fair skins and lived in villages which were laid out in streets and squares. The streets were kept scrupulously clean, and lodges were made of a framework of logs over which earth was piled several feet thick. This mass of earth was shaped into rounded domes. Smoke from their fires escaped from a hole in the roof. They lived more by cultivating their land than by hunting as did other Indians, growing beans, corn, fruits and vegetables.[8]

Though their villages were permanent, they lived in constant fear of invasion by other more warlike tribes, not without reason for before the end of that century the Sioux forced their removal from that area, killing off many of them. A Mandan chief told de la Verendrye that they were the first human inhabitants of that part of the world and that they used to live far to the south, but had been driven north by their enemies. Verendrye felt sure that they must have some trace of European ancestry as one of the Mandans wore a cross and spoke the names of Jesus and Mary. Finally, Verendrye paid them a considerable compliment, coming from a Frenchman: he declared the Mandans were excellent cooks and prepared dishes which would have done credit to a European household. Fascinated by what he had discovered, he left behind him two men to learn the Mandan language.

The fact that these men found 'a few words not unlike the dialect of Brittany' is interesting. The Welsh language has affinities with that of Brittany and several Welsh words resemble those of the same meaning in French, for example *eglwys* and *église* (both meaning 'church').

The next visitor to the Mandans after the Sieur de la Verendrye was Maximilian, another French explorer and friend of Verendrye. He reported that the Mandans were 'rather above medium stature, many of them robust, broad-shouldered and muscular. Their noses, not so long and arched as those of the Sioux, were sometimes aquiline or slightly curved, sometimes quite straight, never broad, nor had they the high cheek-bones of the Sioux . . . Their villages were assemblages of circular, clay-covered huts placed close together. They were surrounded by palisades of strong posts. The huts were slightly vaulted and provided with porticos. The interior was spacious. Four strong pillars near the middle, with several crossbeams, supported the roof. The beds, against the walls, consisted of skins and blankets'.[9]

Maurice Griffith came from Wales to America when he was quite a young man and in 1764 he was taken prisoner in Virginia by the Shawnee Indians. The latter were friendlily disposed and took him on a hunting expedition to penetrate to the source of the Missouri River. High up in the mountains Griffith's party came across three 'white men in Indian dress', with whom they travelled for some days until they arrived at a village where there were others of the same tribe.

'After proceeding with them four or five days' journey they came to the village of these white men, where they found the whole nation of the same colour, all having the European complexion. . . . A council lasted three days and Griffith was present; he had not admitted that he knew their language. It was finally decided that the six strangers should be put to death, and Griffith thought the time had arrived for him to speak. He addressed the council in the Welsh language, said they had not been sent by any warlike nation and that they were actuated by curiosity and had no hostile intentions; that they merely wished to trace the Missouri to its source and they would return to their country satisfied with the discovery they had made without any wish to disturb the repose of their new acquaintances.

'Astonishment glowed in the countenance not only of the council, but of his Shawnee companions who clearly saw that he was understood. Confidence was given to his declarations. The King advanced and gave him his hand and from that moment they were treated with the utmost friendship. Griffith and his five Shawnee companions remained with the nation eight months. As to the history of these people Griffith could learn nothing satisfactory. All they knew was that their ancestors had come up the river from a very distant country. They had intermixed with no other people by marriage and there was not a dark-skinned man in the nation.'[10]

Griffith and his party returned to the Shawnee settlements after an absence of two years and six months, and Griffith himself returned to Virginia where his story seems to have arroused little or no curiosity. Not until May, 1805, was any kind of confirmation found of Griffith's narrative, and then Major Amos Stoddard, author of *Sketches of Louisiana*, met a Frenchman in upper Louisiana. This man had for several years been employed by English traders and his usual station was at the trading house on the Assiniboine, a few days' journey from the Mandans on the Missouri. He also had explored the Missouri and found its source in a large lake from which the Missouri flowed. 'The publication of the narrative of Griffith suggested the propriety of some inquiry relative to the Indians about the head of the Missouri,' wrote Major Stoddard.[11] 'The informant declared (and he sustains the character of a man of truth) that there was a numerous and singular nation of Indians about the lake, who were not in the least tawny, but rather of a yellowish complexion; that they wear their beards and that great numbers of them had red hair on their heads.'

Major Stoddard also quoted Vancouver as having found a people in the vicinity of Columbia River 'speaking a language different from that of their neighbours, and in features resembling the northern Europeans'.

Charles Beatty, the missionary from New York, was the one man in this period who took the trouble to investigate the reports of Welsh Indians and to collect corroborative accounts following on the story he had heard of the Virginian clergyman. His diary, which has been cited by such authorities as Dr. John Williams, Samuel Drake and others, contains detailed narratives of anecdotes he gleaned during his travels.

On one of these journeys, made in 1755, Charles Beatty accompanied by a Mr. Duffield, travelled about four hundred miles south of New York. He came across several people who had spent much time among the Indians during their youth and among these was a man named Benjamin Sutton. Sutton talked freely of his experiences among the Indians, saying that when he was with the Choctaw tribe at a very considerable distance from New Orleans he came across a tribe who were of a different complexion and who spoke Welsh. How he knew that the language was Welsh is not explained: it would seem from Beatty's narrative that Sutton expressed this opinion only after Beatty had cross-examined him on the theory. He then claimed that he had heard one of the Indians converse in Welsh with a Captain Lewis, who was one of their prisoners. According to Sutton, this 'Welsh tribe' then lived on the west side of the Missouri River, 'a great distance above New Orleans'.[12]

The reliability of Sutton's evidence, however, was rather spoiled by his claim that he saw a book in the keeping of the Indians, wrapped up in an otter skin, and which he supposed was a 'Welsh Bible'. This sounds suspiciously like another version of the Virginian clergyman's find, and as the alleged finding of such books occurs quite frequently in some of the accounts of the Welsh Indians, without any book ever being produced as evidence, such narratives can, with about one exception, be regarded as suspect. The only other interesting observations made by Sutton were that both men and women of the tribe kept the rites of Mosaic law; the former 'observed the feasts of the first fruits' and the latter periodically 'separated seven days from the men', it being added that these rites had been handed down to them by their founder 'who had escaped from a land far off after a battle between his brothers for possession of his father's lands'.

Sutton was questioned closely on this statement, for Charles Beatty does not appear to have known at that time any details of the story of Madoc. Sutton replied that the Indians counted the passing of each spring by adding a bead of black wampumon to a long belt that was kept as a calendar. According to the Indians there were 370 beads on the belt which indicated the date of their origin. It was not clear from Sutton's version of this whether this date marked their arrival in this territory or the arrival of their founder from overseas, but he thought it was probably the former.

It is clear from the observations of those like Drake and Dr. Williams, who investigated Beatty's narratives, that Benjamin

Sutton was well known, highly regarded and that he lived at the foot of the Alleghany Mountains in Pennsylvania. Most of these early researchers posed the question of whether the Welsh Indians might have descended from Welsh immigrants who had arrived in America since 1600. It was a fair enough question, but in every case witnesses were certain that this was not possible. The Welsh, when they arrived in America, tended to keep together: it was unthinkable that in less than 150 years they could have lost their identity by being assimilated in an Indian tribe, or that they would not have been able to give a detailed account of their origins. Had any 'Welsh Bibles' been produced, of course, this would have pointed to their origins dating back only to the era of the Pilgrim Fathers.

Charles Beatty's next witness was one, Lewis (or Levi) Hicks, whom he met in the Tuscarora Valley. Hicks had lived among Indians since his youth and knew quite a number of their dialects. He told Beatty that when he once attended a gathering of Indians on the west side of the Mississippi River he heard them speaking a strange dialect which his interpreter, an Indian named Joseph Peepy, declared to be Welsh, 'as he had been acquainted with Welsh people and knew some of the words they used'.

Beatty's journal of these various anecdotes is the most useful of the early narratives of the legendary Welsh Indians, but neither Drake nor Dr. Williams have attempted to find corroborative evidence for the more important statements. Both men touch on the story of the Reverend Morgan Jones, of which they give widely varying versions. Drake even suggests that Morgan Jones promised the Welsh Indians that he would return to Britain, bring back some of his friends and get them to instruct the tribe in Christianity. This is in marked contrast to other reports of Welsh Indians, which suggest they had some inkling at least of the Christian religion. Whether or not Morgan Jones was a charlatan, as some even of his countrymen believed, he certainly lacked missionary zeal in not keeping this promise, if indeed he made it. The most charitable excuse that can be advanced in his favour is that he died after returning to Britain.

Dr. Williams also quotes a 'Mr. Jones' – no relative of Morgan –

who went to Pennsylvania with his family about 1750, and met a Welshman who claimed to have met a Welsh Indian. This friend had a 'house in North Carolina, situated on the Great Indian Road to Charlestown, where he often lodged parties . . . in one of these parties an Indian, hearing the family speaking Welsh, began to jump and caper as if he had gone out of his senses. Being asked what was the matter with him, he replied, "I know an Indian Nation who speak that language and have learned a little of it myself, by living among them," and when he was examined he was found to have some knowledge of it. Being promised a handsome reward he said he would endeavour to bring some of them to that part of the country, but Mr. Jones, soon after returning to England, never heard any more of the Indian'.[13]

About the year 1764 Captain Isaac Stewart, of the Provincial Cavalry of South Carolina, was captured by the Indians some fifty miles to the west of Fort Pitt. Some of his comrades were summarily executed, but the gallant captain appears to have endeared himself to a woman of the tribe who saved him from death by paying for his ransom with a horse. After two years in captivity a Spaniard, who had been sent from Mexico on an exploratory expedition, visited the tribe and requested the chief to redeem Captain Stewart and a Welshman named John David. The chief acceded to the request and Stewart and David set off with the Spaniard, crossing the Mississippi near Red River, up which they travelled for seven hundred miles.

In his personal account of this expedition Stewart stated: '. . . we came to a nation of Indians, remarkably white and whose hair was a reddish colour, at least mostly so. The day after our arrival the Welshman informed me that he was determined to remain with them, giving as a reason that he understood their language, it being very little different from the Welsh.

'My curiosity was excited very much by this information, and I went with my companion to the chief men of the town, who informed him (in a language that I had no knowledge of, and which had no affinity to that of any of other Indian tongues that I ever heard) that their forefathers in this nation came from a foreign country, and landed on the east side of the Mississippi, describing particularly the country called Florida, and that on the Spaniards taking possession of Mexico, they fled to their then abode.

'And, as a proof of what he had advanced, he brought forth rolls of parchment, which were carefully tied up in otter skins, on which were large characters written with blue ink. The characters I did not understand, and the Welshman, being unacquainted with letters, I was not able to know the meaning of the writing. They are a bold, hardy and intrepid people, very warlike, and the women beautiful, when compared with the other Indians.'[14]

That the women were beautiful compared to those of other Indian tribes one can accept not only from Captain Stewart's enthusiastic account of them – 'high-browed, blueish eyes and perfect lips' – but also from George Catlin's paintings of the female members of the tribe. It is also hard to believe that John David would have stayed behind and thrown in his lot with this tribe unless he appreciated their womenfolk, for he was, from all accounts, an enthusiastic and even discriminating hunter of the female sex.

A Welsh seaman named Patrick Watkins made a brief single-handed attempt to revive the Mandan tribe in the early part of the nineteenth century. How he met the tribe is a mystery, as also is the method he used to entice two of their women to set up a colony with him in Charles Island in the Galapagos group – a far cry from Mandan territory. On the east side of Charles Island Patrick's exploits are immortalized in a bay known as Pat's Landing, a more lasting memorial to a remarkable man than that provided by some of the scribblings he left for posterity and the fascinating account of him given in the *Journal* of Captain David Porter, of the United States Navy, published in New York in 1822.

Watkins succeeded in raising potatoes and pumpkins in his *ménage à trois* paradise, where the two women did the work while he lay in the shade and gave orders. These products he generally exchanged for rum, or sold for cash when passing ships hove in sight. He waylaid sailors from these ships when they were rash enough to go ashore on Charles Island and enlisted them as slaves under his command while he lived with his paramours in a state of savage luxury. He was from all accounts a frighteningly ferocious and savage individual, unkempt, with matted red hair and beard, and barbarous in his habits. Yet though a drunken ruffian he appears to have possessed a certain amount of education and a sense of humour. To the outer world he sometimes posed as an Irishman, but more often vaunted his Welsh ancestry, claiming descent from the ancient Kings of Britain. No doubt he was a liar, but his adventures were no work of fiction. By some means he came in possession of an old musket and a few charges of powder and ball. By luring sailors ashore, getting them drunk on the rum with which he plied them and then hiding them until their ships had sailed, he acquired for himself no fewer than five slaves who, being utterly dependent on Patrick, were forced to do his bidding.

Whereas a *ménage à trois* was a manageable proposition, the advent of the slaves ultimately created difficulties. While two of the slaves were apparently carrying out all Patrick's orders without murmur, they were also secretly carrying on with one of the two Mandan women. When Patrick found out, the population of the island was reduced to two, Patrick and the sole surviving woman. By a trick he stole a boat that was landed from one of the English ships and set off in search of a new paradise, leaving behind him the following letter for the captain of the English ship:

From the LAST KING OF THE WELSH INDIANS.
Sir,
I have made many applications to captains of vessels to sell me a boat, but have always been met with a refusal. This time I have taken the law into my own hands. I have spent much time endeavouring to establish my kingdom here and to create a worthwhile life, intending to found a new nation of Welshmen with the two Mandan ladies who because of their own Welsh ancestry when their original King landed in America are the proper material for joining a fellow-Welshmen in plural matrimony, the only course to take when one has to found a new race.

I have no complaints against the women. They worked hard and were pleasant to have intercourse with, having a

very proper regard for the undoubted fact that the act of pro-
creation is something to be prolonged if those indulging are
to get the best out of it. True they have the same bad habit of
all Welsh women that they talk when copulating, but as we
speak much the same language – in part at least – I could
always give the command for silence. Talk on such occasions
only wastes a man's strength for the real purpose of the night.

It was the blackhearted, scurvy English seamen who be-
trayed my good women. For that reason only I must start
again.

You are at liberty to take what I leave behind. There are
potatoes and pumpkins and the hens are good layers.

MANDAN WATKINS, KING.[15]

From Captain Porter's account it would seem that Watkins
returned once more to Charles Island and, for a time, resumed his
old life, though no longer consoled by womenfolk. Once again he
stole a boat and escaped from the island, this time leaving behind
him another letter, signed 'Fatherless Oberlus', and telling the
finder, 'Do not kill the old hen; she is now sitting, and will soon
have chickens.'

He arrived alone at Guyaquil in his open boat and then went on
to Payta, where he joined forces with a tawny damsel, whom he
persuaded to come back with him to Charles Island. But on the
eve of his departure he was arrested and clapped into Payta jail.

Patrick Watkins's contribution to the Welsh Indian history is
perhaps the most amusing of all, even if it is the tallest of the stories.
What is so remarkable is that a seaman with such undoubted gifts
for letter-writing should have had such a beachcombing and disre-
putable career. Perhaps education and rum are not the best ingredients for a seaman.

10

'GENERAL' BOWLES GOES TO LONDON

CHRONOLOGICALLY SPEAKING, the author is indulging in what is rapidly becoming a fourth-dimensional approach to the story of Madoc. There is, one trusts, more method than madness in this form of narrative because it is not always easy to assess what happened in the twelfth century, if one has not already discussed some of the findings of the eighteenth century. Therefore to lead up to a more careful study of whether, where and when Madoc landed in the New World we must first consider in some detail the narratives of those who claimed to have found the Welsh Indians.

This is important if only because contemporary or near contemporary accounts of Madoc's arrival in the New World are too meagre to be assessed on their own. It is only when one examines later findings in America that it is possible to make any kind of judgement.

In the latter part of the eighteenth century reports of the discovery of the Welsh Indians had become so frequent that interest in the Madoc legend was revived in Britain. The *Public Advertiser* and the *Gentleman's Magazine* both ventilated the subject and drew forth correspondence from both sides of the Atlantic.

Theophilus Evans, the author of *Drych y Prif Oesoedd*, a history of Wales, published an account of Morgan Jones's adventures. But there was also another reason for the renewed interest in Madoc. Once again England was at war with Spain, this time the

War of Jenkins' Ear, and so it was fashionable to denigrate the Spaniards' colonizing exploits and to try to prove that America was discovered by a Briton. Later, in 1789, when the Spaniards attacked British settlements on the Pacific coast, it became a matter of honour to claim that Britain reached the New World first.

The *Public Advertiser* of October 8, 1785, published an account of Captain Stewart's findings. Of the language on the roll of parchment Stewart expressed the opinion that it 'seemed like Greek'. He may simply have been using the colloquial 'it seems all Greek to me'; on the other hand some scholars were quick to point out that Julius Caesar had said that the Britons of his day used Greek letters.

Perhaps clergymen had more time for letter-writing in those days, but it is extraordinary how many of them took an interest in this subject. There was a Reverend Mr. Rankin, of Kentucky, concurring in the testimony that the Padoucas spoke Welsh, and the Reverend Humphrey Lynn writing from a Norfolk rectory that 'from letters I have received from Kentucky Madoc must have lived in Florida, Georgia or Carolina . . . I have authentic record of such people as Welsh Indians called the White Panes or Bearded Indians'.[1]

In a letter to the *Gentleman's Magazine*[2] William Owen wrote in 1791: 'Within the last two years I have received no less than three several accounts, perfectly agreeing with one another, proving the existence of an extensive nation of white people, speaking the Welsh language, and we find them even noticed in our common maps under the name of the White Padoucas. . . .

'In consequence of the European colonies spreading over that country, or for some other causes, they (*the Welsh Indians*) removed from the country to Kentucky, where evident traces of them have been lately found; such as ruins of forts, earthenware, etc. It is to be presumed that as their situation was secluded, and not liable to be molested, they left it only in consequence of discovering a more inviting country; and none could be more so than where they finally settled.

'The centre of the country of the Madawgys (*descendants of*

Madoc) and where their villages are most numerous is about 38 degrees north latitude and 102 degrees west longitude of London; but they extend (possibly in detached communities) from about 31 degrees north latitude to 97 degrees west longitude.

'The general name of Cymry is not left among them, though they call themselves Madawgys, Madogiad, Madgiant and Madogian, names of the same import, meaning people of Madawg. Hence the French travellers in Lousiana have called them Padoucas,[3] Montocantes and other names bearing a similitude to what they call themselves, and by which they are known to the native Indians. . . . They are more civilized than the Indians, use horses in hunting; they have irons of which they could make tools . . . their government is on the feudal system.'

This was the first occasion on which an exact location of the Welsh Indians was mentioned.

Among the papers of Lady Fraser, of Cresey House in Lincolnshire, was found a list of notes of possible sources of the Madoc legend. As practically all of these sources have already been quoted in this book there is no useful purpose in enumerating them here, but it is worth mentioning that Lady Fraser described how she was induced to examine this story by 'my reading a book, lent me by a French gentleman about twenty-five years ago. It was translated into English and gave an account of a great nation of Indians within land from Cape Florida that actually speak Welch'.[4]

This was probably a book based on the Sieur de Verendrye's discoveries. A Memoir of the Academy of Paris published about 1765 referred to Welsh Indians 'inland from the coast of Florida', and this may have been translated into English.

It was between 1750 and 1770 that reports of Welsh, or White Indians, were most prevalent. Major Rogers in his *Concise Account of North America*, published in 1765, spoke of the 'White Indians', referring to 'this fruitful country' west of the Mississippi, being 'inhabited by a nation of Indians called by the others the White Indians on account of their complexion, they being much the fairest Indians on the continent. . . . These Indians live in large towns, and have commodious houses; they raise corn, tame the

wild cows and use both their milk and flesh; they keep great
numbers of dogs and are very dexterous in hunting; they have
little or no commerce with any nation that we are at present
acquainted with'.

Accounts of 'White' as distinct from Welsh Indians are given by
such historians, geographers and explorers as Samuel Drake,
Thomas L. McKinney, James Hall and John Filson, the first
historian of Kentucky. Filson, who strongly supported the Madoc
legend and stated that 'of late years the western settlers (in 1874,
when he wrote, the 'west' meant Kentucky and Tennessee) have
received frequent accounts of a nation inhabiting a country a great
distance up the Missouri, in manners and appearance resembling
the other Indians, but speaking Welsh and retaining some ceremonies of Christian worship, and at length this is universally
accepted as a fact.'[5]

Even Thomas Stephens, as mistrustful of the Welsh Indians
reports as he was of the Madoc legend, conceded that the existence
of 'White Indians' had been clearly established. Referring to a
letter dated November 24, 1795, from Morgan Rees, of Philadelphia, and to a document of questions and answers on the Welsh
Indians prepared by the Moravian Mission in America, Stephens
declared 'both documents clearly prove the presence of White
Indians, but the first stops short of proving the Welsh Indian case,
except at third hand, while the second appears to me to be evidence
to the contrary.[6]

Perhaps one of the most celebrated of the witnesses on behalf of
the Welsh Indian case was that son of Wales, who signed the
Declaration of Independence. Francis Lewis, son of a Llandaff
clergyman, emigrated to America at the age of twenty-one and
became a merchant and leading citizen of New York. He fought
in the French–Indian war and was captured by Montcalm in 1757,
when he was taken to Canada with other prisoners. After his
release he was elected a delegate to the General Congress in 1757
by the convention of deputies from several countries in New
York. After the fall of Oswego he was captured by the Indians
near Albany, New York. According to his story of that incident,
he escaped from being tied to a stake and burned alive because he

began talking to the Indians in Welsh; they understood him and he was released.[7]

With due respect to so eminent a man, this story is uncorroborated and not very convincing. As Lewis left no detailed account of the affair one suspects the story may well have been distorted in being passed from one person to another. No reason is given as to why he spoke in Welsh to the Indians, and in any event the locality of the alleged incident is not one from which any other reports of Welsh Indians ever came.

John Filson quoted 'a gentleman whose veracity may be entirely depended upon', one Captain Abraham Chaplain, of Kentucky, who assured him that between the years 1770–75, when he was with his company in Kaskaski, he met some Indians who spoke Welsh. They conversed with two Welshmen in his company and were perfectly understood.[8]

Most reports of Welsh Indians in these years came from the Missouri–Mississippi area, Carolina, Virginia, Kentucky, Tennessee, Alabama, Florida and the surrounding areas. Francis Lewis's report from Albany was exceptional, but one rather more detailed account, presented on an official basis, referred to an even more distant part of America. This is contained in a letter written by George Chrochan to Governor Dinwiddie of Virginia in 1753:

> May it Please Your Honour,
> Last year I understood by Colonel Lomax that Your Honour would be glad to have some information of a nation of people settled to the west of a large river that runs to the Pacific Ocean, commonly called the Welch Indians. As I had an opportunity of gathering some account of these people, I make bold, at the insistence of Colonel Cressup, to send you the following accounts.
> As I formerly had an opportunity of being acquainted with several French traders, and particularly with one that was bred up from his infancy amongst the Western Indians, on the west side of the Lake Erie, he informed me that the first intelligence the French had of them was by some Indians

settled at the back of New Spain; who on their way home, happened to lose themselves, and fell down on this settlement of people which they took to be French by their talking very quick, that there was a large settlement of French on a river that ran to the sun's setting; that they were not Indians, although they lived as Indians; they could not perceive that they traded with people, or had any trade to the sea, for they had no boats or ships as they could see and though they had weapons amongst them they were so old and so much out of order that they made no use of them, but hunted with bows and arrows for the support of their families.

On this account the Governor of Canada determined to send a party to discover whether they were French or not, and had 300 men raised for that purpose. But when they were ready to go the Indians would not go with them, but told the Governor that if he sent but a few men, they would go and show them the country; on which the Governor sent three young priests, who dressed themselves in Indian dress and went with those Indians to the place where these people were settled, and found them to be Welsh.

They brought back some old Welsh Bibles to satisfy the Governor they were there, and they told the Governor these people had a great aversion to the French: for they found by them that they had been at first settled at the mouth of the Mississippi, but had been almost cut off by the French there. So that a small remnant of them escaped back to the country where they were then settled, but had since become a numerous people.

The Governor of Canada, on this account, determined to raise an army of French Indians to go and cut them off; but as the French have been embarrassed in war with several other nations nearer home, I believe they had laid the project aside. The men who furnished me with this account told me that the messengers who went to make this discovery were gone sixteen months before they returned to Canada, so that these people must live at a great distance thence due west. This is the most particular account I ever could get of those people as yet.

> I am,
> > Your Honour's
> > > Most Obedient, Humble Servant,
> > > > George Chrochan.

NB. The Governor agreed with three or four of the back traders to go in quest of the Welsh Indians, and promised to give them 500 [men] for that purpose, but was recalled before they could set out on the expedition.[9]

The phrase 'Welsh Bibles' is almost certainly a misnomer. If there were such books they were probably psalters, missals or some other ancient manuscript. The idea of Madoc taking Welsh Bibles into America centuries before the Bible was translated into Welsh, let alone printed, is so preposterous that one fails to understand how it was accepted by educated men. But no description of any of these books is available, and in the absence of this one must regard this testimony as unsubstantiated.

The letter by Chrochan was written from Winchester, Virginia, a state from which other reports of Welsh Indians had emanated.

Thomas Stephens ridiculed the reports of Bibles and 'sacred books' with which some of these narratives abound. He was, of course, quite right to question such stories when no evidence was produced of the existence of such books or manuscripts. There was the case, quoted by Stephens from Mrs. Campbell's *Tales About Wales*, of an aged man who had been held prisoner by the Cherokee Indians and who was supposed to have obtained from them 'an old manuscript on vellum, very dingy, which appeared to be an old Roman missal'.

If such books existed, the probability was that they had come into the possession of the Indians through itinerant missionaries. If this is the answer to this mystery it is certainly no proof of the Indians being Welsh. Far less likely is the possibility that Madoc took on his voyages ancient manuscripts of the early British Church. Zella Armstrong has put forward an ingenious theory that this might be the explanation of the 'sacred books',[10] pointing out that Giraldus stated that such manuscripts existed in Wales before the defeat of Boadicea, and that there was a manuscript Bible (in Latin) in that country before A.D. 300. Miss Armstrong quoted effectively from Alban of Verulam, who, when suffering from persecution in A.D. 303, told Amphilagus: 'Take thou the hallowed scroll, on which life is written, and flee to the dark forest where thy foes will seek thee in vain.'

Such a theory is of little value when weighed against the absence of the 'sacred books' as evidence. For Madoc to have brought the manuscripts across the Atlantic, and for his descendants to have kept them all those centuries, despite wars, looting, destruction and moving from one place to another, is little more than an exercise in romance.

But, not unnaturally with a race so bibliolatrous as the Welsh, the finding of so-called sacred books became an obsession. With each account of them the story becomes more improbable. In the *Gentleman's Magazine*, that repository of so many observations on the Welsh Indians, Mr. Edward Williams related the experiences of a Mr. Binon, of Coyty in Glamorganshire, who had traded for more than thirty years among the Indians. Mr. Binon told him how about the year 1750 he and five or six others penetrated much farther than usual to the westward of the Mississippi and found a tribe who spoke the Welsh tongue.

'They lived in stone-built villages, and were better clothed than the other tribes. There were ruined buildings; one among them appeared very like an old Welsh castle, another like a ruined church.

'They showed Mr. Binon a book, in manuscript, which they had carefully kept, believing it to contain the mystery of Religion. They told Mr. Binon that it was not very long since a man had come among them who understood it. This man, whom they esteemed as a prophet, told them a people would some time visit them, and explain to them the mysteries in their book which would make them completely happy.

'When they informed Mr. Binon that they could not read it, they appeared very concerned. They conducted him and his companions for many days through vast deserts, and plentifully supplied them with provisions which the woods afforded, until they brought them to a place they knew well; and at parting they wept bitterly and urgently entreated Mr. Binon to send a person to them who could interpret their book.

'A gentleman in company with Mr. Binon at that time, in a letter, confirms the above statement. He says that Mr. Binon declared that these Indians worshipped their book as God, but could not read it. When Mr. Binon said that he came from Wales, they replied: "It was from thence that our ancestors came, but we do not know in what part of the world Wales is."'[11]

This again sounds like an echo of the Morgan Jones story, except for the discrepancy in the dates. Morgan Jones met the Doegs in 1666, whereas Binon learned of the 'man they esteemed as a prophet' ninety years later. Then again the authenticity of this yarn depends on what word Binon used for Wales, an English name for the principality which would not have been used by the followers of Madoc.

By far the most likely explanation of all the 'sacred book' and 'ancient parchment' stories is that they were tribal relics. Parchment records were handed down from generation to generation in some Indian tribes, as is recorded by Catlin and others. Usually they were in too bad a condition to be useful for posterity.

Daniel Boone, the American pioneer and explorer (1735–1820), also knew of the Welsh Indians legend, and from first-hand experience in Kentucky and Tennessee expressed his belief in their Welsh origins. He was impressed by a tribe called the 'Blue-Eyed Indians' and thought these might be 'of the same kith and kin as the Welsh, though I have no means of assessing their language'.

In 1791 a charlatan variously known as 'King', 'Chief' and 'General' William Bowles stepped into the arena of the Madoc controversy. It was a timely and remunerative moment at which to do so, for in England the correspondence in the *Gentleman's Magazine* and the *Public Advertiser* had led to the formation of a modest, but not uninfluential Madoc cult among not merely a few Welsh literary figures, but the missionary movements of some of the Free Churches, the large Welsh colony in London, which had formed a branch of the Cymmrodorion Society, the redoubtable Dr Samuel Johnson himself and Robert Southey who had formed a friendship with Iolo Morganwg. This was the age of a miniature renaissance of Welsh culture and the Madoc story was a focal point for the furtherance of this spirit of literary nationalism. It coincided with a movement among English scholars to rediscover old Celtic legends and to debate these with their Welsh acquaintances.

From a literary point of view it was an exciting period in which to live and one of great activity among the Welsh colony in London. A prosperous furrier of Upper Thames Street, Owen Jones, financed a scheme for sending agents all over Wales in quest of ancient manuscripts and books, and was induced to support Iolo Morganwg's madcap plan of practising Druidical rites on Primrose Hill.

For Bowles this renaissance atmosphere was a superb opportunity. In his Red Indian headgear, which he wore on every possible occasion, he was a picturesque figure, imbued with a considerable amount of charm and panache as he posed as a Red Indian chieftain. He was a consummate liar and far from lending any long-term support to the Madoc legend, which was his aim, managed in the end only to discredit it. Yet while his popularity lasted his mission was a great success. Bowles's true origins are still in doubt. That he was white and an American there is no doubt; he probably had some Welsh ancestry in the not-too-distant past, for when he presented himself in London as a Red Indian chief he was able to convince Welshmen that he had at least a smattering of their language. A Red Indian chieftain was a complete novelty in London in that period and Bowles made an instant conquest, not only in the taverns, where for an ample supply of hard liquor he would regale the customers with colourful accounts of his alleged adventures, but in the literary *salons* to which his baroque personality and gift as a raconteur soon gained him admittance.

David Samwel, a rowdy but erudite, violent but witty naval surgeon, who knew a great deal about Welsh literature, wrote a ballad which admirably describes the tavern-life of the Welsh literary lions of the age:

> In Wallbrook stands a famous inn
> Near ancient Watling-street,
> Well stored with brandy, beer and gin,
> Where Cambrians nightly meet
> If on the left you leave the bar
> Where the Welsh landlord sits,
> You'll find a room where a wordy war
> Is waged by Cambrian wits.
> There various texts they talk about
> In arts, in taste and learning;
> And often solve historic doubts
> With a classical discerning.

Bowles was his own public relations officer, quick to size up the gullibility of his audience and astute enough to know just how to win the Press. On arriving in London he gave interviews to the newspapers and held a conference, proclaiming that he came from the Creek Indians (of which tribe he had given himself the title of Commander-in-Chief) and that the Welsh Indians were based not on legend, but established fact.

William Owen, one of the more easily influenced of the *alumni* who lapped up every shred of evidence about Welsh-speaking Indians, was bemused by the aesthesiogenic Bowles. Soon he was eagerly reporting to the *Gentleman's Magazine* that he and a Mr. Richard Williams had met Bowles and were satisfied with his evidence. Bowles had shown the same adroitness in holding the whole of the Welsh colony in London under his spell as he had in persuading the Creek Indians to admit him to membership of their tribe. Owen wrote to the *Gentleman's Magazine*:

'When Chief Bowles was asked why he thought the white Indians were Welsh, he replied, "A Welshman was with me at home for some time. He had been a prisoner among the Spaniards and worked in the mines of Mexico. By some means he contrived to escape, got into the wilds and made his way across the Continent, and eventually found himself with a people with whom he could converse and stayed there some time."

'Amongst other particulars, he told me that "they had several books, which were mostly religiously kept in skins, and were considered by them as mysteries. These they believed gave an account from whence they had come. These people told the Welshmen that they had not seen a white man like themselves, who was a stranger, for a long time".'

Bowles warmed to his theme, pleading eloquently that his tribesmen needed the consolation of meeting their own kith and kin once again, that it was right that they should be re-united with their ancestors. He told the London Cymmrodorions that his father had had frequent conversations with the Welsh Indians, with whom he talked in Welsh.

The Madoc cult suddenly developed into a campaign for sending an expedition to America in search of the Welsh Indians. Enthusiasm for the idea was at first greatest in London, but it soon spread to Wales itself and to some of the missionary societies. Until this date the missionaries had shown mild interest in the Welsh Indians, but had decided that more proof was required before they could take any action, despite the fact that in 1733 a letter to the British Missionary Society in London had urged the carrying of 'the gospel of peace among our ancient brethren'. This letter, dated, 1 March, stated:

It is not unknown to you that Madoc Gwynedd, a Prince of Wales, did about five hundred years ago, sail westward . . . Some relics of the Welsh tongue being found in old and deserted settlements about the Mississippi make it probable that he sailed up that river. And we, being moved with brotherly love to our countrymen, are meditating to go in search of them, but are discouraged by the distance of the place and the uncertainty of the course we would steer. If you can give us any information and direction together with some help to bear expense we shall find men adventurous enough to undertake the expedition, having no other end in view than to carry the gospel of peace among our ancient brethren;

and believing it will be to the enlightenment of the British empire in America and a proof of prior right to the whole continent should we happily succeed.

> We remain, gentlemen, your loving
> countrymen,
>
> (signed)   John Davis,
>   David Evans,
>   Nathaniel Jenkins,
>   Benjamin Griffith,
>   Joseph Eton.[12]

Without doubt this letter combined religious fervour with empire-building.

Bowles had an answer for the most sceptical of his listeners. Were these Welsh Indians the Doegs, as Morgan Jones had indicated? he was asked. He did not fall into that trap; no, he replied, they were the Padoucas, a tribe living on the Missouri River. The Padoucas, he plausibly explained, were the 'Men of Madoc', and Padoucas was simply a corruption of their original name of Madawgwys.

William Owen became one of the leaders of the campaign to send an expedition in search of the Welsh Indians, and soon he was supported by Iolo Morganwg and Thomas Pennant. Iolo, perhaps the cleverest literary forger of his age, may have been carried away at first by his own enthusiasm; it is possible that he never believed an expedition would ever start. Perhaps he was too wrapped up in his zealous claim to have rediscovered the ancient ritual of the Druids, or earning too much money from Owen Jones by producing 'lost' manuscripts. Whatever his motives, when the time came for an expedition to be launched Iolo declined to join it.

11

JOHN EVANS'S STRANGE QUEST

IN 1791 IOLO MORGANWG was a bardic hero to his countrymen, a
self-educated stonemason who by dint of hard study had made
himself the chief living authority on ancient literary history and
the early Welsh bards. No one had yet suspected his gift for
forging ancient odes, so his support for the expedition to find the
Welsh Indians was considered a good reason for contributing
funds for the project.

Yet the man who was to make the expedition was then only an
unknown twenty-one-year-old from the village of Waunfawr,
just outside Caernarvon. His name was John Evans.

The picture one gets of Evans from his contemporaries is that of
a poor but pious young man from a family of Welsh Methodist
preachers, filled with a burning ambition to preach the gospel
overseas. It is a facile portrait of a complicated character, with
ambiguous aims and devious quirks in his make-up, based partly
on his family background and partly on the fact that his village
schoolteacher is said to have been Dafydd Ddu Eryri (David
Thomas), another famous Welsh poet of his day. Those who have
written about John Evans up to date encircle him with a halo of
honesty and, almost, martyrdom, but the truth is that from the
day he decided to seek his living in London young Evans showed
signs of being an opportunist, an adventurer and one more fond of
money than the Gospel.

In London, Evans sought out William Bowles in the taverns,

having already shown a liking for hard liquor which does not altogether go with teetotal Welsh Methodism. Possibly he was
excited at the prospect of joining an expedition to find the Welsh
Indians; possibly, too, he may originally have had ideas of converting them to Christianity, though this suggestion is not
supported by any evidence. It is much more probable that Evans,
with one eye on adventure and the chance of free travel and the
other on the scope such an expedition provided for making
money on the side, determined to offer his services. He had
ingratiated himself with the London Welsh, notably with Iolo
himself, and, when Iolo finally decided not to make the trip,
Evans immediately offered to undertake the quest for the Welsh
Indians single-handed.

The truth was that funds did not warrant an expensive expedition, so Evans's proposal to tackle the expedition on his own
weighed in his favour with the organizers. Thus at the end of the
summer of 1792 he sailed for America, with various letters of introduction to Welshmen who had settled in Philadelphia and elsewhere, including William Pritchard, a bookseller, and Dr. Samuel
Jones. Evans seems quickly to have discarded the theories of
William Bowles and Morgan Jones and certainly he received very
little encouragement from the Welsh settlers who strongly urged
him to abandon the idea of such a quest, mainly on the grounds
that the Indian tribes were savage and dangerous.

He next appeared in Baltimore on October 10, 1792, taking a
job as a clerk in a store in that city. For the winter at least it was
more profitable than searching for Welsh Indians. None the less,
to do him credit for pertinacity, when spring came round Evans,
despite further warnings from his new-found Welsh friends,
insisted on making the quest. He had made up his mind that, if
there were Welsh-speaking Indians, they were probably either
the Padoucas (or *Commanches*, as the French called them), or the
Mandans. From what he had learned everything pointed to the
Mandans.

By this time Evans must have been somewhat disillusioned by
his fellow-countrymen, which may explain his subsequent conduct, for Mr. Arthur T. Halliday, of Baltimore, writes: 'My

great-grandfather knew John Evans and was always interested in the theory of the White Indians. In some old papers and letters of his which I came across I found the following note:

"'John Evans had little help or encouragement from Welsh settlers in Philadelphia and Baltimore. He had been promised assistance, but it was never forthcoming. I think the reason he didn't find the Welsh Indians was that he didn't intend to help them [his fellow-countrymen] any more when funds were not forthcoming. His whole idea seemed to me to be to keep what he found to himself and, for some mysterious reason, to capitalize his findings by selling his discovery to somebody else."'[1]

A cryptic observation, but it begins to make more sense as the story unravels.

Evans studied his maps and decided that the Indians he sought were somewhere far up the Missouri River. To find them he could either go north to Canada and link up with the Canadian fur-traders who made trips to the Missouri, or travel south into Spanish territory and sail up the river. That he carefully considered both routes is evident by the fact that he asked for letters of introduction to the Governors of Canada, but ultimately he chose the route from the south. In March, 1793, Evans crossed the Alleghany Mountains and reached the Ohio River, down which he sailed for seven hundred miles until he reached the point at which it joins the Mississippi. Then by river craft he went up the Mississippi for a further two hundred miles to that mighty river's junction with the Missouri at St. Louis.

International politics now enter into our story as a major factor. For in the fading years of the eighteenth century four nations were still battling for the right to rule the North American continent. There was the young American nation, anxious to hold what it had so recently won through its Declaration of Independence; the British, who held sway in Canada and the north, where the Hudson's Bay Company had been formed to trade in furs with the Indians; the French, who had also settled in Canada and who had built the town of New Orleans; and the Spaniards who were still powerful in the south, especially in St. Louis. This situation had, however, undergone a change during the Seven

Years' War when France and Spain had allied against England. France had ceded to Spain all land west of the Mississippi, thus making New Orleans and St. Louis Spanish territory. England, through Wolfe's action at Quebec, had made Canada a British possession, and the United States' growing power threatened to drive France and Spain out of the American continent. Yet, though perturbed at the newly formed United States stronghold in the central and eastern states, both France and Spain regarded England as the larger menace. All English moves were mistrusted as being activated by espionage, or attempts to win more territory: it was an age in which 'Perfidious Albion' was regarded as a power who made treachery a mode of policy.

The Spanish Government, however, differentiated between Celts and English. They regarded Scots, Welsh and Irish as potential enemies of England and therefore ready-made material for employment in the Spanish espionage service. Spain's chief aim at this period is made very clear in an article by A. P. Nastair in the *Missouri Historical Review*:

'In the last decade of the eighteenth century opportunities for private gain and a desire on the part of Spanish officials to check British encroachment upon Spanish territory . . . made the wish of the Government of Spain to open the vast country contained in the watershed of the Missouri River.'[2]

The Lieutenant-Governor of St. Louis was Don Zenon Trudeau, an able and energetic administrator, who in co-operation with the Governor of New Orleans, Baron Carondelet, wanted to find a route across the Rocky Mountains which would link up the Mississippi Valley and California. Along this route they planned to build a series of defence forts. It was a mission which called for great secrecy and a concerted effort to prevent spies of Britain or U.S.A. from ascertaining details of their plans.

Such was the unpropitious moment at which John Evans arrived in St. Louis. Here was an inquisitive stranger, without visible means of support, crossing into Spanish territory with some wild and unlikely story of looking for Welsh Indians. It sounded improbable to most, but the Spanish officials, conscious that British spies would give much to learn their plans, decided that

Evans was an English agent rather than a harmless crank. He was promptly clapped into jail and remained there for a considerable period. Exactly how long he remained in captivity is not known. Some state he was in prison for nearly two years; other sources suggest that, though kept under surveillance in St. Louis, he was eventually allowed out on parole.

David Williams, the chief authority to date on the story of Evans's expedition, writes: 'It must have been a cruel disappointment for him. At last Trudeau was persuaded by an influential American judge to set him free.'[3]

But the cruel disappointment was only temporary. The Spaniards were determined to find out more about Evans's aims, and eventually they came to accept that his mission was simply a quest for Welsh Indians, that he had received little help from Welsh settlers in America and that here was a potential ally who was embittered by lack of support and had no particular love of the English. Could Evans be won over to the Spanish cause, and, if he could, would he be useful to Spain? What impressed the Spaniards was that by now Evans had lost interest in the Padoucas and was more intent on finding the Mandans. For one of the objectives – indeed a prime objective – of the Spaniards was to seek out and win over Mandan territory. How better to achieve this than to employ a man who possibly had some kinship with the Mandans, and, better still, who spoke their language? By this time the Spanish officials had checked what they regarded as Evans's quixotic quest against their own inquiries about the Mandans. These suggested that Evans's story might be genuine. So Evans was cajoled and coaxed, bullied and then flattered into becoming an agent of the Spaniards.

This does not at all resemble the portrait of Evans supplied by his admirers: here fact belies biography. The popular story has it that a Spanish agent, James Mackay, a Scotsman, met in Cincinatti a Welsh Baptist minister, Morgan John Rhys, who knew all about John Evans. Rhys, after trying to distribute Bibles among the cut-throat Revolutionaries of Paris, had lost some of his fervour for the Bible, but gained a great deal more for the radicalism of the Revolution. Returning to Wales, he founded a radical periodical, but his countrymen were rather more devoted to the Bible than to radicalism, so, restless as ever, he emigrated to America with the object of creating a settlement for Welshmen who were prepared to fall in with his advanced views. It was on Rhys's advice that James Mackay sought out John Evans.

That, at least, is one story. But it is based solely on the word of Mackay, a Spanish agent. Mackay's own account of the matter is as follows: 'On my way from New York to Louisiana in 1794 I met a worthy gentleman, Doct^r. Reis [sic], who, after informing him of my intended expedition, furnished me with a small vocabularly of the Welch language written by himself, and informed me respecting a Mr. John Evans from Wales, who was gone to Illinois with the intention of travelling westward to see the supposed Welch tribe.

'Having arrived in Louisiana, I got ready for my voyage to the west. I sent for, and engaged for my assistant Mr. Evans, who spoke and wrote the Welch language with facility.'[4]

There is something that smacks of falsehood about these statements. They were written after the turn of the century, several years after the events described and after Evans's death. In 1794 Evans was in prison in St. Louis, and Morgan John Rhys certainly would not have known of his whereabouts unless told of them by Mackay. It seems much more probable that the Spaniards had asked Mackay to make inquiries about Evans and that Mackay had been given Rhys's name as a reference by Evans himself.

Mackay's finding of Evans was certainly not nearly as fortuitous as Mackay himself suggested. James Mackay in company with other fellow Scots had worked as a trapper in Canada and had had a great deal of experience in pioneering new routes and organizing expeditions. The Spaniards, having heard all about these activities, first secured his services and then, impressed by his ability and knowledge of the terrain, gave him Spanish nationality. They soon found him to be a faithful employee and gave him the title of Principal Explorer and Director of Indian Territory in the Missouri Company, which had been established by the Spaniards to build the new line of forts. Before the forts could be set up the new territory had to be thoroughly explored and charted, and the

Spaniards hoped that, by following the Missouri River to its source, they might eventually find a tributary flowing down to the Pacific. Earlier Spanish expeditions had failed to achieve this; in 1795 it was hoped that Mackay's expedition would enable them at last to succeed. It was almost a last, despairing bid and this more than anything else encouraged the Spaniards to gamble with the services of John Evans. Mackay knew perfectly well that Evans had no experience as an explorer, but felt that, if the story of the Welsh-speaking Indians was true, Evans would be the man to win them over and act as interpreter. Rhys would merely have confirmed that Evans was not an English agent.

It is true that Mackay's expedition was going in the same direction that Evans himself wished to go, but he could have been under no illusions that the Spaniards wished to use him as an agent and an anti-British one at that. He was appointed second-in-command to Mackay, surely a most unusual appointment for one who had no experience of exploring the terrain. But the offer of this post was not made as a tribute to his merits but as a bait to ensure his loyalty to the Spanish cause. 'One of the objectives of Mackay's expedition,' wrote A. P. Nastair, 'was to drive the British out from among the Mandans, where they had established a fort. He [Mackay] instructed Evans not to deliver, nor show anything regarding his discoveries to any human save Mackay, Clamorgan, or other representatives of the company in the presence of the Lieutenant-Governor.'[5]

Before he had encountered the Spaniards Evans's reports were always suggesting that he expected to meet the Welsh Indians any moment; one could almost picture his waiting in a tent for them to appear miraculously out of the woods. Always he had met somebody, never named, but vividly described, who had talked with them. Or he had actually discovered the exact location of one of their villages. Yet after this captivity and his joining Mackay's expedition (which, incidentally, he always misrepresented as his own expedition) there was silence and doubt. The change of tone was remarkable.

The truth was, of course, that Evans was under Spanish orders; as an agent of their government he was only allowed to say what they wished him to say. Under the encouragement of James Mackay he quickly changed his allegiance from England to Spain – 'sufficiently,' states Mrs. Penelope J. Allen, 'to cause the British flag to be lowered and to hoist that of Spain over the British fort in Mandan country.'[6] What anguish this knowledge would have caused the Tudor historians, Dr. Powel, William Owen and the Cymmrodorion Society of London!

Mackay and Evans set forth up the Missouri in August, 1795, taking with them thirty men and boat-loads of goods to be traded with the Indians. It was an exhausting first leg of their trip, rowing against a swiftly running river in extremely hot and humid weather, often in torrential rain. By the beginning of November they reached a village of the Omaha Indians, whose chieftain, Black Bird, was one of the most formidable warriors in the area. With winter approaching, Mackay knew that there was no other course open to his party than to remain where they were, buy the Indians' friendship with gifts of cloth, tobacco and firearms and hope for the best. When food became scarce Mackay sent out John Evans – or Don Juan Evans, as the Spaniards now called him – with a band of Indians to hunt buffalo.

Then came news that a French–Canadian named Jessaume, in the service of the British North-West Company, had arrived in Mandan territory and set up a British post there on the Missouri River. This was discouraging intelligence for the Spaniards, who were alarmed at the prospect of the British establishing a post on their planned line of communications. Evans was ordered to lead a small party of Spaniards to remove Jessaume from his post.

This expedition had two purposes: first, to dislodge the British, and second, to plot the route and make a detailed survey of the territory. Evans was told to make notes of everything of interest on their journey, a description of the Indian tribes encountered, their languages and religion, and to draw a map of their route as they went along. All land must be claimed in the name of King Charles IV of Spain and the natives must be told that the King was 'the protector of all white and red men'.

But after travelling for three hundred miles Evans's party were forced to turn back to escape from the Sioux Indians, one of the most savage of all tribes. They had no alternative but to return to their base camp at Fort Charles. Mackay's next step was to draw up a manifesto, dated May 27, 1796, in which Spain claimed all land along the Missouri River and warning off all foreigners. This alone is full proof that Evans now regarded himself as a servant of the King of Spain.

Evans set off on his next expedition on June 8, 1796. From the skilful map which he drew of his route it would seem that he went by boat along the Missouri; at any rate after travelling for some nine weeks he and his party reached the Arikara Indians, seven hundred miles from their base. This was the farthest point yet reached by any Spanish exploration team. *En route* they were met by Cheyennes with whom they traded; then, late in September, Evans became one of the first white men to cross the territory of the Sioux and the Arikaras and to reach a Mandan village.

The date was September 27, 1796, a day which marks a singularly abject betrayal of his native land by a man who had been financed originally by his fellow-countrymen. Evans distributed medals, flags and other presents to the Indians in the name of the Spanish King and even delivered a speech extolling the country of his new masters. Taking possession of the fort, which had been established by British traders, he tore down the Union Jack and hoisted the flag of Spain in its place. Within two weeks of this incident Spain had declared war on Britain. By joining the Spaniards Evans was now guilty of treason. He had passed the point of no return; there could be no question of his returning to his native land without suffering the severest penalty.

Making friends with two Mandan chieftains, Big White Man and Black Cat, Evans spent many evenings conversing with the Indians during his six months' sojourn among them. His sole talent as an entertainer was that he played the flute, which fascinated the natives who in return provided him with detailed knowledge of the Missouri River beyond the point he had reached. What is not easily explained, however, is how Evans was able so easily to persuade the Mandans to come over to the Spanish side. True, the Indians could be bribed by gifts, but on the other hand the Mandans were a rich tribe and, unlike most other Indians, well supplied from the crops they grew. They were courteous, hospitable, even humorous and high spirited, but there is a good deal of evidence that they really preferred to deal with the British and Canadians than the Spaniards. Yet Evans was able to do almost anything he liked with them. This does not, of course, prove that they were Welsh Indians, but it at least suggests some affinity between them and Evans, despite the fact that he had no knowledge of Indians or their dialects. The test came when the Canadians tried to hit back; it was in the depths of winter, and Evans was practically living alone with the Indians and unable to get in touch with either Mackay or the other Spaniards. He had nothing left with which to trade and was almost completely at the mercy of the Mandans.

There are several curious features about this expedition. Why, in the first place, did not Mackay himself take charge of it? Why, as leader of the exploration trip, did he leave so important a task to Evans, then still very much on trial, unless he had reason to believe that with Evans as leader more co-operation could be obtained from the Mandans? This suggests that Mackay might have believed in the Welsh Indian story.

The Mackay Notes in the archives of the Missouri Historical Society reveal that he knew all about the Welsh Indian reports. But the extraordinary thing is that he linked the reports solely with the Padoucas and not the Mandans. The omission of any reference to the Mandans in this connection is as curious as Mackay's neglect to mention that Evans had been imprisoned by the Spaniards. This is what Mackay had to say about the Padoucas and their alleged Welsh connection:

'The Paducas Tribe (who live South of Cheyenne River and on the headwaters of Delport and Missouri) does not seem to be of the same race with those nations around them from whom they differ in almost everything. They are more honest, peaceable and sincere in all their transactions, friendly to each other and courteous to strangers. Their manners more approaching civilization, their skin more fair, their countenance more open and agreeable in their features in a Great Degree, resembling that of White people.

'About the time I had in view to ascend the Missouri, a number of well-informed persons of both Europe and America believed the probability of a tribe of Welch descent's being somewhere near the headwaters of the Missouri . . . The name Paduca was considered as synonymous with Madoc, a Welch Prince who about six or seven hundred years ago sailed from Wales towards the west with a number of vessels and people . . . it was supposed that the Paducas were the remains of Prince Madoc's Colony.

'Tho, during my former tour in the north west and upper parts of the Missouri, I had heard nothing of a Welch Tribe, *I believed the possibility of their existence and considering the light such a discovery might throw on the History of America was determined to use all means in my power to unravel the mystery.*'[7]

The italics are my own, but they merely emphasize the fact that Mackay was keenly interested in the Welsh Indian theories. He went on to say that he and Evans had a sufficient opportunity to prove that the Paducas could speak not one word of Welsh, 'nor anything similar thereto'.

There is also the extraordinary fact that when Jessaume, the Canadian, returned with plenty of goods to trade with the Indians, the Mandans saved Evans's life when Jessaume threatened to kill him. Jessaume retreated and Evans stayed on in the village until spring. When the Welshman returned to Fort Charles he found the Missouri Company which employed him had become bankrupt, for Mackay had also become short of trading goods and the Indians had turned against him when he made a trip into Nebraska.

Having travelled 1,800 miles in sixty-eight days, Evans arrived back in St. Louis in July, 1797. David Williams writes that 'it is probable that he had intended to return to Wales when his work was done. But the Spanish authorities, who thought very highly of him, offered him a post as land surveyor'.[8] Yet it is inconceivable that Evans had any such intention, especially as he had committed treason, and he conveyed no such suggestion in the curt letter he sent to Dr. Samuel Jones, of Philadelphia.

The lynch-pin of Thomas Stephens's arguments against the existence of the Welsh Indians was the fact that, according to him, Evans searched far and wide for such a tribe, but never found them. This supposition, rationally enough, was based on the letter sent to Dr. Jones in 1797, in which Evans wrote:

'In respect of the Welsh Indians, I have only to inform you that I could not meet with such a people, and from intercourse I have had with Indians from latitude 35 to 40 I think you may with safety inform our friends that they have no existence.'[9]

This, coupled with Mackay's notes already quoted, was the *coup de grâce* to the theory of the Welsh Indians as far as the Welsh were concerned. If a Welshman as enthusiastic as John Evans had been could only report failure, that must be the end of the matter.

Yet the very brevity and finality of Evans's letter, and the fact that he never returned to Wales, make this negative report strangely suspect. Mr. Arthur T. Halliday's great-grandfather was convinced that 'Evans never returned to Philadelphia because he lied to his friends about the Indians'. Nastair, and even such an authority on Indian and particularly Cherokee history as Mrs. Penelope Allen, tell another story altogether about Evans and his motives. Mrs. Allen points out that Evans made his report after a search of only about six months and that in some of his earlier reports Evans 'appeared to be none too careful of the truth and inclined to boastfulness.'[10]

There seems little doubt that, for better or worse, Evans had decided to stay with the Spaniards, and that at their behest he wrote the letter stating that no Welsh Indians existed. What better evidence was there to rebut a British claim to Mandan territory than the statement of a Welshman who had come to America solely to discover the Welsh Indians?

Mr. Halliday's great-grandfather added a postscript to his memoranda on this subject by stating in 1803 that Evans 'when heavily in strong liquor bragged to his friends in St. Louis that the Welsh Indians would keep their secret to their graves because he had been handsomely paid to keep quiet on the subject. He added that in a few more years there would be no more trace of any Welsh ancestry or language as time and disease would eventually remove all traces.'

This in itself is not proof that Evans was a liar, for, if he were, then Mackay also comes into the same category. Yet the fact remains that Mackay, as a Spanish subject, had even more reason than Evans to lie, and it is odd, to say the least, that Mackay should go out of his way in his Notes to pay such a tribute to Evans. 'Mr. Evans was a virtuous young man of promising talents, undaunted courage and perseverance.' Courage he may have had, but Mackay was certainly not unaware of his defects, and to call Evans 'virtuous' was to paint a false picture.

Evans was intelligent and he could draw maps, but it seems far more likely that the generous treatment he received from the Spaniards was due to his refuting the Welsh Indian story than for any other services. They certainly did not remunerate him because of exceptional abilities, as has been suggested, for Evans's efficiency had long been impaired by a growing craving for strong liquor and fondness for the bordellos. He was already an alcoholic, sometimes lying stupefied in the brothels for days at a time. This alcoholic condition is not just gleaned from idle gossip; his contemporaries mention the fact in detail. By 1797 he was in such a poor state of health that he must have been a liability to the Spaniards – the more so as he appeared to talk too freely when in his cups – and his only use to them was what he could achieve in propaganda and especially in denying the existence of the Welsh Indians. The Spaniards were convinced that the English would capitalize on this legend for their own ends unless firmly discouraged. This, and almost entirely this factor, must have weighed with the Spanish officials who offered Evans employment as a land surveyor, an assurance of security for life and down payment of the equivalent of two thousand dollars in cash, a very large sum in those days for an almost unemployable drunkard.

Just as in the seventeenth century the Spaniards had searched for traces of the Welsh Indians in the Georgia–Alabama–Tennessee area, so once again they sought to examine the whole question. The new Governor of New Orleans, Don Manuel Gayoso de Lemos, who had asked Evans to map out the frontier between Spanish and British and United States possessions, had declared that 'it is in the interests of His Catholic Majesty that the reports of British Indians in Mandan country be denied once and for all. If, however, as seems possible, the subject of associations with the

Mandans is not mentioned by the British, it might be more expedient to refrain from referring to this tribe, but to relate the denial only to the Padoucas who have already been said by the British to have an association with the Welsh.'[11]

What more proof could be needed? Don Manuel's statement not only underlines Spanish intentions on the subject, but also throws new light on Mackay's strange omission of any specific mention of the Mandans, but emphasis on the Padoucas.

Having written his letter to Dr. Samuel Jones, Evans continued on the downward path. He became a cheat as well as a drunkard, and was involved in trouble when he took for himself land which had been intended for others. He went to live in Louisiana for a time, and then, through a recommendation from his friend Mackay, became a member of the household of Don Manuel, who, when Evans was sober, urged him to continue with his map to determine Spain's frontiers in America. That this map was completed is established by a letter which President Thomas Jefferson wrote to Captain Meriwether Lewis on January 13, 1804, in which he stated: 'I now enclose a map of the Missouri as far as the Mandans. It is said to be very accurate. It was done by a Mr. John Evans by order of the Spanish Government.'

It was probably the last service which Evans rendered to the Spaniards, for on May 20, 1799, Don Manuel wrote to Mackay, saying, 'Poor Evans is very ill. I perceived that he deranged himself when out of my sight, but I perceived it too late. The strength of the liquor has deranged his head; he has been out of his senses for several days, but with care he is doing better, and I hope he will get well.'[12]

Before the end of that month Evans had died in New Orleans at the early age of twenty-nine. A chapter of exploration which had opened so full of bright promise and even sturdy patriotic hopes had ended on a squalid note of failure and treachery.

12

REPORTS FROM TRAVELLERS

MADOC IS VARIOUSLY reported as having landed in America at such widely separated places as Alabama, Florida, Newfoundland, Newport (Rhode Island), Yarmouth (Nova Scotia), Virginia, the mouth of the Mississippi, the Gulf Coast, Yucatan, the Isthmus of Tehuantepec, Panama, the Caribbean coast of South America, a number of islands in the West Indies and the mouth of the Amazon.

At the same time the Welsh Indians are said to have been located in British Columbia, and other parts of Canada, Alabama, Tennessee, Georgia, Mississippi, Missouri, Kentucky, Virginia, North Carolina, the Ohio Valley, New York State, North and South Dakota, Oregon, Mexico and Peru, and even this list could be extended to include a few marginal reports.

There are extravagant accounts that Madoc and his companions reached Mexico and established the Aztec Empire, and then travelled on their all-conquering way to found the Mayan civilization and the Empire of the Incas in Peru. It has even been suggested that because there are red-haired people in the Galapagos group that they eventually sailed on there. For good measure there is the legend that one of them named Mormon lived to write their story which was duly handed down to Joseph Smith, who founded the Mormon religion. This may have originated in the fact that many Welshmen were among the Mormon pioneers. Brigham

Young told Captain Jones, one of his lieutenants, of a Welsh settlement on the Rio Colorado and that he believed that the Moquis were descendants of Madoc.

Bernard de Voto wrote that 'at least thirteen actual tribes were at one time supposed to be Welsh Indians. Besides these at least five imaginary tribes with names made to fit were designated, and at least three not named, but vividly described'.[1]

One can quickly dismiss the more extravagant claims. Tryggui Oleson mentions that the ancient stone at Yarmouth, Nova Scotia, has suggested that Madoc may have landed there because of some strange characters inscribed on it.[2] But these are certainly not Welsh and are more likely to have been links with the Norsemen. Kathleen O'Loughlin also refers to this story, and mentions as alternative landing places Rhode Island, Stony Brook in Weston or Cape Cod. The Reverend Benjamin F. De Costa, probably the most respected authority of his time on pre-Columbian voyages to America, acquiesced in the Madoc legend and retained his belief, borne out from anthropological and archaeological studies, that Madoc landed somewhere in this area of the eastern seaboard of the U.S.A. Under the pen name of Mishawun he put forward the idea that the ancient fortifications and earthworks at the mouth of Stony Brook on the Charles River, Massachusetts, were built by Madoc.[3]

These earthworks were surveyed in 1885 by Professor E. N. Horsford and Dr. Davis, engineer of the local waterworks. De Costa even claimed that the fortifications were so similar to remains at Ruabon and Llangollen, North Wales, that they must have been constructed by the early Welsh settlers in the twelfth century. 'The spirit of this work on the Charles,' wrote de Costa, 'is noticeably ancient and does not bear the slightest trace of French military architecture of the sixteenth century. It is distinctly British that is to say, Welsh.'[4]

That there was a great resemblance to the Cefn Bank earthworks near Llangollen is not disputed, and it was even remarked upon at the time in *Archaeologia Cambrensis*, and the origin of a circular fortress at Newport, Rhode Island, was also said to have been of ancient Welsh design. But careful probings produced no more findings, and it is surely significant that there have been no reports of Welsh Indians from this vicinity.

Similarly certain ancient houses at Montezuma in Arizona have been compared to Welsh castles by some vividly imaginative tourists.

The only possible support for the story that Madoc may have landed in Canada or the northern part of America lies in an extraordinary error in one edition of Sir Thomas Herbert's book, *A Relation of Some Yeares' Travaile*. But this error, one that even misled the astute Thomas Stephens, will be dealt with in a later chapter to which it more appropriately belongs. Dr. Powel's version about Madoc leaving Ireland to 'farre north' may have caused Benjamin Bowen and others to think it meant he sailed north of Ireland, when in fact the sentence almost certainly implies that he sailed south-west and left Ireland far to the north. Meiron quoted Brechfa as saying that 'Madoc directed his ship to the south-west in the hope of gaining fair winds and helpful currents, for that was the advice given him by the astronomers'.[5]

But, as the Boston area has been suggested by an eminent American source, the reports of Welsh Indians in the northern part of America are worthy of examination. Oddly enough they nearly all come from the western side of the continent which does nothing to help de Costa's theories. As a general rule Indian tribes did not move far afield, but it is possible that a tribe who had assimilated early foreign settlers might have been more enterprising and, driven constantly northwards by the arrival of Europeans, travelled far from their original encampments.

In August, 1947, the Associated Press of America carried a story which stated that the Kutenai Indians of British Columbia had been identified as descendants of Madoc. This report owed much to records which had been kept by Mr. John Pritchard, of Invermere, during his many years' close contact with the rapidly diminishing Kutenai tribe. The language of the Kutenai is distinct and separate from all other Indian dialects and in some respects unique. it is neither guttural and rasping like many Indian dialects, but soft and musical with an upward lilt at the end of a sentence rather like the Welsh. But the tribe is not markedly different physically from other Indians except that some of them have brown, curly hair, but their origins would appear to be Mongolian.

The whole question of their alleged Welsh origin was raised as recently as 1946 when some strange markings were found on a rock at a place called Spuzzum. The markings were identified as resembling Ogham, a form of Runic writing said to have been found in parts of Wales. In fact the writing had more in common with the ancient Scandinavian ornamental Runic.

An attempt was made at the time to prove that there was a close resemblance between Welsh and Kutenai. It was pointed out that Kutenai numerals from one to ten are simply Welsh words with Indian suffixes, for example:

	Welsh	*Kutenai*
1.	Un	Un–oakwa
2.	Dau	Dau–as
3.	Tri	Tri–cates
4.	Pedwar	Pedwar–chato
5.	Pimp	Pimp–yiko
6.	Chwech	Chwech–enmista
7.	Saith	Saith–wisdalla
8.	Wyth	Wyth–wychge
9.	Naw	Naw–kititwa
10.	Deg	Deg–ettowa.

Numeral comparisons between one language and another are not particularly helpful in proving anything. Far too many languages have similarities in their respective numerals. This particular comparison is remarkable certainly, but the trend is not confirmed by the rest of the dialect.

The Cherokee tribe is one that has been frequently linked with the 'Welsh Indians', so the statement of a Cherokee seeress in modern times is at least of some interest. Billed under the name of 'Princess Wahletka' when she appeared in a Cardiff theatre in August, 1921, she told the *Liverpool Daily Post*: 'I am a firm believer in the Madoc theory. All our Indian tribes believe in it, since one in particular, the Seneca tribe, living in the north-west of the United States, is credited with Welsh descent. Unlike all other tribes the Seneca people have pale, compelling eyes and other features that characterize them as being not wholly Indian. Moreover it is a tribal tradition that many centuries ago a fleet of foreigners landed on our shores and, becoming friendly, later intermingled and even married the native.'

Here was one Cherokee who did not support the theory that this tribe was composed of 'Welsh Indians'. In fact, as will later be seen, the Cherokees were their enemies.

In 1865 a Lieutenant-Colonel Samuel Tappan, who had lived and served as a soldier in Colorado and New Mexico for several years, made a report on the Navajo tribe some two hundred and fifty miles south of Santa Fé. They were, he said, 'the most hopeful of all Indians . . . their language is almost pure Welsh; a Welshman can understand them at once . . . the blankets which they make so beautifully are made in precisely the same way as the domestic blankets in South Wales'.[6]

On the strength of this information a request was sent to the Smithsonian Institution in Washington for the history of the Navajo to be looked into.

Three years previously the American Ethnological Society had officially expressed the opinion that there was considerable evidence not only for the Welsh Indian theory, but for the Madoc story as well. In 1863 the American Antiquarian Society, to which a benefactor had presented a supposed relic of the Welsh Indians, rather more cautiously said 'the future must decide this question'. In 1865 the Smithsonian Institution still regarded the Madoc story as an open question. George Gibbs, in his reply to the query about the Navajo, however, offered little hope of confirmation. 'The character of the language of the Navajos,' he replied, 'is well known. Vocabularies, more or less extensive, have been obtained from time to time by various officers of the army, government agents and by Mr. Bartlett[7] himself. From these the late Professor Wm. W. Turner demonstrated long since its affinity with the great Athapascan or Chepewyan stock, a family occupying the northern part of the continent, next south of the Esquimaux, and extending from the shores of Hudson's Bay to those of the Pacific . . . In fine, the Navajos and Apaches are offshoots of an extreme northern race who have wandered southward, just as the Comanches are a branch of the Shoshonees or Snakes of Oregon. . . . As regards the blankets, they are the common pattern of Mexican *sarape*, made, it is true, exceedingly well.'

Captain William Clark and Captain Meriwether Lewis, Private Secretary to President Jefferson, inspired by the President's keen interest in exploration of the Missouri country, made an attempt to locate the Welsh Indians in 1804. This was not their prime intention, as Thomas Stephens seems to have imagined, but purely incidental to their discovery that the River Missouri was divided into three tributaries, nearly all of equal size, more than two hundred miles from its source. They decided to make a survey of the area and map it. At the same time they were curious to see whether there was any truth in Captain Stewart's remarkable yarn. No doubt, too, they were prompted to look into the matter by having been given a copy of the map drawn by John Evans. They followed the most northerly of the three tributaries and returned the same way, but found no trace of the reputed Indians. This, opined Stephens, again threw doubt on the existence of such a tribe, but Major Stoddard took a very different view. He believed that Clark and Lewis chose the wrong tributary and that the earlier travellers who had encountered Welsh Indians in this region had explored one or other of the two tributaries. In the case of Captain Stewart the details of his journey would suggest that Major Stoddard's guess was correct. The same can also be deduced from a study of the itineraries of Charlevoix and Griffith.

It was in the same year as the Clark–Lewis expedition that the story of Maurice Griffith was printed in the *Palladium*, a Kentucky newspaper.[8] This aroused fresh interest in the whole question of the Welsh Indians. Publication of the story produced a whole crop of reports of Welshmen having been seen in the state of Kentucky. Albert James Pickett, in his *History of Alabama*,[9] declared that 'there are evident traces of the Welshmen having formerly inhabited the country around Kentucky, particularly wells and ruins of buildings, neither of which was the work of Indians'.

For many years after 1804 the bars and smoking-rooms of

Ken.tucky resounded with stories about people who boasted of having met Welsh Indians. Many were pure fantasy, or in the category of 'fishermen's tales', but others were so carefully detailed that one either dismissed them as the zanier efforts of an irrepressible raconteur, or as something calling for further research. One such was the extraordinary anecdote of Lieutenant Joseph Roberts, which was printed in the *Public Advertiser* – of Louisville, Kentucky, not of London – on May 15, 1818.

Roberts was in the smoking-room of a hotel in Washington in the year 1801, when he had cause to rebuke a young servant, a native of Wales, for having brought him a glass of brandy with warm instead of cold water. Roberts, half jocosely and half reproachfully, told him in Welsh: 'I'll give thee a good beating.'

The detail of the story is such that, if one is to follow every twist and turn in the narrative, it must be quoted in full, as it appeared in the newspaper interview with Roberts. It should, however, first be pointed out that Roberts, who came from Hawarden in Flintshire, originally dictated his story to a Welsh magazine, *Greal*, which first published it in 1805–6. Stephens, who cited this, described it as 'tolerably stiff testimony'. Its obvious defect is that it was not told until at least four years after the incident described and may in the telling and with the passing of time have been considerably embroidered, or possibly laced with some more brandy.

'There happened to be in the room at the time,' the story continued, 'one of those secondary Indian chiefs, who, on my pronouncing those words [in Welsh], rose in a great hurry, stretching forth his hand, at the same time asking me in the ancient British tongue, "Is that thy language?"

'I answered him in the affirmative, shaking hands at the same time, and the chief said it was likewise his language and the language of his father and mother and of his nation.

'I said to him, "It is also the language of my father and mother and also of my country." Upon this the Indian began to inquire from whence I came, and I replied, "From Wales",' but he had never heard of such a place. I explained to him that Wales was a principality in the Kingdom called England. He had heard of England, but never of such a place as Wales.

'I asked him if there were any traditions amongst them whence their ancestors had come. He said that there were and they had come from a far-distant country, very far in the east and from over great waters. I conversed with him in Welsh and English, but he knew better Welsh than I did, and I asked him how they had come to retain their language so well after mixing with other Indians. He answered that they had a law or established custom in their nation forbidding any to teach their children another language until they attained the age of twelve years and after that they were at liberty to learn any language they pleased.

'I asked him if he would like to go to England and Wales; he replied that he had not the least inclination to leave his native country and that he would sooner live in a wigwam than a palace. He had ornamented his naked arms with bracelets and on his head were ostrich feathers.

'I was greatly astonished and greatly amazed when I heard such a man who painted his face yellowish-red and of such an appearance speaking the ancient British language as fluently as if he had been born and brought up in the vicinity of Snowdon. His head was shaved except around the crown and there the hair was very long and plaited, and it was on the crown of his head he had placed the ostrich feathers, which I mentioned before, to ornament himself.

'The situation of these Indians is about 800 miles south-west of Philadelphia, according to his statement, and they are called the Asguawa, or Asguaw nation.

'The chief courted my society astonishingly, seeing that we were descended from the same people. He used to call upon me almost every day and take me to the woods to show me the virtues of the various herbs which grew there, for neither he nor his people were acquainted with compounded medicine.'

Lieutenant Roberts may have meant the Osage tribe, a branch of the Iroquoian, like the Seneca, Cherokee and Tuscarora Indians.

Of the tribes who were at various times mentioned as being, or containing among their number, Welsh Indians the following may be mentioned: Tuscaroras, Doegs, Mandans, Shawnees, Padoucas, Cherokees, Omans, Creek, Osage, Navajo, Hopi and Modoc. As F. W. Hodge wrote in his *Handbook of American Indians North of Mexico*, 'the myth of a tribe of Welsh Indians . . . placed them first on the Atlantic coast, where they were identified with the Tuscarora, and then farther and farther west until about 1776 we find "Welsh" or "white" Indians on the Missouri, where they appeared as the Mandan, and later on Red River. Later still they were identified with the Hopi of Arizona, and finally with the Modoc of Oregon, after which they vanish.'[10]

Hodge, who regards the subject as a 'popular fallacy' dismisses the whole question rather cursorily and strangely omits to mention those areas from which most reports of the Welsh Indians came – the south-east Atlantic states and around the Mississippi.

The Padoucas were better known in earlier days under their French name of *Commanches*. By all accounts they were a particularly savage tribe, notorious for the barbaric and sadistic tortures they imposed on their enemies. Yet James Mackay, as recorded in the previous chapter, gave a remarkably contrasting description of them: 'honest, peaceable and sincere in all their transactions, friendly to each other and courteous to strangers'. It is hard to believe they could have changed so much in the course of fifty years. It is, however, now generally accepted that the Padoucas could not have been Welsh Indians.

Some authorities deny the existence of the Doegs, mentioned both by Morgan Jones and Paul Marana, though even the sceptical Stephens seems to accept their reality, declaring that they probably belonged to the Delawares, who lived lower down Ohio's Delaware River. But, until the middle of the eighteenth century at least neither the Padoucas nor the Doegs were known by the English, and only the French had close acquaintance with them. It was almost certainly through French sources that Paul Marana heard about the Doegs. If the Doegs were part of the Delaware tribe, they belonged to the Iroquoian group, which comprises the Iroquois proper, Hurons, Tuscaroras and Cherokees among others. If so, they spoke Iroquois and not Algonquin, as Stephens suggested. But there is no firm evidence for the Doegs as a tribe, though they may have been a sect within a tribe.

One of the early fallacies about the Indians was that they were a nomadic people, and this was used to try to explain how Welsh Indians appeared in so many different places in America. The Indians were not, generally speaking, nomads. They invariably laid claim to a certain district, the boundaries of which were well understood, if not clearly defined, and they kept to those areas. But there were exceptions, notably among the Athapascan and Algonquin tribes of the far north, and, of course, when a tribe had intermingled with foreigners, extremely rare though this may have been in the earlier centuries, persecution by the orthodox Indians may well have forced them to keep on the move. By the beginning of the twentieth century the Indian was often a mongrel, with not enough aboriginal blood to be distinguishable in the features. In 1910, in Oklahoma, for example, the tribal rolls contained thousands of names repudiated by the former tribal courts, and there were cases in which individual 'Indians' had only a sixteenth and in some instances one sixty-fourth of Indian blood.[11]

Nevertheless a gradually diminishing number of reports of individual Welsh Indians trickled back to the big cities until the mid-fifties of the nineteenth century. There was a Mr. Gilman who reported red-haired Indians speaking Welsh in 1857, which was cited by Thomas Stephens. This account seemed to bear out the narrative given to Major Stoddard by a Frenchman travelling in Upper Louisiana in May, 1805. He explored the Missouri for the purpose of extending trade, and learned of the presence of 'a singular nation of Indians, who were not in the least tawny, but rather of a yellowish complexion; they wear their beards and great numbers of them had red hair on their heads.[12]

An unsigned story about the bearded Indians, alleged to be Welsh, also appeared in the *Medical Repository* of 1805.[13] A Captain Davies told of finding Welsh Indians in Illinois, and John P. Brown, author of *Old Frontiers*, who believed that the Muscogee (Mexo-Ilgee, Mexican people) were linked with the descendants of Madoc, stated that they 'settled along the Mississippi River and its far-reaching tributaries as far north as Illinois and as far south and east as the Gulf of Mexico'.

As reports of these mysterious Indians became fewer, and as more detailed information on the structure and sociology of Indian tribes was processed into something resembling a science, so interest in the story waned, at least among most modern historians and anthropologists. Madoc and the Welsh Indians do not fit neatly into their carefully worked out theories and analyses of the Indian tribes. It has become to them just another legend, so that in 1950 Marshal T. Newman, then on the staff of the Smithsonian Institution, wrote an article entitled *The Blond Mandan*, in which he stated: '. . . this review indicates that the blondism and other non-Indian characteristics reported for the Mandan of the eighteenth and early nineteenth centuries are much more plausibly explained by inter-tribal and individual variability in pigmentation and facial features, augmented by recent white admixture, than by pre-Columbian miscegenation with European exploring parties.'[14]

That may be an anthropological case, but it is certainly not an historian's findings. While the pattern of racial development after the Spaniards' landings excluded any integrated element in most areas, in Mexico a mixed race began to predominate. Miscegenation was far more likely in earlier centuries, when exploring parties were small, than in later years when the larger European groups who emigrated in units tended to keep to themselves.

What is of most importance is the evidence of men who lived in an era when reports of Welsh Indians could still be assessed. Historians who had heard this evidence either first hand or second hand were better able to pass judgement. Thus Stoddard had a completely open mind on the question and inclined to the belief that there was something in the Madoc theory. Stoddard was a sober recorder of facts, and he was disappointed that so little effort was made to track down the Welsh Indians. 'Some enquiry,' he wrote, 'ought to be made into the origin and language of this singular nation, and the trouble and expense of making them a visit, if properly managed, would be inconsiderable. If they spoke the Welsh language forty or fifty years ago, it no doubt still prevails among them. The lapse of more than six centuries, the occasional admission of strange idioms, the revolutions in dress, pursuits, and modes of life are sufficient to change, and even destroy the vernacular dialect, not only of the Welsh colonists, but of every nation on the globe.

'. . . Travellers describe certain private societies among the Indians, which apparently resemble our lodges of Freemasons. Their rules of government and the admission of members are said to be nearly the same. No one can be received as a member of the fraternity, except by ballot, and the concurrence of the whole is necessary to a choice. They have different degrees in the order. The ceremonies of initiation and the mode of passing from one degree to another would create astonishment in the mind of an *enlightened* spectator. Is not this practice of European origin? In the early periods of English history the knowledge of freemasonry was mostly confined to the druids; and Wales was more fruitful of this description of men than any other part of Europe. They were almost the only men of learning in those days. . . .

'Our principal aim in this chapter is to excite a spirit of enquiry . . . it cannot be too often revived, nor too strictly investigated.'[15]

John G. Palfrey accepted the Madoc theory in 1858, as well as that of the Welsh Indians. Even Justin Winsor, as an historian a man who weighed every doubt against each disputed fact and made a habit of disbelief, declined to rule out that Madoc might have discovered America. Some school text-books in America still insist that Madoc reached the New World first.

Nevertheless the purpose of this chapter is to administer a corrective rather than a stimulus, to point out fallacies and let some of the wilder, uncorroborated reports speak for themselves. Beyond that it is to reject some of the more fanciful theories and to narrow down the area in which one can usefully search for the Welsh Indians and the landing place of Madoc. Benjamin de Costa's claims to Massachusetts, and Kathleen O'Loughlin's brave efforts to suggest that Vinland was really Gwynetland are as unreal as some of the ancient poems already quoted from patriotic Welshmen.

Leïf Eriksen may have reached Labrador; whether he did or not,

Newfoundland and Labrador, and possibly Nova Scotia, form the area which was vaguely called Vinland. Professor Kittridge has referred to Layamon's 'Round Table' narrative in which he wrote 'A Zung non be of Winet-londe come', claiming that 'Winet-londe' meant 'Gwynedd-lande'. Out of such similarities in words are romances created. Sir Thomas Herbert, who felt so sure that Madoc must have heard the tales and prophecies of Seneca, may have taken the same view, and argued that Erik's Vinland was really Gwynedd-lande, or Wineda, and that Erik had been confused with Madoc. *Ergo* Madoc arrived in Newfoundland. It is ingenious, but it has one obvious flaw: Erik did discover a land which he or his descendants, or scribes, named Vinland some centuries before Madoc's day.

It simply will not do to support the claims of Madoc by trying to decry or deny those of Erik.

13

WILLEM THE MINSTREL

BY THE EARLY seventeenth century there was a tendency among inquiring historiographers to link the fabled Vinland with Madoc's voyages and to suggest that the early Welsh explorers on one of their trips sailed on a northerly route.

Much of this theorizing was based on the Arthurian legends, and as many of these were developed and written in the twelfth century it is not unrewarding to take an objective look at them. What we are mainly concerned with at this distance in time is establishing probability rather than possibility, and possibility rather than straining after an unattainable truth. The Arthurian legends have for centuries been regarded as fictitious stories which an earlier generation had built into falsified history. Today that viewpoint is slowly being eroded. Eugene Vinaver, professor of French language and literature at Manchester University and the acknowledged expert on Sir Thomas Malory, has recently given his opinion on the significance of the discovery of an early fifteenth-century chronicle of King Arthur and his knights in the library of Alnwick Castle, Northumberland. 'The real significance of this find,' he suggests, 'could be that in the Middle Ages the distinction between fact and fiction was very slight indeed. Until now scholars and historians have made artificial distinctions between "chronicles" and "romances".'

Willem the Minstrel's work on Madoc is described as a 'romance'. In that age the word meant a narrative, and however much these narratives were gilded in the course of retelling, their basis invariably was factual. It would be highly irrational to link the Madoc legends with those of King Arthur, as some have done, but it would be equally unwise not to examine them for clues.

One can fairly safely assume that Arthur was not a king, but a sixth-century military leader, fighting for the Britons against the Saxons, and later lovingly and cleverly built up into a literary figure as glamorous as Charlemagne on that consistent medieval British principle of whatever the French can do, we can do better. It is not improbable, if one delves into ancient genealogical trees, to find that through Uther Pendragon Madoc was descended from Arthur. Equally it is possible that centuries ago the Madocian and Arthurian legends became inextricably interwoven and that some narrators ignored the discrepancies in time, gaily mixing sixth- and twelfth-century narratives.

But it is not irrational to examine how these legends became interwoven, as here lie some real clues to the story of Madoc as told by his contemporaries, or at least by his near contemporaries. The Arthurian legends are based on three certain sources: English manuscripts such as those at Alnwick Castle, discovered as recently as 1965; the continental versions such as those of the French on which Malory drew for his *Morte d'Arthur* and the Flemings who brought the stories from Wales to Holland at the end of the twelfth century and early in the thirteenth century; and, finally, the Welsh sources of Taliesin and Geoffrey of Monmouth.

Geoffrey of Monmouth may have been more responsible than others for creating what seemed like a link with the Madoc legend. Geoffrey was Bishop of St. Asaph, which was in the kingdom of Gwynedd, and wrote his *Historia Britonium* in the latter part of the twelfth century. In this work he claimed that King Arthur went to Iceland and conquered that country, a most unlikely proposition, but then Geoffrey was a romancer. What, however, is important is that Geoffrey expected to be believed and because there had been British and Danish links with Iceland long before the twelfth century, such a claim then would not have seemed improbable. Benjamin de Costa was convinced that Madoc expected to find

Vinland when he sailed west because of his contacts with the Danes in Ireland. He cited Adam of Bremen, stating ninety-five years before the voyage of Madoc that 'a region had been discovered by many in that [Western] Ocean which was called Winland because vines grew there spontaneously. This we know not by false rumours, but by certain testimony of the Danes'.

Certainly by testimony of the Danes, but also, and probably even more certainly in Madoc's case, by the Icelanders who had made Lundy their base.

The Flemings were chroniclers in a sober Dutch manner; they collected, arranged and narrated legends rather than embellished them, and, this being their technique, they were as much interested in true life contemporary adventure as in legends that had been gleaned in Wales by talking with bards and priests. A large number of Flemings returned from Wales and the border counties between 1185 and 1220, faithfully transmitting to the Continent the Arthurian legends and much other Celtic folk-lore. But the Flemish versions of many of these stories have unhappily not always been committed to paper; far too often they were simply turned into songs by itinerant minstrels to gratify the romantic yearnings of the lonely wives of the Crusaders. About 1255 a Brabantine minstrel translated Walter Map's *Lancelot du Lac* at the command of his master, Lodewijk van Velthem, and Jacob van Maerlant produced several 'romances' dealing with Merlin and the Holy Grail. Among these Flemings was Willem, a shadowy figure, variously described as minstrel, poet, priest and scholar. His origins are vague; it is clear that he lived in Wales for a lengthy period, probably on the Welsh borders around Herefordshire, as he was known to Walter Map, himself a Herefordshire man.

His best known work was undoubtedly *Van den Vos Reinaerde* (Reynard the Fox), the prologue of which introduces him as *Willem, die Madocke makede* (Willem, the author of Madoc). In his introduction to his critical examination of *Vos Reinaerde*, Professor J. W. Muller asks: 'To whom do we owe this masterpiece? When and where was it written? . . . a certain Willem in the first line of the prologue called himself a poet who had earlier written a work about one Madoc, a work which has often been mentioned by more recent authors, and seems to have been very popular at one time, but now, alas, is lost.'[1]

Dr. Muller speculates on the basis of what little is known of this 'lost romance' and chronicle of Celtic and Welsh origins, in the shape of a fantastic account of the voyages of an ancient explorer. Another author who has written about *Vos Reinaerde*, J. D. Wolters, surmises that the work on Madoc can 'only be guessed at'. A British romance? A description of an ancient voyage of discovery in the style of Brandon? Is *Madoc's Dream* mentioned by Maerlant the same work? Who was this Willem? Was he a priest? His literary education and wide reading, his geological knowledge (he knew about Thuringen, Saksen, Ardennes, etc.), his erudition, his intimate acquaintance with the law, all seem to suggest this. He must have been someone not afraid to give his own independent opinion about the world, with a smile of understanding and without making the impression of a schoolmaster.[2]

One suggestion is that at some time Willem must have been a praemonstratenser from the Abbey of Drongen near Ghent, a cloister with estates near Hilst and Hulsterloo in Dutch Flanders. A *Willelmlus clericus* lived near Hulsterloo in 1269, but everything remains uncertain about the man as far as his native Holland is concerned. An unrelenting search at the Amsterdam University Library and all the principal libraries and museums in Holland produced no further clues. Yet such was the quality of his *Reinaerde* that speculation about him continues. All he revealed of himself in that work was that his name was Willem and that he also wrote *Madoc*. Dutch writers who have inquired into the identity of Willem have gained what information they could not in Holland, but in England and France.

There are fascinating scraps of information about him here and there. Walter Map, whose *De Nugis Curialium* was comprised of legends, gossip and anecdote, referred somewhat satirically to the 'jongleur-bardh Willem, proud as eny pecok, and singe, y-wis, as eny nightingale'. This makes Willem sound more like a troubadour than a priest, and indeed in one important respect his work differs from that of other Flemings; he retained the gift of sober chronicling, but added to it a facility for employing words and phrases that brought out the colours of his narrative, interspersing fact with legends which appear to give his own interpretation of those facts.

Walter Map returned to England after completing his education in Paris in 1161, so he must have met Willem sometime between that date and about 1200, when, one assumes, Willem was a young man. There is no mention of Madoc in *De Nugis Curalium*, but one must remember that the latter was said to have been compiled at the request of Henry II, to whom neither a Welsh hero, nor a renegade Fleming would make sweet reading.

The only other clue given by Walter Map was that Willem went to the court of Marie of Champagne, daughter of the wife of Henry II. M. Edouard Duvivier, of Poitiers, who has made a study of the chronicles of the Troubadours, helped to supply the next link in the quest for Willem by declaring that *Les Romans de Guillaume le Jongleur* were current in Provence and in Champagne in the thirteenth century.

'Willem is certainly one of many *auteurs inconnus*, who, with Audefroi le Bâtard, Chrestien de Troyes and Gace Brûlie enshrined the ancient legends and *pastourelles* in the courts of the twelfth and thirteenth centuries. He has been forgotten for two reasons. First, because he was a foreigner, and secondly because his *Reinaerde* was almost certainly not discovered until long after he was dead. I think he probably died before 1240 and that Dutch searchers for facts about his life have been looking for them in the wrong period.'

Yet M. Duvivier insists that it was his lost work of *Madoc* which was, strangely enough, for centuries the best known. 'It is said to have been obtained originally through Willem's knowledge of Welsh, to have been translated first into Latin, then into French, and probably not at all into Flemish.

'A reputed copy of a French manuscript of the work was found in Poitiers in the seventeenth century, and, having inspected this closely, I am convinced that it must have been translated not later than the end of the fourteenth century and quite possibly much earlier.'[3]

It must have been a habit of Willem to announce himself as the author of another work, for here he is described as 'Guillaume qui fait Reynaud'. The manuscript is probably only a précis of *Madoc*, but the language is undoubtedly medieval French as the following lines will show: '"*Laise," fait Madoc, "com mar fui ne! J'ai laxiet ma serour an la valee . . ."*' and the odd phrase applied to a ship as though it were a woman, '*cointe et jolie*'.

There is an autobiographical postscript in the text which explains that the narrator, Willem, had been both a minstrel and a soldier, originally attached to the Flemish mercenaries fighting the Welsh, but that his fondness for the latter and their bards made him change sides. He lived for a while in an island called 'Ely', had travelled widely in the Low Countries and in France and was especially interested in stories of early discoveries of land in the west from 'Seneca to Madoc'.

First there is a prologue which tells how Willem learned his stories from 'bards and men of the sea', how he had been told to keep the story secret from the English who would go out in search of Madoc if they knew the facts. There is no mention of Owain Gwynedd, but Madoc is 'the scion of a noble family, driven into exile', a minstrel like Willem himself. Though no bards are mentioned by name, the reference to *chansons manavitiennes* seems to indicate them. This phrase could refer to songs or odes of the Manawyddan tradition, to be found in the *Mabiogion*, which, though faded from current usage in Wales in the twelfth and thirteenth centuries, had, curiously, found popularity in Lundy Island. This poses the question as to whether Willem lived in Lundy at some time. For 'Ely' was the name given to Lundy by the Normans, and it is far more likely that this was the island referred to by Willem than that of the same name in the Fen District. The original church on Lundy was named after Elen, a Welsh saint, and Ely was derived from this.

The history of Lundy provides some other support for the theory that Willem lived there. In the Pipe Rolls it is recorded that in 1197 the sum of '100 marks was paid to the Walensian infantry', who were employed to defend the island. Willem may have been one of these mercenaries. Then again the Welsh called Lundy Ynys Wair, described by Taliesin, compiler of the *Mabio-*

gion, as the mythical 'Isle of Youth'. In the records of Lundy there is a manuscript by Taliesin which tells of *Caer Sidi*, the 'Fortress of the Fairies':

> *Seemly is my seat in Caer Sidi;*
> *Neither Age nor plague for him that liveth there:*
> *As Manawyddan and Pryderi know,*
> *Three organs play before the fire there,*
> *And around its corners the ocean currents go.*[4]

All this provides a further pointer to the departure point of Madoc's second expedition as well as indicating fairly positively that Willem knew Lundy. Benjamin F. Bowen stated that Madoc on his second voyage left from 'a small port five miles from Holyhead on the Isle of Angelsey'.[5] This was believed to have been a now forgotten place named Ynys Yr. It will be recalled that Isaac Taylor suggested that the departure point was Ynys Hir not far from where Port Madoc is today. Both Ynys Hir and Ynys Yr resemble Ynys Wair, and in searching their atlases for this name later researchers may not have realized this was the Welsh name for Lundy. Meiron, of course, depending on the narrative of Brechfa, positively asserted that the second expedition left from Lundy.

Willem tells of Madoc's fame as a sailor, which was explained by his grandfather being 'half a Viking', and how he went to the Court of Louis VII of France, disguised as a monk as an envoy of his race. This would certainly seem to identify Willem's Madoc as being a son of Owain Gwynedd, for Owain sent two Welsh monks with letters to the French king, offering his support against Henry II. One gathers that Madoc was inspired by the stories of 'The Fountain of Youth', enshrined in ancient legend and variously described as 'an island populated by the loveliest of virgins' and as a 'mighty new land where wine flowed like water and there was plenty for all'.

Willem, probably adopting the customs of the age of courtly love, introduced a romantic note into his narrative, without which no doubt the ladies of the Court of Champagne would have become restive. Madoc's loved one is not named: here Willem was obscure and from the manner in which he wrote she may have been a real person, or simply an idealized myth. This mysterious maiden was named the 'River Nymph', who was likened to a mermaid because she encased her legs in fish-nets, which surely makes her the originator of fish-net stockings! Willem probably borrowed from Taliesin again here, for the mermaid of the rivers and lakes was a constant *motif* in Welsh folk-lore. Almost certainly the 'River Nymph' is at least a semi-fictitious element in the story, though Willem insists that she and the bards urged Madoc to seek out the 'Fountain of Youth', which at first he thought was the Isle of Ely, but later decided must lie much farther out to sea.

There is at this stage a gap in the narrative and an indication that some folios of it are missing. Then follows the statement already referred to in Chapter 8 of Madoc undertaking his voyage because of a penance inflicted on him by the 'conscience-stricken bard', who wanted him to discover the 'Fountain of Youth' and used the penance as a subterfuge. This is mentioned in the vaguest terms, but it could refer to Llywarch as it tells how the bard was saddened by what he had done.

The remainder of Willem's story relates how Madoc found *'paradis ravi par le soleil, resplendissant com fruits de mer'*, how he returned to 'Wair for two new ships' for another voyage to found a new kingdom of 'eternal youth, love and music, where all should share in the abundance of good things'. There is also a reference to the expedition being armed with 'ten painted pearls to probe the rivers' of, presumably, *paradis*. This is a literal translation, which M. Duvivier considers means the coracles, painted silver possibly, so that they could be seen from afar, and used by the expedition for trips into the interior. Could the reference to 'ten ships' have been a confusion with the dispatch of ten coracles aboard two ships?

Willem, like most good Dutchmen, must have had his feet firmly planted in reality, for his mood, though prone to picturesque extravagances of fancy, is always cognisant of hard facts. Thus Madoc sought in 'Ely' the 'seaman's magic stone', which would ensure a safe return to his new-found heaven – that *pierre laide*, used by the Icelanders. This must be interpreted as a reference to the magnet, for Willem stated that it 'guided the seaman on his course, providing he ensured the safety of his craft with nails of horn'.[6]

Apart from confirming the story of the use of stag's horns as nails in the *Gwennan Gorn*, Willem also gives an entirely new explanation for this. By linking the use of the magnet, or lodestone, with the provision of nails of horn, he presumably meant that ordinary nails might have affected navigation. That such a belief was held in medieval times was demonstrated by John Ruysch, compiler of the Rome Map of 1508, who mentioned that in building ships wooden nails were sometimes used as iron nails were dangerous because of the magnetic attraction of some rocks.

Guiot de Provins, one of the Troubadour poets, wrote in 1181 of the usefulness of the magnet to the mariner:

> *Un art font qui mentir ne peut*
> *Par la vertue de la marinière . . .*

Necker, Abbott of Cirencester, who died in 1217, was also acquainted with the use of the compass, so there does appear to be ample testimony that navigation as distinct from pilotage had been developed among a few Western mariners in the twelfth century.[7]

The Viking raiders came to Lundy in the ninth century, and gave the island its present name, bringing their long boats with them. Not only are the Icelanders said to have used the lodestone in the eleventh century, but Icelandic ordinances were found in the archives of Lundy and the island is mentioned in the famous *Orkneyingers Saga* (Vikings' History).[8]

There is just a hint in Willem's narrative that Madoc had not found all he was searching for, that the *paradis ravi par le soleil* was not his final goal, but that this might be 'six days' distant from a treacherous garden in the sea' – *La Mer Dégringolade*, he called it. From the description of this mysterious 'garden' in the ocean, 'which no storm could ever dissipate, and which swallowed up ships', it would seem to be the Sargasso Sea, which stretches from the Gulf of Mexico north and east past Florida almost to the Azores. The weeds of the Sargasso were, of course, never dense enough to impede the passage of ships, but their presence would have been sufficient to frighten the superstitious early mariners, many of whom told highly imaginative stories about the fate of ships which strayed into the Sargasso. Willem could hardly have invented this story and equally he could not have heard it from other mariners, for the Sargasso Sea was not officially discovered until Columbus reported it in the *Journal* of his first voyage to the West Indies. In this Journal Columbus implied that he had evidence of earlier voyagers through this weed-infested area. Columbus wrote of the Sargasso that 'the weather was that of Andalusia in April' and the sea had 'large patches of very green grass', a description which is very similar to that of 'the warm sea in which plantes do grow' of Cynfric ap Gronow.[9]

Willem's is a strange narrative, filled with imagery and vivid description, yet interlarded with a great deal of material which, if not comprised of facts learned at first-hand, could only have been gleaned from contemporaries of Madoc. It would certainly seem to be based on what Willem had been told and was not a work of fiction. Legend was undoubtedly blended into the story, but the accounts of envoys to the court of King Louis, the description of the Sargasso Sea, the extremely accurate references to Lundy, the mention of 'nails of horn', the quotations from Taliesin and the corroboration of two voyages made by Madoc all point to an attempt to chronicle a true-life adventure.

Lundy had far closer association with Wales in the twelfth century than with England, as the Welsh ordinances dealing with the island show.[10] The Icelandic Sagas covering the period 1139–48 also tell of a 'Freeman from Wales' who descended upon Lundy and appears to have been a power to be reckoned with: 'he ran away to that Isle which is called Lund' and often sailed to 'the Southern Isles'.[11] The Freeman may not have been Madoc, but it is yet another instance of Welsh influence in the island, and it is clear from the Sagas that the long boats of the Norsemen used Lundy as a base for their forays to the south-west and against the English coast.

The 'Fountain of Youth' and the mysterious paradise in the Atlantic Ocean were to be found equally in Welsh, Irish,

Icelandic and Danish legend. It is not quite clear in Willem's narrative whether Madoc did not find the 'Fountain' on his first voyage, or whether he visited it briefly and intended to return again. Willem certainly hinted at the discovery of an island, surrounded by enormous, strange fishes, which promised to be worth a second look, seeming to hint that the expedition had little time in which to explore it. This he names as 'one of the Isles of Llion'.

Madoc may have returned to Lundy by accident on his return voyage. The currents would have brought him somewhere near the Scillies and from there he might easily have mistaken the broad approaches of the Bristol Channel for those of St. George's Channel. On the other hand he may have gone deliberately to Lundy to find out first how the situation was in Gwynedd. Then again he may have returned briefly to North Wales, but been forced to set sail again on account of Dafydd's hostility. It is therefore quite possible that his second expedition may have had an international flavour, being comprised of Welsh, Irish, Danes, Icelanders and even Flemings. There is the extraordinary coincidence that one report of the 'Welsh Indians' in America describes them as being called 'Welegens', and *Welegen* was a term used by the inhabitants of Lundy in referring to a Welshman.

When the chronicles of St. Brandon's voyages were examined by experts more than two hundred years ago it was alleged that they were purely fictitious and derived from the *Arabian Nights*. Since then new evidence suggests that the converse is true, and that the story of the giant fish which Sinbad mistook for an island was plagiarized from the narratives of St. Brandon.[12] Further than this the notes on the Piri Reis Chart of 1513 substantiate this theory. Note XIV states that 'in ancient times a priest by the name of Sanvolrandan (Santo Brandon) travelled on the Seven Seas, so they say. The above-mentioned landed on this fish. They thought it dry land and lit a fire upon this fish. When the fish's back began to burn it plunged into the sea, they re-embarked in their boats and fled to the ship. This event is not mentioned by the Portuguese infidels. It is taken from the ancient *Mappae Mundi*'.[13]

It is unfortunate that Piri Reis did not identify the exact map from which it was taken. It could have been the lost *Fortunata* map. In the Ferdinand Columbus Library in Seville there is a curious reference both to this map and to the oddity of 'moving islands'. The actual text states: '*Et Inventio Fortunata narra, sarsi mentione di due altre Isole, volte all' occidente l piu Australi, . . . che de Isole de Capo verde; le quali vanno sopra l'acqua nutamdo.*' This reference, dated 1571, is to two islands – 'towards the west and a little southward of Cape Verde', which 'skim along the water'.

One of the most eccentric characters who flitted around the Elizabethan court was the mathematician and astrologer, John Dee (1527–1608). Dee drew up a genealogical table in which he claimed to be 'Roderick, Prince of Wales'. Whatever his motives in doing this, Dr. John David Rhys asserted that he was descended from the ancient family of Dee of Nant-yr-Groes, Radnorshire.[14] His links with Wales were strong and, like Sir Thomas Herbert, he had access to the valuable collection of manuscripts in Raglan Castle, seat of the Earl of Pembroke, before they were all destroyed during the Civil War. Both he and Herbert may have learned something of Madoc's voyages from these, as some of the Brechfa odes were believed to be housed there. After leaving Cambridge University, where he is said to have studied eighteen hours a day, becoming a Fellow of Trinity College, he went to the Low Countries and on his return brought back with him an astronomer's staff of brass from Gerard Mercator.

Astronomy alternated with astrology and magic in the career of John Dee and he was nearly all his life suspected of being a black magician. Two informers accused him of trying to take Queen Mary's life by poison or magic. Nevertheless he was an immensely erudite man and on his own initiative procured copies of famous manuscripts and old maps at the Vatican, Florence and Vienna. At the command of Queen Elizabeth he wrote an astrological calculation respecting 'a fit day for Coronation'. In 1580 the Queen, having desired to know her title to countries discovered in different parts of the world, Dee drew up a hydrographical and geographical description of such countries on two large rolls.[15] He travelled far and wide, visiting St. Helena and going to Prague and Russia, where the Emperor offered him £2,000 a year for his services.

Dee was a strong protagonist of the Madoc claim to the discovery of America and went to some pains to establish this more positively than some of his Tudor contemporaries. No doubt his Welsh patriotism encouraged him to do this. Hakluyt consulted him frequently and cited him as a source of information on more than one occasion. But Dee had a passion for secrecy and kept a great deal of his knowledge to himself, committed only to his 'Secret Book', which he is said to have showed to Queen Elizabeth when she visited his library at Mortlake. But, alas, a mob, inflamed by stories of his black magic and incited by his enemies, broke into his house and looted many of his books and manuscripts.

In the field of navigation he was a pioneer who developed his theories with mathematical precision, though his own definition of navigation was simplicity itself: 'the art which demonstrateth how by the shortest way, and in the shortest time, a sufficient ship . . . be conducted.'

Dee not only collected maps, but navigational data and information about ocean hazards from travellers, and his cartographical notes suggest that he had based many of his statements on the *Fortunata* map. But the mystery remains as to what exactly this map was, who saw it, and whether there were two or three versions of it. Benjamin F. de Costa, who delivered an address on the subject to the American Geographical Society,[16] attributed two works to the Carmelite monk, Nicholas of Lynne, who is said to have made a voyage to lands near the North Pole in about 1360. One work was an astronomical calendar, adapted for purposes of practical navigation, the other, which is lost, was the *Inventio Fortunatae* map and book, a copy of which he presented to King Edward III. The earliest allusion to this map was contained on the margin of John Ruysch's Rome Map of 1508. Ruysch wrote: 'It is written in the Book of Fortunate Discovery that, under the Arctic Pole, there is a high magnetic rock, thirty-three German miles in circumference. This is surrounded by the fluid surgenum sea, that, as a vase, pours out water by four mouths from below.'[17]

This almost allegorical description of Nicholas's alleged discoveries contains an echo of much similar thought at a much earlier age. The fear of magnetic rocks was strong in the early Middle Ages, as we have seen in the suggestion that wooden or horn nails be used in ships. It was also to be found in ancient legends, but in these the fear does not refer to the Arctic Circle but to an island far out in the Atlantic and especially to what Willem calls the 'treacherous garden' in what must have been the Sargasso Sea.

Dee based his arguments in favour of Madoc's voyages of discovery on several sources. He cited the *Fortunata* map, which he claimed Nicholas had based on a much earlier map made by the Icelanders, and said he had secured much information about Madoc from James Cnoyen, of Bois-le-Duc, a Dutch explorer. Cnoyen's book, *Belgica Lingua*, is also lost, though both Dee and Mercator made extracts from it. Dee asserted that Cnoyen had in his possession a map dating back to before 1400, based on information from Nicholas of Lynne, Willem of Ghent and 'a priest of Brittany who had an astrolabe'. This showed the track of the voyages of both Nicholas and Madoc and indicated far out in the Atlantic an island called *Gwerdonnau Llion*, discovered by Madoc. Dee was of the opinion that this island was somewhere 'close to the sea of weed' and that it must therefore have been either 'Bermoothes or an islande in the Bahamas'. By Bermoothes Dee meant Bermuda, 'the still-vexed Bermoothes', as Shakespeare refers to the island in *The Tempest*.[18]

Gerardus Mercator supplied some more background to these statements: 'Touching the description of the north partes I have taken the same out of the voyage of Iames Cnoyen, of Hartzeman Buske, which allegeth among the rest he learned of a certaine priest in the King of Norwaye's Court in the yeere 1364. This priest was descended from them which King Arthur had sent to inhabit those islands. He sayd that those foure indraughts were drawne into an inwarde gulfe or whirlpoole, with so great a force, that the ships which once entered therein could by no meanes be driven back againe and that there is never in those partes so much winde blowing as might be sufficient to drive a corn mill.'[19]

Dee's view on this statement was that Mercator had confused his facts. He believed that Mercator had been told of Madoc's voyage and what the priest mentioned was descended not from King Arthur, but from one of Madoc's party who had returned to Europe after the first expedition. He also thought that Mercator had confused reports of whirlpools in the Arctic Circle with a factual account of the risks of being becalmed in the Sargasso Sea. Bringing imagination and logic to bear in his analyses of these early voyages, Dee thought it possible that no absolute proof of Madoc having discovered the Isle of *Gwerdonnau Llion* could be established because it was probable that this was one of several islands in the Atlantic Ocean which were known to disappear beneath the sea from time to time.[20]

'Disappearing islands' greatly worried the early explorers, and, in an age when there was no seismographical expert to re-assure the navigators that each year a few islands in different parts of the world disappear altogether as a result of earth tremors in the ocean, they assumed that either the islands actually moved – 'skimmed the waters' – or they were gigantic fish. The St. Brandon legend can best be explained by this phenomenon. During a cyclone in January, 1945, one of the small islands of the Carados Group, 250 miles north-east of Mauritius, disappeared for a few days as a result of a cyclonic swell. These islands are normally only a few feet above sea-level, and are not inhabited as a general rule, but at times groups of fishermen are left there, using the main island of Saint Brandon for the purpose of fishing and drying fish. The fact that the name of Saint Brandon was given to one of them is in itself an interesting commentary on past legend.

14

LANDFALL IN ALABAMA

IF ONE ACCEPTS that Madoc made two trips to America, one
must equally assume that it is highly improbable that he would
land at the same place, or even in the same region, on each
occasion. In the twelfth century that would have been navigationally impossible, except for a miraculous coincidence.

Therefore it is probable that Madoc founded two colonies in
different parts of America after each voyage. It is, however, highly
improbable that his companions fanned out in various directions
from each place and that this is the explanation of the Madoc
legend developing in various parts of the American continent.
In the first place, not only would Madoc have landed a relatively
small number of people on each occasion, but it seems obvious
that had two such small parties split up their chances of survival
would have been negligible.

In trying to assess where Madoc landed on his first expedition
one must assess the evidence of the previous chapters on the Welsh
Indians. A large number of the reports of their existence can be
ruled out as, at best, unproved, or worst, untrue. A pattern begins
to emerge from the reports and this appears to show that the
majority of reliable reports come from those areas close to the
Missouri and Mississippi Rivers. Admittedly this covers a vast
area, but, having considered reports from the whole North
American continent, it is a step forward to have narrowed the
search even thus far.

There is also the testimony of almost every authority that Madoc probably landed somewhere between the West Indies and the Gulf of Mexico in the south and Virginia in the north. If Welsh Indians were found in areas around the Mississippi and Missouri Rivers one would have expected their ancestors to have landed in the Alabama–Florida region. The majority of early writers suggest one or other of these areas. Hakluyt, it is true, opined that Madoc landed in the West Indies, and indeed he may well have done so before reaching America. Harcourt alone suggested Guiana, and those who supported the theory of a Mexican landing based their theories almost solely on the evidence of Cortes. The remainder thought it must have been Florida or Alabama, though they gave no specific reasons for saying so.

The main reason for suggesting the Florida–Alabama region would be that in the sixteenth and seventeenth centuries most mariners, knowing the probable routes, would have been likely to have given this advice to the writers. Examining the question entirely on a navigational and scientific basis, one is bound to come to the conclusion that Madoc, if he had unconsciously taken advantage initially of the Canaries Current, would have sailed with the North Equatorial Current and the Gulf Stream up the coast of Florida. When in 1513 Ponce de Leon went in quest of the 'Fountain of Youth', he was borne on the Gulf Stream until he discovered Florida instead. Madoc could hardly have missed the advantages of the North Equatorial Current and the Gulf Stream, despite his complete ignorance of the existence of either. From the North Equatorial Current his ship would have reached the head of the Gulf Stream somewhere between Florida Keys and Cuba, where it is ninety-five miles wide and from surface to sea-bed a mile deep. In parts of the ocean at least, weather conditions permitting, the colour of the Gulf Stream would be such a contrasting shade of blue that it would give him a course for long distances ahead. Almost any early mariner would have been drawn irresistibly to follow the warm, azure highway of the current.

Hakluyt was very cautious in hazarding his personal opinion that Madoc probably landed in the West Indies. He may possibly have based this theory on the fact that there was a small island named Mona, off Puerto Rico, lying in the stormy Mona passage which is the gateway from the Atlantic to the Caribbean. This island was known as Mona in Hakluyt's time and has been mentioned by him. It also happens to be the ancient Welsh name of Anglesey. Kathleen O'Loughlin cites this as possible evidence of a landing place by the Welsh, but there is nothing to support the theory and it is more likely that Mona is a contraction of Madonna.[1]

One of the curious features of Sir Thomas Herbert's *A Relation of Some Yeares Travaile* is that he was at such pains to revise the section of the book dealing with Madoc that, after three editions, the version of the story is markedly different in certain important respects. Unless one reads all the editions of this work, to rely on Herbert's narrative is in the nature of a lottery. Some of these discrepancies in various editions have already been pointed out, such as Abeyvile, Abergwili and Abergele. I find in a later edition of the book this extraordinary disclaimer in the text of what is still a book full of printer's errors: 'I shall . . . redeeme an errour formerly by a printed mistake of *David* for *Madoc*, of whom wee treat of.'

On the same page of the text he writes: 'We may entertaine some lights out of authentique Story, and peradventure whereby at first *Madoc*, and his brother *David*, adventured upon those Discoveries.'

Yet later in the book Herbert makes it clear that Madoc made his return trip to America with his brothers 'Edwal and Eneon' (Einon). It is impossible to believe that Herbert, a scholar, having already acknowledged his debt to such sources as Dr. Powel and Hakluyt, would confuse Madoc with Dafydd. This must have been, as he claims, a printer's error. It also looks as though the printer, having made one correction, immediately perpetrated another error (possibly by misreading Herbert's handwriting) in the very next paragraph which, presumably, should read: '. . . whereby at first *Madoc*, and his brother *Riryd*, adventured upon these Discoveries.'

If one accepts this probability, then Sir Thomas Herbert's version more closely approximates to that of Ieuan Brechfa and Meiron.

But, apart from correcting mistakes in later editions, Herbert made quite a few amendments and additions to his text on Madoc. Stephens and Kathleen O'Loughlin both cite the edition in which he says that Madoc 'first reached Newfoundland'. Stephens no doubt felt the mention of Newfoundland showed that the early authors were just guessing at Madoc's landing place, while Miss O'Loughlin felt it helped to confirm her own theories that he might have landed in the region of Cape Cod. But in two of the later editions of the book, if not positively the last two, Herbert states quite clearly and unambiguously:

'. . . after long saile and no less patience, blest with some happy winds, at last they descried land in the Gulph of Mexico, not farre from Florida, a land affording health, aire, gold, good water and plenty of Nature's blessing, by which Prince Madoc was overjoyed and had reason to account his happy estate, superiour to that his brothers strive for, so eagerly emulating with ambitious hate and bloud each other even for a little Territory, incomparable to that good destiny allotted him, being a vast and weal Kingdome, obtained in some part without opposition, and able to satiate the most covetous.'[2]

In this 'happy estate', said Herbert, Madoc 'planted, fortified some advantagious places'. This item of information was added by the author to later editions of his book, but he gave no authority for this statement, though from the general sources he cites it was probably Cynfric ap Gronow, or from Portuguese travellers with whom Herbert had considerable correspondence. He owed much in his writings to information he received from Portugal. There are no signs of primitive fortifications of an unusual character in Florida, but there are quite a few examples in adjacent Alabama, Georgia and Tennessee, and it was some few years before Herbert wrote his travel book that the Spanish authorities organized their expeditions for the *gente blanco* in these territories, one of the main reasons for which was the discovery of the mysterious ancient forts. When the Sieur d'Iberville located the site of Mobile in 1701, he and his French companions discovered the remains of ancient dwellings for which they could not account.[3]

There are at least three forts in Alabama, Georgia and Tennessee which archaeologists have testified are of pre-Columbian origin. They are primarily defence works, intended to give protection to small communities. All three are believed to have been the work of the same group of people and built within the period of a single generation. What is most remarkable about these fortifications is that they have outlasted many defence works built by the European explorers of the sixteenth century.

The three forts are the Old Stone Fort, seventy miles west of Chattanooga, in Tennessee; the fort on the top of Lookout Mountain at De Soto Falls in Alabama, forty-five miles south of Chattanooga, and Fort Mountain in Georgia, seventy miles southeast of Chattanooga.

John P. Brown, author of *Old Frontiers*, writes that 'there has never been a satisfactory explanation for the fortifications such as Fort Mountain and Old Stone Fort. It is apparent that the people who built them were in deadly peril, or they would not have undertaken tasks involving such tremendous labour. Indians might have erected picket stockades, but it is not possible that they built the heavy stone fortifications so skilfully planned from an engineering standpoint.[4]

The forts have been the subject of studies by Lucian Lamar Knight (*Landmarks, Memorials and Legends*), John Haywood, the Tennessee historian, and Albert James Pickett in *his History of Alabama*. Opinion is unanimous that the forts were built a few hundred years before the arrival of Columbus and that they are quite unlike any known Indian constructions. The Old Stone Fort in Tennessee consists of an irregular triangle of rather more than fifty acres, formed by high bluffs rising from the tributaries of the Duck River, walls of stone and flint, which rise to as high as twenty feet in places, and a moat. In Haywood's time he stated that the moat was twenty feet deep and, with the walls, presented an effective and skilfully designed defensive system. In almost all respects it is almost identical with ancient remains in Wales, the arrangement of walls and moat and the single gateway as entrance being typical of descriptions of such works in Gilbert Stone's *Wales*.

At some time in the distant past seeds must have been dropped in earth which had filled a hollow at the top of one of the walls. Out of this hollow grew a tree which was cut down on August 7, 1819, by a Major Murray. When dendrochronologists examined the stump of the tree they calculated by its 337 annular rings that it dated back to 1482.[5] The fort must have been built long before this date.

But before making a further examination of these fortifications it is perhaps an appropriate moment to examine the claim that Madoc landed at Mobile Bay in Alabama, as this is the one place where a tablet has been erected to commemorate the alleged feat. Credence has been given to this not only by the Daughters of the American Revolution, but by the Fort Morgan Historical Commission.

If Madoc had followed the ocean currents, they would have brought him first of all close to the swamps of southern Florida, an unpromising vista for any explorer. Entering the Gulf of Mexico, he would have sailed on in search of a suitable landing place, and Mobile Bay would almost certainly have attracted him as much as it did such later explorers as Ponce de Leon, Pineda and Hernando de Soto. When the Spaniards landed here and took it over from the Indians Mobile was called Echuse by the native tribe. All these explorers, and Americus Vespucius, who dropped anchor here in 1497, paid tribute to Mobile Bay as a perfect natural landing place. They called the bay Bahia del Espiritu Sancto, meaning the 'Bay of the Holy Spirit' because it gave them refuge from the stormy Gulf of Mexico. Today, despite modernization, it is still a delightful retreat, well protected by the hills in the background, but in Madoc's day it must have been a veritable paradise after the swamps of Florida. De Soto's scribes painted a grim picture of Florida, referring to it as 'a land full of bogs and poisonous fruits, barren and very worst country that is warmed by the sun'. Most of the early explorers in these parts, after taking a quick look at Florida and a cursory examination of the coast, seem to have given it a wide berth and to have passed on towards Mobile Bay, which provided an excellent anchorage.

The chief documentary evidence in support of Mobile Bay as the place where Madoc first made landfall in the New World is to be contained in two old letters in the Ayers Collection in the New-berry Library, Chicago. When Major Amos Stoddard was pre-paring material for his *Sketches of Louisiana*, he wrote to John Sevier, Governor of Tennessee, seeking information. This letter, dated August 30, 1816, was as follows:

'As I am an utter stranger to you, I should not venture to address you on the present occasion, were I not in some measure encouraged to do so by your old friend, Governor Claiborne, who has just left this place.

The object of this communication is to request a statement of particulars of a story, which Governor Claiborne thinks you detailed to him some years ago. According to his account, you once saw an ancient book in the hands of a Cherokee woman which you supposed was written in the Welsh characters, said to be given to her by an Indian from the west side of the Mississippi, and which was afterwards burned with her house.

'I have been some time collecting material to prove the existence of a Welsh colony on this continent, which landed here, according to the testimony of history, as early as 1170. If you can call to mind the circumstances to which I have alluded, and will be so good as to communicate them to me, I shall feel myself under many obligations to you.

Signed:

AMOS STODDARD, Major
2nd. Corps, U.S.

John Sevier served as Governor of Tennessee for two terms and has justly been called the founder of that state. A prominent states-man of the Territory of the United States South of the Ohio River, which existed between the era of the State of Franklin and the creation of Tennessee, he had served in the King's Mountain and other Revolutionary campaigns. He fought against the Indians in the Tennessee Valley for more than thirty years, and his prestige among the tribes was such that, though his military prowess caused him to be feared, he was ultimately loved by them. As proof of this devotion they adopted his daughter Ruth and made her a princess of the tribe, teaching her their own Cherokee language. Ruth Sevier served as an interpreter for her father and accompanied him on many of his expeditions, and by this means he learned more of the Indians' secrets than they would reveal to any other white man.

Governor Sevier replied to Major Stoddard in these terms:

Knoxville, October 9, 1810.

Sir,

Your letter of August 30 ult. is before me.

With respect to the information you have requested, I shall with pleasure give you so far as my memory will serve me, aided by a memorandum taken on the subject of a people called the Welsh Indians. In the year 1782 I was on campaign against some part of the Cherokee [this would be in the Chattanooga area]; during the route I had discovered traces of very ancient, though regular fortifications. Some short time after the expedition I had made, I took the opportunity of inquiring of a venerable old chief called Oconostota, who was then, and had been for nearly sixty years, the ruling chief of the Cherokee Nation, if he could inform me what people it had been which had left such fortifications in their country, and in particular one on the bank of the Highwassee River.

The old Chief immediately informed me: 'It is handed down by the Forefathers that the works had been made by the White people who had formerly inhabited the country now called Carolina; that a war had existed between the two nations for several years. At length it was discovered that the Whites were making a large number of boats which induced the Cherokee to suppose they were about to descend the Tennessee River. They then assembled their whole band of warriors and took the shortest and most convenient route to the Muscle Shoals in order to intercept them on their passage down the river. In a few days the boats hove in sight. A warm combat ensued with various success for several days.

'At length the Whites proposed to the Indians that if they

would exchange prisoners and cease hostilities, they would leave the country and never return, which was acceded to; and after the exchange they parted friendly. That the Whites then descended the Tennessee down to the Ohio, thence down to the Big River (the Mississippi), then they ascended it up to the Muddy River (the Missouri) and thence up that river for a great distance. They were then on some of its branches, "but," said he, "they are no more White people; they are now all become Indians, and look like other red people of the country".'

I then asked him if he had ever heard any of his ancestors saying what nation of people these Whites belonged to. He answered he 'had heard his grandfather and father say they were a people called Welsh, and that they had crossed the Great Water and landed first near the mouth of the Alabama River near Mobile and had been driven up to the heads of the waters until they arrived at Highwassee River'.

Many years ago I happened in company with a Frenchman who had lived with the Cherokee and he said that he had formerly been high up the Missouri. He informed me that he had traded with the Welsh tribe; that they certainly spoke much of the Welsh dialect, and though their customs were savage and wild, yet many of them, particularly the females, were very fair and white, and they frequently told him that they had sprung from a nation of White people. He also stated that some scraps of old books remained among them, but in such tattered and destructive order that nothing intelligent remained in the pieces or scraps. He observed their settlement was in an obscure quarter on a branch of the Missouri running through lofty mountains. His name has escaped me.[6]

The Chief Oconostota informed me [that] an old woman in his Nation, named Peg, had some part of an old book given her by an Indian living high up in the Missouri, and thought he was one of the Welsh tribe. Unfortunately before I had an opportunity of seeing the book, the old woman's house and its contents were consumed by fire. I have conversed with several persons, who saw and examined the book, but it was so worn and disfigured that nothing intelligible remained; neither did any one of them understand any language but their own, and even that, very imperfectly.

I have thus, Sir, communicated and detailed the particulars of your request, so far as I have any information on the subject, and wish it were more comprehensive than you will find written here,

Signed:

JOHN SEVIER.

This is the only mention of Mobile Bay as having been the landing place of Madoc to be found in American sources, but it fits into the pattern of other reports covering the Alabama – Georgia – Tennessee triangle and those from the Mississippi-Missouri areas that the Welsh landed at the lower end of Mobile Bay, where Fort Morgan is today, and made their way up the Alabama and Coosa Rivers to the country around Chattanooga before fanning out farther north. Even without there being any corroboration of the statement contained in the Sevier letter, the siting of the ancient fortifications alone appears to give a clue to their movements. Ramsay and Haywood, historians of this area, and the reports of the Bureau of Ethnology to the Smithsonian Institution are all agreed that the remains of the old forts were in the Chattanooga country on the Hiwassee River and the Chickamauga Creek. Referring to archaeological remains found in this district, the Ethnological Bureau in 1898 reported: 'Sewanee on the north bank of the Hiwassee River is a fort of the same name five miles above Conesauga Creek, and Columbus in Polk County in Tennessee. Here are extensive remains of an ancient settlement and a cemetery and, also, seventy years ago, a square enclosure or fort of undressed stone.'[7]

The three principal forts already mentioned are located on the route which the Welsh settlers would have followed, according to Chief Oconostota's statement. It is a consistent northward route from De Soto Falls in Alabama. Thus, though the Sevier evidence is second-hand and vague in some particulars, it is corroborated by later findings in some important points. Benjamin F. Bowen described how in the year 1854 he talked with an old Indian, who told him that a race of white people had lived on Conesauga Creek many years previously. They had cleared the land, ploughed it, raised grain and introduced the honey-bee. The old Indian said that the tribe were known as Welegens.[8]

Once again in Sevier's testimony one hears of the inevitable scraps of paper and ancient books, which always turn out to have been lost, mislaid, indecipherable or, as in this instance, burned. The mysterious books recur so frequently in the reports of the Welsh Indians that one wonders whether there is some strange psychological explanation for the phenomena. Could it be that the Indians divined that the white explorers were fascinated by such finds, and that they produced any scraps of parchment they might possess? The fatal flaw in this argument is that often the manuscripts or books were not produced and that, when found, nobody seems to have taken the trouble to examine them carefully. There was the testimony of George Chrochan, who claimed that the three young priests who went in search of the Welsh Indians 'brought back some old Welsh Bibles to satisfy the Governor they were there'. Yet he made no mention of whether the books were examined, or what they contained.

Interesting light on the subject of the mysterious books is provided in a letter to the author by Mr. Coles J. Pearman, of Cincinatti. Mr. Pearman is on his mother's side descended from a Welsh family who settled in Virginia in the fifties of the seventeenth century. The name was Jones, which does not help very much, and they came from Bangor. The original emigrant was one Merfyn Jones, who was a dissenting preacher.

'Merfyn Jones,' writes Mr. Pearman, 'moved from Virginia to Kentucky, in common with many other Welsh people, and lived on the borders of that territory and what is now known as the State of Tennessee. He had brought with him from Wales copies of the New Testament in Welsh – very crudely printed copies, of which I have one in my possession now. It is an interesting document because in the margins of the book there are handwritten notes in a language which seems to be part Indian and part

Welsh. It is as though he has taken a text in the original Welsh, which he has underlined, and scribbled in the margin exactly what the text would be in the Indian dialect. In one or two instances there are slight differences in spelling, but the translation is almost identical; in others there are basic words in common, but also some differences in words. On the whole it would seem that the Welsh and Indian version are very much the same. An expert who has examined this believes that the Indian handwritten matter is similar to the Mandan dialect, though not sufficiently to warrant a firm declaration to this effect.

'The story handed down in my mother's family is that Merfyn Jones discovered a tribe of Indians who spoke a dialect very similar to Welsh and that he was able to converse with them in a mixture of his own language and theirs. He set out on a journey in 1663 to take a set of New Testaments in Welsh to these people, but never returned. I have often wondered whether the mysterious books referred to in reports of the Welsh Indians could have been the New Testaments he carried with him.'[9]

This might explain one, or possibly two cases of the 'sacred books', but it is stretching probability too far to suggest it is the solution to every case.

A pamphlet by H. P. Biggar, entitled *Precursors of Jacques Cartier*, published by the Ottawa Archivist,[10] is illustrated by a copy of an old map made by Diego Ribeiro in 1529. On this map, close to Newfoundland, are the words *Tierra de los Bretones*, and this has been cited by some as indicating that it was discovered and occupied by the 'Britons', or Welsh. Such a claim shows an ignorance of history. Cabot discovered Newfoundland and Nova Scotia in 1496, reported the excellent fishing to be obtained there, and from then onwards it was fished regularly by the Portuguese and Bretonese. *Tierra de los Bretones* refers to the Bretons, who also gave their name to Cape Breton in Newfoundland.

Ribeiro, however, who was cosmographer and chart-maker for the Spaniards, made several charts, his earliest being based on the celebrated *Padrón Real*, the official record of discoveries drawn by royal order in 1508, and in one of these, the *Sevilla* chart of 1519, now in the Ibanez Cartographical Collection in Seville, there are the words *Tierra de los Gales* with a thin line pointing to Mobile Bay, and a short line, at right angles to this, pointing slightly inland. Whether this was information obtained from the *Padrón Real* map of 1508 one does not know, as no authenticated copy of this map now exists, but it is accepted that Ribeiro is the chief source of what little we know about it.

This is perhaps the earliest proof that the Spaniards had heard of the mysterious Welsh in the vicinity of Mobile long before the expeditions were sent out in quest of them, for *Gales* is unquestionably the Spanish for 'Welsh'.

Chief Oconostota's statement that the Welsh Indians landed at Mobile Bay was so positive that it calls for closer examination, if one is to anticipate some legitimate criticisms of his evidence. Mobile was the name given to the bay in 1711 by the Sieur de Bienville when the French took over Dauphin Island, chosen because this was the title of the Mobilian or Mauvilian tribe of Indians. It has been suggested that the actual name of Mobile would be unknown to Oconostota and that it must have been 'inserted' into the Indian chief's evidence by Governor Sevier. Apart from the fact that Sevier was a stickler for the truth and not addicted to embellishment in his reports, Oconostota had actually visited Mobile and knew the locality well. He was invited by the French envoy among the Cherokee Indians to visit Mobile and went there about 1736. John Stuart, the British Agent among the Cherokees, also lived at Mobile for several years. Oconostota's grand-daughter Elizabeth, the daughter of George Lowery and Ocaloosta, daughter of the chieftain, after her marriage to Sevier's son, Joseph, declared that Oconostota saw a coracle at Fort Serof, which he declared to be identical with those used by the Welsh Indians and that he believed this to be proof of their story.

'The whole tradition of the Welsh Indians,' she told James Farson, 'was passed down in their tribe from one generation to another, though in my grandfather's time it had dimmed considerably. My grandfather was quite certain that they described their landing place accurately once he had visited Mobile, for they gave him details of the bay itself, of the island (Dauphin Island) and the three rivers running into it. The first clue that he had that it must be Mobile Bay was when they mentioned the Mobilia tribe. As to my grandfather stating that they were Welsh, this was based on their saying that they came from a land called Gwynet far across the seas, and James Stuart told him this must mean Wales.'[11]

This Indian testimony on the Welsh Indians I regard as the most factual and detailed of the early evidence of their existence. Oconostota's grand-daughter effectively filled in some of the gaps in the narrative and answered questions that needed to be posed. Elizabeth Sevier felt sure that somewhere, some time 'the tribe had committed some of their history to paper and that in some way the ancient parchments must be connected with this. There had been something that might have been a map,' she added, 'a very primitive one, and nobody could read it'. She thought that this might be contained in the book kept by the old Indian woman named Peg. More significantly, she added, 'the white people would tell my grandfather that they had "lost" a great deal of their language. They said that many of the words used by their fathers and grandfathers were now forgotten and so they had no records of much of their past.'

15

IN THE FOOTSTEPS OF THE WELSHMEN

SPECULATION AS TO what happened to the first expedition by Madoc is not greatly assisted by documentation. Almost the only statement we have is that of Sir Thomas Herbert, telling how Madoc, on his return, 'found many of his Britaines dead, caused by the Natives' villany, or alternation of the clime, which notwithstanding he digested patiently, and . . . bettered the first intention, living with content, and dying in no less distance from Heaven than when at home, unhappiest in this that their own Nation forgot them quite either judging them lost, because never after hearing from them, or because their own Beings were turned topsie turvy'.

This must have been pure surmise on Herbert's part, for if Madoc did not return to Wales again, how could anyone know that he found many of his followers dead. How, indeed, can they be sure that he landed in the same place, or that he even reached America the second time?

There can be no certain answer to the last two questions. It could even have been that Madoc was lost at sea on his second voyage, as some odes and legends suggest. If eventually he reached Mobile Bay, he might not even have caught up with his fellow-adventurers of the previous voyage. By that time they may have moved some distance inland. Herbert may have based his surmise about Madoc finding a depleted number of Welshmen on his return on Ponce de Leon's accounts of his visits to Florida. The latter stated that wherever he landed he 'found the natives hostile', a comment which led Edward Channing somewhat illogically to suggest that it pointed 'irresistibly to the presence of earlier Europeans in that region'.[1]

Zella Armstrong put forward the idea that Madoc might have made three trips to America – 'as is sometimes stated,' she added. She did not say where it is thus stated, but remarked that 'Several accounts, including Hakluyt's, intimate that Madoc made a third journey to America, but careful research indicates that the last trip was made by some of his followers rather than Madoc himself. So far as is discoverable in available references, Madoc by that name is not mentioned again in any record after his landing at the end of the second journey'.[2]

I have found no trace of any evidence to this effect, and can only conclude from the absence of any precise references by Zella Armstrong, that her theory is based on Herbert's suppositions of what Madoc found on his second trip. If Madoc had returned to Wales a second time, there would certainly have been fuller accounts of his activities. If he had been lost at sea not far from the Welsh coast on his second voyage and news of the disaster had filtered back to his countrymen, this might have been a prime cause of the death of the original legend about his discovering America. The stories of his first trip would probably have been greeted by disbelief, whereas the news of his loss at sea would linger much longer in the minds of his countrymen.

One can fairly safely assume that, if Madoc was not lost at sea on his second voyage to the New World, he would have followed more or less the same route as before. Borne by the same currents, he would again have approached the Gulf of Mexico. This time he might either have been carried north by the Gulf Stream along the coast of Florida, or to the Bahamas or other islands in the Caribbean, or to the coast of Mexico. One suggestion is that he might have reached Guadeloupe, as Antonio de Herrara, the Spanish historian recorded that Columbus found the remains of wrecked ships at Guadeloupe and could not account for their origin.[3]

A second suggestion, put forward by many writers, is that on

George Catlin, painter and student of the Mandans

Mah-To-Toh-Pa, chief of the
Mandans

Portrait of a Mandan woman, Me-
Nwek-E-Sunk-To-Ca, by Catlin

the second outward voyage Madoc might have landed in Mexico. This proposition was originally put forward by some Spaniards and eagerly followed up by the Tudor historians. Hakluyt, who cautiously considered that the West Indies was where Madoc first landed, may have given some attention to the Mexican theory for a second voyage, for in the third volume of his *Discoveries* he quotes an extract from a work of Antonio de Epejo written in 1583, which stated that 'The Spaniards along the Rio del Norte, latitude 37 degrees upwards, found the Indians there far more civilized and having a better form of government than in any other part of Mexico'.

In the seventeenth and eighteenth centuries attempts were made to show that there were similarities between the Mexican and Welsh languages. The Isle of Curacoa was said to be similar to the Welsh *groesaw*, meaning welcome, a ridiculous contention on any grounds other than a faint phonetic resemblance. The Reverend John H. Parry went so far as to claim that the double-l in Mexican was not derived from the Spanish alphabet, but from the Welsh double-l, completely ignoring the contrast in pronunciation of the respective double-l in each language. But this is almost as large a piece of nonsense as his other suggestion that Madoc was in reality Manco Capac of Peru and that Mamma Ocello was his wife (Ocello being, according to him, a corruption of the *Uchel*, meaning 'highest'). Thus, he argued, Mamma Ocello was 'the Highest Mother in the Land'![4]

There is indeed no resemblance of any importance between the Mexican and Welsh languages. The letters B, D, F, G, R, S and W have no place in Mexican, while Q, X and Z, so frequently found in the latter language, have no place in Welsh.

The Tudor historians, Sir Walter Raleigh among them, pointed to several words heard in Mexico which, they argued, could only have a Welsh origin. Sir Thomas Herbert summarizes some of these when he wrote: 'It could be no other than Madoc [who found his way to Mexico], confirmed by the records yet extant, writ by Cynfric ap Gronow and Gutten Owen, and no less orthodoxall, by that language left by the Cambrians to Birds, Rivers, Rocks, Beasts and the like.

'Some of which words are these *Gwrando*, signifying in the Cambrian speech to give eare unto or hearken; Pengwyn, with us a white head referred to by the Mexicans, to a Bird so-called, and Rockes complying with the Idiom. Some Promontories had like denominations, called so by people to this day.

'Such are the Iles Corroeso, the Cape Barutaine of Britaine, the floud Gwyndowr or White Water; Bara, bread; Mam, mother; Tate, father; Dower, water; Byrd, time; Llwynog, a fox. . . .'[5]

It is odd that the Mexicans should adopt the word *pengwyn*, meaning literally 'white head', for the penguin which has a black head. As for *mam*, this is merely an abbreviation for the Mexican *Mamma*, which has its root in Spanish. As for *dower*, this is much more likely to have been a corruption of the Spanish *agua*. It was the later Tudor explorers and historians who tried to read Welsh influences in Mexican words, and by that time most probably many Spanish words had been adopted and adapted by the Mexicans and would, of course, be used when they conversed with any white, or European explorer. Even the Spaniards who believed that Madoc might have been in Mexico did not claim that the Mexican language had traces of Welsh.

Yet, despite all these objections, it is possible that Madoc may on his second voyage have landed in Mexico. There is no proof that he did, and it is unlikely now that any will be forthcoming, but the testimony of Cortez, Peter Martyr, Hornius, Biud de Haro, and even Prescott in his *History of Mexico* does abundantly point to the arrival on these shores long before Columbus of people from far across the ocean. But only Peter Martyr suggested that the Welsh had left 'several old British words among the inhabitants'. This is a very different matter than to assert they had given the Mexicans a completely new language.

The Mexicans may have built up their mysterious visitor into a heroic figure, or a kind of god. If Madoc left, promising to return, this might be the explanation of their legend. To the ancient Mexicans he could have become like Bonnie Prince Charlie, 'the King over the water'. But it is impossible to accept that Madoc, with a relatively small party, could have conquered the entire Mexican nation and established himself as an Aztec King, and that

the Montezuma encountered by Cortez was descended from
Madoc.

John P. Brown went further than this, claiming that the
Quetzalcoatl of Aztec legend and worship was in fact Madoc.
'The god was white and he had a beard. He was certainly no
Indian. How would the Indians have known of such a person
unless he existed? The legend contributed largely to the compara-
tive ease with which Cortez conquered Mexico . . . The god really
existed and he may have been Madoc, who arrived in Mexico on
the second of his voyages, earned the affection of the Indians,
taught them, and eventually left them, but promising to return . . .
The Indians thought that the Fair God, Quetzalcoatl, had returned
to them when Cortez came. The winged serpent of Mexico also
has never been explained. It may have derived from the Griffin of
Wales.'[6]

Torquemada also testified that the memory of Quetzalcoatl
was honoured as that of a white man who had come from the far
north. He said that Quetzalcoatl stopped the Mexicans from
shedding blood in sacrifice, but taught them to offer bread and
flowers and burn incense instead. Other Spaniards, as we have
seen, insisted that there were traces of Christianity and such relics
as the Cross to be found in Mexico when they arrived there.

The most searching investigations in Mexico have, however,
not revealed any Welsh traces in what was an ancient, and
unique, if cruel form of civilization. There were even in the last
century some twenty different dialects in Mexico and of these
fourteen were studied in detail and analysed. The suggestion that
the Moquis tribe of Mexican Indians were descended from the
Welsh has already been refuted. Purchas mentioned that the
Pueblos on the Rio del Norte might have originated with Madoc
and his followers, but this again has been substantially denied by
most experts. The Gachupines were descended from people born
in Europe, though after Columbus's day, while the Mestizoes
come from a mixture of white and Indian stock, again dating from
after 1500. All archaeological discoveries here point to Mexican
and Peruvian civilization and not to any European influence.

Yet even if Madoc landed in Mexico for a brief spell and then sailed away, the legend of the strange white man from far across the sea would have lasted as much as if a visitor from Mars had dropped from the skies into the Sahara Desert in the same period. With such a superstitious people as the Mexicans the legend would naturally grow into something larger and more mysterious than it was. When confronted by the Spaniards for the first time, the natives would all wish to praise and deify their previous visitor from across the ocean.

More than this I think it would be unwise to speculate. The chief argument in favour of Madoc having been in Mexico is undoubtedly the testimony of the Spaniards who had nothing to gain from telling the truth. While it could be argued that the Tudors exploited this story, the Spaniards were most unlikely to have invented it.

Some of the speculation about further expeditions by Welshmen in the pre-Columbian era can be attributed in part to the multifarious reports of the existence of Welsh Indians over so wide an area. Earlier investigators of the legend may have come to the conclusion that, if all these reports were true, several expeditions would have been necessary for so many of Madoc's descendants to have been located in so many places. One can therefore dismiss such speculation on two counts; first, that some of the reports were either faked or the brain-children of Munchaussen-like minds and others were based on false surmises, though otherwise genuine; secondly, that if there had been more than two expeditions, much more would have been known about them by contemporary scribes.

There are some reasons to believe that Madoc may, on the way back from America after his first voyage, have sought refuge from a storm in the Bahamas, probably at the island of Bimini. The Ribeiro map of 1529 shows, somewhat inaccurately, to east-north-east of the coast of Florida an island marked *Tierra de Bimini*.[7] Now the Spaniards never troubled much about the Bahamas, despite the fact that Watling Island was probably the island sighted by Columbus shortly before reaching the New World. The Spaniards learned of the existence of Bimini from the mainland Indians who gave it this name. It was from the Indians that the Spaniards learned that the 'Fountain of Youth' which Ponce de Leon sought was none other than the Isle of Bimini. They had learned of its existence from 'Matec', according to Peter Martyr.

The 'Fountain' on Bimini is little more than a legend now, though at one time its healing properties enjoyed a considerable reputation. The island inspired Heinrich Heine to write:

> *In the Isle of Bimini*
> *Blooms the everlasting springtime and again*
> *In the Isle of Bimini*
> *Springs the all-delightful fountain.*

The 'Fountain of Youth' was enshrined in Welsh legend long before the twelfth century. If Madoc and his men had found such a fountain, that could have kept the legend alive. That they returned to Wales and spoke of their discovery could have been the explanation of Willem's references to the 'Fountain of Youth'. Willem told of an island surrounded by strange fish of enormous size: these could have been the giant tuna, the blue marlin swordfish and other big-game fish with which Bimini still abounds. It is not beyond the bounds of possibility that the *Gwerddonau Llion* (the legendary Isles of Llion) shown on the Fortunata map was meant to be Bimini, though it is shown to be in the middle of the Atlantic and not in the Caribbean. But there is no evidence that the Welshmen tried to settle on the island.

When the Spaniards first landed in Mobile Bay, their ships had to anchor some distance out as much of the bay was too shallow for large vessels until eventually a channel was dredged. But it was an ideal anchorage, and it may well have been, as later evidence will suggest, that the Welshmen used coracles to get ashore. By the time the Spaniards arrived Indian tribes were in possession of the immediate interior and for some years presented a hostile front to the settlers. In 1519 Pineda erected a huge Christian Cross at Mobile and Catholic services were held here for the first time. Nine years later when Narvaez landed all of his followers except four were massacred by the Indians. The Indians were almost certainly of the Creek tribe.

If one follows the line of the ancient forts through Alabama, Georgia and Tennessee, it is possible, by extending the line down to Mobile Bay, and, starting from there, to retrace the steps of Madoc's followers on their journey inland. They probably arrived in the deep water behind the point where Fort Morgan is today, and then explored the whole of Mobile Bay before venturing up a small stream known as Dog River.

One or two modern maps even call this stream 'Mad Dog River', such is the cult of Madoc in this part of Alabama. There is no justification for this. The stream was called Rio del Perro by the Spaniards, meaning 'River of the Dog', and its name was possibly changed to Dog River some time after the Treaty of Paris in 1763, when the British took over Alabama under the title of British West Florida. On the other hand it is claimed that when the Sieur Pierre le Moyne d'Ibervile came to Mobile in 1701, it was know as Dog River then. I find this hard to believe, as indeed is Peter Brannon's suggestion that Madoc was known as 'Madog or the Dog' and that the name of the river was derived from this.[8]

Again using coracles, which they almost certainly brought with them on the voyage, the Welshmen would then have progressed up the Alabama, Coosa and Hiwassee Rivers. Whether they met resistance at this early stage one cannot say. Their instincts as Welshmen would certainly impel them to make their way up any river. But they would almost certainly have made their base on the shore of the bay. Don Tristan de Luna Arellano, who commanded the Spanish fleet which came here to colonize the coast in 1559 reported that 'the port of Ochuse is one of the best to be found in the discovered part of the Indies. The lowest water it has at the entrance is eleven cubits, and inside it has from seven to eight fathoms . . . ships can anchor in four or five fathoms, a cross-bow shot from land. There were some few Indian huts which seemed to be for fishing'.[9]

De Luna also reported that there was much game and wild fowl, and many fish of numerous varieties. The initial experience the Spaniards had of the Indians was that they were friendly as long as they thought the invaders were only there for a short stay. They provided burden-bearers and gave their services without any charge, but the moment they discovered the Spaniards wished to stay permanently they became hostile. A similar situation may have beset the Welshmen; on the other hand they may not have found the Indians until they went some way up the Alabama or Coosa River, as natives did not appear in great numbers along the coast until the Spanish invaders arrived. The Spaniards found that all the 'towns' in the territory were on the banks of the rivers; the rest of the land was so densely forested that population was scanty.

The Welshmen's route was undoubtedly up the Alabama River, not the Tombigbee River, to the point where it joins the Coosa River, deep into Alabama and close to the borders of what are now Georgia and Tennessee. Here is situated Look-Out Mountain, part of the Alleghanian chain, rising to a height of about one thousand feet and close to the waterfall which takes its name from De Soto, where the first of the fortifications was established.

Unhappily, during the past hundred years the remains of the fortifications on Look-Out Mountain have been tampered with, and the walls have been robbed of stones for the building of summer cottages. All that is left is a hump covered by the mould of dead leaves.

But in 1833 it was still possible to get a clearer picture of the original fort, and Josiah Priest then gave the following account of his explorations here.[10]

'The top of the mountain is mostly level. On this range, not-withstanding its height, a river has its source, after traversing it for about seventy miles, plunges over a precipice (De Soto Falls). The rock from which the water falls is circular, and juts over consider-ably. Immediately below the falls, on each side of the river, are bluffs which rise two hundred feet. Around one of these bluffs the river makes a bend, which forms a peninsula.

'On top of this peninsula are the remains of what is esteemed to be fortifications which consist of a stone wall built on the very brow of this tremendous ledge. The whole length of the wall is thirty-seven rods and eight feet, including about two acres of ground.

'The only descent from this place is between two rocks, for about thirty feet, when a bench of the ledge presents itself, from

Routes followed in the U.S.A. by the 'Welsh Indians'

two to five feet in width and ninety feet long. This bench is the only road or path up from the water's edge to the summit. But just at the foot of the two rocks, where they reach this path, and within thirty feet of the top of the rock, are five rooms, which have been formed by dint of labour. The entrances of these rooms are very small, but when within, they are found to communicate with each other by doors or apertures . . . Twenty men could have withstood the whole army of Xerxes, as it was impossible for more than one to pass at a time and might by the slightest push be hurled 150 feet down the rocks.'

There are quite marked similarities in these remains to those of pre-Norman castles in North Wales. Mr. Arthur F. Griffiths, a Kentucky surveyor, made a detailed sketch of the De Soto remains some years ago and, on a visit to Wales, was able to compare it with a plan of what the original Gwynedd castle of Dol-wyddelan must have been like. He noted that in the arrangement of the ditches, on the inner side of which rocks were piled up and mixed with dirt, and in the pattern of the stonework, the mode of construction was almost identical. 'One must remember that most castle remains in Wales today are of Norman origin,' stated Mr. Griffiths. 'It is not easy to reconstruct completely what Welsh fortifications were like in the twelfth century. The Normans took over several such forts, including Dolwyddelan, and remodelled them. But one can study the general methods then used. They show that the Welsh had during the Dark Ages and the attacks by the Danes lost the building arts of the Romans and by the twelfth century they were only just beginning to develop their own methods, which could be summed up as crude, but effective, primitive but strategically well planned. At Dolwyddelan the plan was not only similar to that at De Soto Falls, but the siting almost identical – the same placing of the fort on a high, precipitous rock, the emphasis on inaccessibility, the smallness of the entrances and, more significant, the use of materials. Both in Wales and at De Soto the materials used were the natural, shattery stones of the country, well squared and with a hard mortar.'[11]

It is almost certain that this was one of the forts discovered by Sevier during his Cherokee campaigns. It had been hidden for years when Priest stumbled across it, and outside the immediate locality of De Soto Falls its actual site is not well known today. Priest surmised that it was 'the work of an unknown people who must later have been overwhelmed by the Cherokee Indians'.

What Governor Sevier did not make completely clear in his letter to Major Stoddard was that his own itinerary during the Cherokee campaign of 1782 was in itself corroboration of what Chief Oconostota had told him. Haywood has given this itinerary in some detail: across the Tellico River on the Hiwassee Trace, then across the Hiwassee River to Vann's Town and Bull Town at the head of Chickamauga Creek, and afterwards up the Coosa to the Tennessee River. Thus Sevier followed almost the identical trail of the white Indians.

Close by the De Soto Fort are caves in the cliffs which also show signs of having been adapted for living in, for rooms have been carved out in the interior. It was at first thought that the fort and caves were built by De Soto and his men, as the Indians told the early settlers that this was the work of 'a white people who wore clothes, who had beards and were fair skinned'.[12] But there is nothing remotely Spanish about these works, and De Soto himself reported finding at least one fort in this territory.

From De Soto Falls the wandering Welshmen, possibly by this time constantly threatened by hostile tribes, presumably made their way north-east along the Coosa River into Georgia. For here at Fort Mountain in the Cohutta Range, south of Chattanooga, is another fortification built on top of the mountain. Once again it is apparent that the people who built it intended to create a bastion secure against all attacks. The same skilful defensive system as at Stone Fort, already mentioned, is evident. That it was hastily constructed, more so perhaps than some of the other fortifications, is also apparent, for the boulders have been put together without any cementing substance. The walls are built in a succession of angles, each forming a pit capable of sheltering half a dozen men.

This is the highest of all the forts, nearly 3,000 ft, and the main defensive wall is 855 ft. long, obviously intended to protect its builders from a powerful invading force. Hughes Reynolds in *The Coosa River Valley* gave his opinion that 'at one point there was a gateway which led to a spring. The wall was built with the skill of military engineers with such angles that all parts of the wall could be defended. Such a defensive work was fully up to the standards of early European military science and far beyond the ability of the Indians to construct unaided. The Cherokee legend is that it was built by people with pale faces whom the Indians overcame and chased out of the country, but that is very far from a solution of the builders. It is unlikely that the builders were in any way related to the Mound Builders, for a number of reasons, one being that the Mound Builders were not stonemasons.

'Another conjecture is that it was built by de Soto and his soldiers. However, a comparison of the time consumed by them in crossing from the headwaters of the Savannah River to their camp at Chiahi proves it impossible for them to have stopped long enough to build any such defensive works. Moreover they were not on the defensive; they were completely on the offensive.'

It is perhaps worth noting here that the reference to Mound Builders concerns the mounds built by the ancient Indians for burial or religious purposes. Such mounds are to be found in many states, but they were earthworks quite unlike these stone fortifications. The Cherokee Indians are believed to have penetrated to this territory in about the thirteenth century, so it could have been about this time that the forts were built. Lucian Lamar Knight, the Georgian historian, declared of Fort Mountain that 'a former occupancy of this region by Europeans is strongly intimated if not unmistakably proved'.

The Welshmen may have remained at Look-Out Mountain for a considerable time and attacks against them were probably rare at first. Once they had been dislodged from one place, however, the Indians returned to the assault more frequently. It is a long step from the first fort at Look-Out Mountain to that at Fort Mountain. Afterwards forts were more often and seemingly more hastily erected. Either this was the beginning of a long retreat or else it was an attempt to make a last stand by setting up a ring of forts in the Chattanooga area. The next settlement was at Hiwassee River, the Savannah Fort in Polk County, Tennessee, where there are extensive remains of fortifications today.

Judge John Haywood, the Tennessee historian, writing early in the last century, stated that there were 'five forts in the Chattanooga area which had been built by white people living there before the Indian occupation'.[13] He based his opinions on prolonged investigation of the various forts, on cross-examination of Indians and a search in the Spanish archives of the territory. Haywood claimed that an ancient system of cementing unknown to any archaeologist was employed in building these defence works.

Could this have been the 'lost secret' of cementing at Conway Castle, to which Mrs. Wilde referred? Haywood named the five sites of the forts as:

(1) a point at the mouth of Chickamauga Creek on the outskirts of what is now Chattanooga; (2) on a site now covered by Chickamauga Lake; (3) a site twenty miles from the mouth of Chickamauga Creek; (4) on the Hiwassee River; (5) Pumpkintown. The fort on the Hiwassee River is the one spoken of by Sevier and Chief Oconostota and mentioned in the nineteenth annual report of the Bureau of Ethnology.

Finally, after ringing Chattanooga with defence works, the fort builders came to Old Stone Fort, at Manchester, Tennessee, on the Duck River. This, together with the forts at Look-Out Mountain and Fort Mountain, comprise the only fortifications still remaining today in anything approaching a worthwhile condition. Most of the ancient sites have long since been covered over by other buildings, like the fort which was on the Tennessee River at Hamilton, and is now the site of the County Court House.

16

MAINLY ON THE MANDANS

IT IS WHEN we come to the Old Stone Fort at Manchester, Tennessee, that the trail of the Welsh Indians becomes indistinct and least easy to pick up. For suddenly the defence works cease. Speculation inevitably takes over. Either the Welshmen were wiped out by the hostile Cherokees or some other tribe, or, hard pressed by their enemies, they started on a long trek in search of safety, never staying long enough in one place to make it worth while building a fort.

One theory is that Madoc's colony was slowly eroded by incessant attacks and disease until the few remaining Welshmen were assimilated by Indian tribes, to whom they introduced traces of a primitive Welsh culture. It is argued that they were forced northwards down the Ohio Valley and became mound-builders. Certain facts, admittedly, point to this. Other historians have pointed to the mounds and earthworks on an island near the Falls of Ohio as an indication of their burial ground after thousands of them had been killed in a vast battle, and that the survivors went down the Ohio River, started up the Mississippi and came to the mouth of the Missouri. In 1710 it was rumoured that they had withdrawn beyond the Mississippi. Mound building seems to coincide with the periods in which the tribe were relatively untroubled by their enemies. Mandan mound building was quite distinctive from that of other Indian tribes and from the descriptions of Verendrye, La Chapelle, Catlin and Jabez Halliday such constructions resembled the 'motte and bailey castles' of the earth mound and palisade type such as the one at Twt Hill, Rhuddlan, North Wales, built in 1073 by Robert of Rhuddlan.

Certainly they must have been assimilated. The only questions which are difficult to answer are, firstly, how soon were they absorbed by other tribes, and, secondly, to what extent did they retain a distinctive culture. The Muscogee (Mexo-Ilgee) Indians, driven out of their own country by the Mayas and the Toltecs, are believed to have landed at the mouth of the Mississippi in the eleventh century, which was about the date of the coming to power of the Aztecs in Mexico. But at the beginning of the thirteenth century the Cherokees pushed the Muscogees southwards and followed on into Tennessee. It must have been at some stage in the thirteenth century – possibly somewhat less than one hundred years after Madoc landed – that the Cherokees and the Welshmen clashed.

Thus the assimilation of the Welshmen could have started as early as 1250, but more probably did not begin until much later. If one accepts only a third of the reports of their existence made by European explorers, the preponderating evidence is that they managed to survive for some few hundred years, sadly depleted, but more or less a co-ordinated community, and that they made their way to territories around the Missouri River.

One strong argument in favour of the ancient forts having been built by the Welshmen is that the Cherokees had by the middle of the thirteenth century spread throughout Tennessee and as far south and east as the Gulf of Mexico and Alabama, and they were essentially mound-builders and never made stone fortifications.

For several weeks, possibly even for several months, the Welshmen could have held out in their forts against the savage tribesmen. But eventually sheer force of numbers and an effective blockade would have defeated them. Then they either had to yield, come out and be killed or make a truce with the invaders by promising to go away. The trend of the history of Indian tribes suggests the third method was the one adopted.

Chief Oconostota, relating the history of his people as handed down to him by his forefathers, spoke of a great battle between the 'white men' and the Cherokees. When the Welshmen were defeated a treaty was called at Muscle Shoals, where the white men agreed to leave the Chattanooga area at once. This may explain why axes, hoes and other metal utensils were found around the abandoned fort on the Hiwassee River. It is very difficult to fix the date of this battle and the ensuing treaty, but it was probably nearer to the seventeenth century than to the thirteenth.[1]

Judging from the many reports of Welsh Indians which came from Kentucky, the survivors of Madoc's colony probably moved north into Kentucky and, at some time or other, into Carolina in the next stage of their long trek across America. Robert Durrett testified that stories of the Welsh colonists were to be heard around every fireside where pioneers gathered in the eighteenth century.[2] There was an old Indian trail which led from the Old Stone Fort to Nashville in Kentucky.

But by the early eighteenth century it is very doubtful whether many traces of Welsh ancestry remained. Certainly these would not be discernible to anyone who did not possess an intimate knowledge of the Welsh race. But it is easy to see how any slight semblances of essentially Welsh characteristics would become magnified to Welshmen coming across the survivors, and they would be tempted to exaggerate the similarities. When Frenchmen or Spaniards came across the Welsh Indians they merely remarked on the purely European characteristics. The question remains: by whom were the Welshmen assimilated, or, alternatively, into what Indian tribe did they eventually evolve through miscegenation? One can eliminate the Padoucas, despite all claims to this effect. Many other tribal claimants have already been eliminated in preceding chapters, including the Tuscaroras, though there is not sufficient evidence about the Doegs to make an absolute decision one way or another. It is just possible that there may have been some assimilation by the Cherokees, though here again the evidence is mainly against any such assumption. History invariably points to the expulsion of the 'white men' by the Cherokees, not their absorption.

One interesting point about Chief Oconostota's testimony, which was very thoroughly followed up by later historians, is that the chief was insistent that the Welshmen had been the first people to come to Alabama. This could explain how so small a group survived as long as they did. If they had only thirty years in which the territory was theirs alone, it would be sufficient a period to enable them to increase their population, assuming that some women were among their number.

In tracking down the further route of the Welshmen, two points need to be considered. Several reports refer to 'bearded Indians'; I have counted no less than fourteen positive stories to this effect, and they cannot all be faulted even though the term 'bearded Indian' is in itself a misnomer. There are no bearded Indians. Therefore if early settlers came across such a phenomenon, the person found was certainly not a pure Indian. And if he were a half-caste he would not be likely to be confused with a Welsh Indian, nor would he have told a story about ancient ancestors who came from far across the seas. The other point is that raised by Burder about the Mobilians, a tribe who lived to the west of the Mississippi, which he and other historians thought might be the missing link in the Welsh Indian story. The Mobilians spoke the languages of many tribes, yet their own was said to be unlike any other Indian tongue. The evidence is that the Mobilians had come from the south; they may have taken their name from Mobile and been descendants of the Mobilia, or Mauvilia. In this case their association with the Spaniards probably explained their own bastard dialect and their ability in understanding other languages.

The one tribe which from all accounts is the most likely to have evolved from the Welshmen, or to have absorbed them, is the Mandans. They dwelt alongside tributaries of the Missouri River, the area from which most reports of the Welsh Indians came. For the best part of two hundred years after Columbus discovered America they remained practically unknown and away from all contact with Europeans. The Sieur de la Verendrye heard about them and in 1735 decided to explore Mandan territory, taking a French expedition inland from the lakes down the Missouri. Eventually he received an invitation from a Mandan chief to visit the tribe.

De la Verendrye was fascinated by what he saw. In his journal he

A Mandan Indian in full dress sketched by Catlin

Contemporary sketch of a Mandan Koorig, showing shape, base and thwart. Its length was 4 ft. 10 in.

Method of carrying a Welsh coracle in 1820; from a drawing by George de la Motte

recorded that the Mandans were 'white men with forts, towns and permanent villages laid out in streets and squares'. He found eight villages, which were kept extremely clean, well defended and sited on the headlands of the Missouri River.[3]

There was no lack of detailed description in Verendrye's narrative. He described the dome-shaped houses, built to a regular plan, in which the Indians lived, how their lodges were made of a framework of logs over which earth was piled several feet thick. They claimed to be the first human inhabitants of that part of the world. They lived well, had totally different customs from other tribes, and practised agriculture more than hunting. Neatly laid-out fields of Indian corn, beans, melons and pumpkins testified to their agricultural skill.

Verendrye mentioned the remarkable fact that whereas all other Indians he had encountered were clean-shaven, some of the Mandans grew beards. He also spoke of the 'grey hair' of the older Indians, a significant point because Indians do not have grey hair. Indeed, the very fact that Indians were beardless and never had grey hair has led many ethnological experts of the orthodox schools to condemn reports of bearded and greying tribesmen and dismiss them as inventions. There are, however, far too many of such reports over a long period of years for them to be summarily dismissed. The lack of such reports in the past hundred years merely means these particular Indians have died out.

The meticulous narratives of Verendrye cannot be disregarded; they are corroborated by other French travellers, and Reuben Thwaite recorded that 'a tradition of white bearded Indians was rife among the French traders and explorers in the eighteenth century . . . The variation of colour of complexion, hair and eyes among the Mandans led to various theories of their origin, among them that of Welsh derivation gained much currency . . . The colour of these Indians is sometimes reddish, sometimes a less dark copper colour. In some it is greyish brown, in others yellowish. After a thorough ablution the skin of some of them appears almost white and even shows colour in the cheeks. There are whole families among them with grey hair'.[4]

The Mandan villages in la Verendrye's day were obviously

permanent settlements and there was every indication that the Indians had been in the vicinity for a very long time. The villages were designed primarily as peaceful communities, but there were also signs of defence works. La Verendrye referred to the existence of walls and trenches, and Bougainville, another early French explorer, mentioned the villages being surrounded by moats.[5]

There never was any suggestion by the early explorers that the Mandans were not Indians. The emphasis was mainly on the fact that they were much more nearly white than other tribes and that in many respects they had European characteristics. Maximilian, Prince of Wied, who followed Verendrye to the Mandan villages, gave a detailed account of their physical characteristics – the 'ethereal beauty of the women, the robust, broad-shouldered men, with noses not so long and arched as those of the Sioux . . . sometimes aquiline or slightly curved, sometimes quite straight, never broad, nor had they the high cheek-bones of the Sioux'.[6]

It was the savage Sioux tribe who eventually forced the Mandans to withdraw from these villages. The date of this withdrawal was certainly long before the end of the eighteenth century. George Catlin, the artist and historian, who made first-hand acquaintance of the Mandans at a much later period, put the date at about 1760. At any rate the Mandans withdrew and managed once again to hide themselves away in unexplored territory. Neither the French nor the Spaniards were able to locate them again for many years, the latter not until the Mackay–Evans expedition.

The critics still point to the evidence of Mackay and Evans as the ultimate *coup de grâce* to the theory that the Mandans were the Welsh Indians. But, as we have seen, both men's evidence is suspect and Mackay specifically applied his testimony to the Padoucas not the Mandans. It is true that the critics can rejoin that only eight months after Evans left the Mandans they were visited by another Welshman who did nothing to support the story. But in the first place it is almost certain that David Thompson was not told about John Evans by the Mandans, for in the account he wrote of the tribe he made no mention of his fellow-countryman. It is also equally certain that Thompson had never heard either about Madoc or the stories of the Welsh Indians, otherwise he would surely have confirmed or rejected the reports. He did neither. Finally, David Thompson did not speak Welsh and indeed knew nothing about Wales. His grandfather had been David ap Thomas, but when his father went to live in London he changed the name to Thompson, obviously desirous of completely anglicizing himself. David Thompson was born in London and his father died when he was a child. He was apprenticed to the Hudson Bay Company at the age of fourteen and went to Canada.

But if Thompson knew nothing of the Welsh language or customs, he arrived at the conclusion that the Mandans were a fair-skinned race with many European characteristics.

The next visitors to the Mandans were Meriwether Lewis and William Clark, who record that the tribesmen told them of their perpetual war with the Indians over the centuries. Clark said the Mandans made it plain that they regarded all other Indians as 'foreigners' and their enemies. By this time Napoleon had acquired from Spain all her territories west of the Mississippi and had sold them to the United States. William Clark, who was later promoted to General, retained to the end of his days a lively appreciation of the Mandan women. Starnes in his *Missouri Historical Review* recalled the general at the age of seventy speaking with 'youthful fire' of the Mandan women as 'the handsomest in the world'.

Many travellers speak of the Mandan maidens with equal enthusiasm and pay tribute to their blue eyes, fair skins and light-brown hair. George Catlin was so moved by their beauty that he used them as models and painted many portraits of them, all of which show a remarkable distinction in their faces, and in each picture he emphasized the blue eyes.

Thomas Stephens, who dismissed most reports of the Welsh Indians as 'rubbish', admitted quite frankly that George Catlin was 'the most respectable witness on behalf of the story'. He could hardly do otherwise for Catlin has given us the most detailed picture of this tribe which has been compiled by anybody. Catlin was a remarkable man by any standards. Talented, erudite, a trained observer with a flair for detail, painstaking, with a picturesque touch about his writing that was even more evident in his private letters than in his books, he was in his way an American Gauguin. A more romantic life than Catlin chose to lead it would be hard to imagine. Born at the beginning of the nineteenth century in Wyoming, he started life as a law student in Connecticut, giving this up after three years to study painting in Philadelphia. Painting entranced him and claimed more and more of his time. Then one day some Indians came to town. Catlin painted them and became fascinated with their womenfolk. It is only fair to say that he was equally excited about the tribal way of life, their customs and history. The sudden enthusiasm became an obsession, the obsession became a call which he could not turn down. He wanted to carry out an expedition to their lands, not only to paint, but to write the Indians' history as a record for posterity before, he said, 'it was too late'.

But nobody would support his scheme, financially or otherwise. He met with marked hostility. So, just as swiftly as he had fallen in love with the Indians, he gave up everything – his career, his parents and his wife. In 1832 he set out on his quest.

George Catlin was the last white man to have had any close contacts with the Mandans. There were very few of them left in the eighteen-thirties, and by this time traces of their original ancestry must have been almost obliterated. If in 1782, when Governor Sevier was negotiating with the Cherokee chiefs, Oconostota was relying on his memory of what was already distant history, in 1832 the remaining Mandans would probably not have any knowledge of the Welsh tradition. Only a man who was prepared to spend a long time studying every detail of their lives and talking with them could expect to acquire any worthwhile information on the subject. This is what Catlin did. Whereas John Evans spent only six months among the Mandans, Catlin lived with them for eight years, winning their confidence, painting their portraits, making sketches of their homes and equipment and compiling copious notes for his two-volume history of the North American Indians, which contained several chapters on the Mandans alone.[7]

This was followed in later years with a highly successful lecture tour in Britain and an exhibition of Indian articles in London, where he presented an Indian chief to Queen Victoria.

Perhaps Catlin etherealized and refined the Mandan women in his portraits. This was not an uncommon technique among painters of his age. His Mandan maidens are unquestionably beautiful. He had the gift of making colours talk, and the Indians with their ceremonial attire provided him with every opportunity to indulge in an orgy of colours. His portrait of Me-Nwek-E-Sunk-To-Ca reveals an exquisitely chiselled face, with large attractive blue eyes, a well-shaped, rather long nose and cupid's bow lips that would have graced the salons of Versailles. Her hair hangs over her shoulder in long, dark brown, perfectly straight plaits. She is plump, and the artist made no attempt to disguise this, but if one took away the Indian clothes and gave the hair a coetaneous coiffeur, with her fair colouring she would have passed for a European. Catlin's male portraits vary from that of Chief Ha-Na-Tah-Nu-Riah, who was pale-faced but distinctly more Indian-looking in his features, to Mah-To-Toh-Pa whose eyes were also blue and whose colouring was even fairer than that of the Mandan woman already mentioned. Mah-To-Toh-Pa had the features and looks of a northern European.

Catlin was especially interested in the fact that La Verendrye had come across one male Mandan who wore a cross and spoke the names of Jesus and Mary, but found no traces of Christianity among them. But by this time the Mandans were half-breeds, or quarter-breeds, and miscegenation would have removed their most ancient traditions of a spiritual nature. It is therefore all the more interesting that Catlin, who had no Welsh blood in him, and no special reason for pursuing the Madoc theory, persisted in searching for evidence to confirm his own belief that they were descended from the Welsh Indians. At no time, not even on his lecture tours in England, did he make exaggerated claims about this theory, but insisted that he merely wished the facts to speak for themselves. He stressed again and again the Mandans' complete distinctness from other tribes. Many of them, especially the women, had blonde and reddish hair. Their villages, even in Catlin's time, were much better built than those of other tribes.

Catlin descended the Missouri River from the Mandan villages of St. Louis, covering a distance of 1,800 miles, and during this expedition he made careful search of the banks for traces of earlier occupation. He found occasional traces of sites of villages, which the Mandans had been compelled to abandon by other tribes. It soon became obvious to him that the tribe had been gradually weakened over the years and that as they moved north so their fortifications became less formidable and their defences more inadequate. Constant attacks had broken their spirit.

'They continued to make their repeated moves,' he wrote, 'until they arrived at the place of their residence on the upper Missouri. Ancient fortifications on the Missouri, some of which being built on the banks of the rivers with walls in some places twenty or thirty feet in height, with covered ways to the water, evince a knowledge of the science of fortifications, apparently not a century behind that of the present day and present incontestable proof of the former existence of a people far advanced in the arts of civilization, who have for some cause or other disappeared and left these imperishable proofs of their former existence.'[8]

Catlin did not go far enough to find the fortifications in the Alabama – Georgia – Tennessee area, and, probably because of this, he expressed the belief that Madoc entered the Mississippi at Balize, or landed 'somewhere in Florida'. He was certain from his researches that the Mandans reached the Ohio River, where they cultivated fields and established a flourishing colony until attacked by other tribes whose numbers were vastly superior to their own. When he came across the surviving Mandans they indicated to him where their earlier habitations had been, and from this information he was able to find the sites of villages they had set up sixty miles away some seventy years previously, probably about 1760. From the number of houses in the earlier sites he thought there must then have been three times as many Mandans.

'Near the mouth of the Big Shienne River, two hundred miles below their last location, I found still more ancient remains and in as many as six or seven other places between that and the mouth of the Ohio River, each one, as I visited them, appearing more ancient, convincing me that these people, wherever they might have come from, have gradually made their moves up the banks of the Missouri to the place where I visited them.'[9]

Catlin's glowing tributes to the beauty and fair complexions of the Mandan women are borne out by many others. General Clark's account of them is almost identical, while Verendrye was even more emphatic not only about their European looks but their civilized habits and semblance at least of culture. Rued Hjalmar Holand declared that 'all archeologists are agreed that the Mandan Indians have been in prehistoric contact with Europeans. Their frequently recurring blue eyes and their blonde complexion and their superior culture prove this.'[10]

La Chapelle, one of Verendrye's henchmen, whom he left behind to study the Mandan language, paid rather more attention to his love-life than to his researches. Unashamedly he confessed that he never mastered the language, but that he had learned a great deal about their amorous customs which were, he declared, 'a remarkable combination of primitive, lascivious ceremonies and a romantic code of behaviour that had a flavour of the troubadours'.[11] He mentioned that the erotic rites they practised attracted many visitors among the European traders, and that they were accompanied by the music of an instrument that resembled a primitive harp. One gathers that the harp was not an instrument in general use among them, but was brought out only on ceremonial occasions. They had love songs which were plaintive and melodious.

George Catlin thought it possible that the name Mandan might have been a gradual corruption of Madoc, Madocan or Madawgan. But he revised this opinion somewhat when he learned from the tribe that their own, original name for themselves was *See-pohs ka-nu-mah-ka-kee*, meaning the people from the land of pheasants. This was 'probably the name of the primitive stock before they mixed with any other people, and to have got such a name it is natural to suppose that they must have come from a country where pheasants existed, which cannot be found short of reaching the timbered country at the base of the Rocky Mountains, some six or eight hundred miles west of the Mandans, or the forest of Indiana and Ohio, some hundreds of miles to the south and east of where they last lived. . . . This is, I think, conclusive proof that they formerly occupied a country much farther to the south, and that they repeatedly changed their locations'.[12]

Catlin found there was a possibility that the name Mandan had been given to the tribe by the Ricarees, though eventually he discarded this theory on the grounds that they were known as Mandans in Verendrye's time. He speculated briefly as to whether a nasal intonation had changed the word *madder* into Mandan, this being the name applied to a species of red dye. John P. Brown referred to the nasalizing of vowels by the Cherokees. *Ga-da-gi* (Battle Ground, or bloody ground) was pronounced *gan-da-gi*. But such speculation is apt to be sterile, as also is Catlin's claim that *mandon* was the Welsh word for the woodrook, a species of madder used as a red dye. Stephens rejected the idea that *mandon* had any such meaning in Welsh, insisting that it referred solely to dandruff. Other Welsh scholars, however, believe that there were rare instances of *mandon* being used in the sense of a red dye substance.

Catlin was, however, adamant from his personal inspection of old Mandan sites that they came from the banks of the Ohio, and 'brought with them some of the customs of the civilized people who erected those ancient fortifications. I am able to say that the numerous specimens of pottery which have been taken from the graves and *tumuli* about those ancient works (many of which may be seen now in the Cincinnati Museum and some of which, my own donations, have so much surprised the inquiring world) were to be seen in great numbers in the use of the Mandans, and scarcely a day in the summer when the visitor to their village would not see the women at work with their hands and fingers moulding them from black clay into vases, cups, pitchers and pots and baking them in their little kilns in the sides of the hills or under the bank of the river'.[13]

Some of the Mandans retained their tribal purity, but many more, when attacked, saved their lives by inter-marriage with other tribes. They developed a close association with the Ricaree tribe in their later years. The Ricarees settled alongside them and gradually took over the Mandan villages as the population of the

Mandans dwindled. In the summer of 1838 the Mandans were almost wiped out by smallpox, introduced by the fur-traders. Some forty of the tribe survived and were adopted by the Ricarees as slaves. Finally the Ricarees and the Sioux clashed in battle and the Mandan slaves either committed suicide to avoid capture or laid down to die.

It was a pitiful end to the tribe. Some Mandans were so weary of their lot that they implored the Sioux to kill them; others killed themselves by jumping head-first from a thirty-foot ledge of rocks in front of their village. Catlin recorded how Chief Man-To-Tom-Pa watched his family die and then wandered off into the forest to starve himself to death. After six days he returned and laid down beside his dead family. Three days later the last of the Mandans – in that area at least – was no more.

'So have perished the friendly and hospitable Mandans,' sadly commented Catlin, 'from the best accounts I could get, and although it may be possible that a few individuals may yet be remaining, I think it is not probable. One thing is certain, even if such be the case, that as a nation, the Mandans are extinct.'

Thomas L. McKinney and James Hall estimated that the total survivors after the smallpox epidemic was about 125–145. A few sought refuge in Fort Barthold, and in 1870 a reservation was set aside for them along the Missouri River and the Little Missouri, which belies Stephens's contention that there was no trace of them in an area of the Missouri River in 1858.[14]

17

A LANGUAGE CONUNDRUM

So far the question of any similarities between the Welsh language and the dialects of Indian tribes has merely been mentioned in the most cursory manner when isolated cases have been quoted. To have attempted any scientific examination at an earlier stage in this book would have been to theorize without possessing the full facts.

It is now necessary to review the two extremes of opinion which have already been put forward. The abundance of the evidence so far is on the side of that view which states that the dialects of some Indian tribes were identical with the Welsh language. There is Morgan Jones's story of how speaking Welsh saved his life, a story echoed by many others, including so distinguished a witness as Francis Lewis, the signer of the Declaration of Independence. Then again there are the adventure of Stedman, the sailor, the saloon-bar encounter by Lieutenant Roberts and the old Indian, and Captain Chaplain's account of Welsh-speaking Indians. Without question the evidence for this extreme view is more prolific than that amassed by its opponents.

But quantity is one thing and quality is quite another. Apart from the fact that much of the evidence in favour of Welsh-speaking Indians was probably exaggerated to make the story sound better, the quality of it is marred by the fact that few people followed up their experiences by producing incontrovertible proof.

The other extreme view is that there is no trace of Welsh in any known Indian dialect today, that there never was and that any similarities are only coincidental and isolated.

One must concede that there is no trace of Welsh in any Indian dialect today. As far as the Mandans are concerned, they have been more or less extinct for well over a century, and their dialect died with them. The Kutenai tongue, with which we have already dealt, sounds impressive when presented with a few numerals, but does not stand up to any further examination. Therefore, one can also concede, in respect of some dialects, the argument that similarities are coincidental and isolated, something that applies to many languages when comparisons are made.

It is the second and extreme dogmatic view that there never was any trace of Welsh in Indian dialects that one must subject to a much closer test.

Indian languages are so completely unlike those of Europe both in the construction of sentences and in sound that it is not surprising that misconceptions arose about them before they were fully understood and studied. But because of this general *dissimilarity*, any similarities in any one dialect would have been noticed much more quickly. It may well be that, with those of British descent, there was a tendency among some to imagine an occasional likeness to Welsh. This tendency might well have been enhanced if people had heard stories about the Welsh Indians. Thus, when they came across an Indian name like Nantikoke, they would immediately see in this a resemblance to the Welsh *nant-y-cwch*, a curved brook or river. Then again the discovery of such a place as Madoc's Creek in Virginia would excite more speculation. This kind of discovery could explain some of the stories mentioned, but it is no answer in the case of Welsh-speaking people who claimed to have conversed with Indians in their own language, unless one dismisses them as liars, and there are too many of them to put them all in this category.

Thomas Stephens examined the language conundrum in some detail, though without going to America and without examining all the evidence on the other side. He made a superficial study of no less than eight dialects – Algonquin, Iroquois, Sioux, Catawba,

Cherokee, Uchel, Natchez and Mobilian (a bastard tongue in any case). He pointed out that the letter 'l' was, with one exception, not to be found. The letter 'l' is, in fact, to be found among the dialects of the Indians of Central America, and may, or may not, have been introduced by the Spaniards. Stephens also stressed the fact that the letter 'f' is rarely used. Double-f and double-l are frequently to be found in Welsh. There were also no pronouns and no abstract terms, he added, concluding emphatically that nowhere could he find any resemblance to Welsh.

What similarities there were in individual words, such as those already mentioned in this book, he either dismissed as coincidence or implied that they were far-fetched comparisons.

Why, however, did Stephens pay scant attention to the Mandan dialect when he admitted that Catlin was the most respectable and respected witness for the Welsh legend? It is true there was no handbook on the Mandan dialect; it had not even been studied then to any great extent other than by Catlin himself, for the Mandans had been decreasing numerically for years and had been so constantly on the move that few Europeans had come in contact with them in recent times. Also, when Stephens wrote his celebrated essay, the Mandans had been practically extinct for nearly twenty years.

In view of Stephens's conviction that the Indian dialects had no pronouns, he should have revised his opinions when confronted with Catlin's testimony. The Mandan dialect not only had pronouns, but they were very similar to the Welsh. An examination of the following table should establish this:

English	Mandan	Welsh	Pronunciation
I	Me	Myfi	Mifi
You	Ne	Chwi	Chwe
He	E	Efo, Hwn	Efo, Hoon
She	Ea	Hi, Hon	He, Hon
It	Ount	Hwynt	Hooynt
We	Noo	Ni	Ne
They	Eonah	Hwna	Hona.[1]

Stephens, however, made no concession where surely a most

marked exception to his general rule called for one. He argued correctly that in Welsh there was no neuter personal pronoun, and that *hwynt* was not really 'it', but they. *Hwna*, he said, was a form of the demonstrative pronoun 'that', or this. Yet he disregarded that Mandan for 'Those ones' was *Yrai Honah*, which is almost identical to the Welsh equivalent of *Yrhai Hyna*.

Catlin, said Stephens, had an 'imperfect knowledge of the Welsh tongue'. Maybe, but Stephens also had a lack of knowledge of the Mandan tongue. Whereas almost all other Indian dialects differ completely in every respect from European languages, in the Mandan dialect there is a distinct resemblance in certain of the sounds. The gutturals, palatals, labials and dentals, with their mutations, are often completely identical. Catlin, on a visit to Britain, brought with him a long list of Mandan words and sentences, and discussed these with Welsh scholars. They found that while the majority of Mandan words were unlike those of Welsh, there was an astonishing similarity when some whole sentences were translated into Welsh, and that a pattern of similarity existed. What convinced Catlin that Mandan might have derived from Madoc was when he heard the Indians exhorting the aid of the 'Great Spirit of the Race': *Madoc Maho Paneta am byd*, which in Welsh would be *Madoc Mawr Penarthur am byth* ['Madoc the Great Spirit for ever'].

Somehow *Madoc Maho* was associated with their ancestral 'Great Spirit', though the Mandans could not explain the reason for this.

Catlin, in a letter to Mr. Lewis Edward, of Washington, after his return from London, wrote: 'I must confess some disappointment that, after conferring with other Welsh scholars, I find that modern Mandan is basically different from Welsh, but at the same time there is no doubt at all that the similarities which do exist are of a pattern and so pronounced that there must be a link between the two languages. I now see Mandan as a two-tier, possibly a three-tier language. It consists of a language within a language, and it would seem that the more ancient part of that language is cherished for certain special occasions and for certain functions of everyday life. Quite often I found that where there were two or more words with one meaning, one of those words would be the equivalent of Welsh. The Mandans themselves invariably explained that some of the Welsh-sounding words had almost gone out of use. The tragedy is that someone did not make a study of their dialect a century previous to this.'

It will be noted that the Mandans had a similar word to the Welsh for head, or chief – *pan* as compared with the Welsh *pen*. When they wanted to say that something was missing, or 'not there', they said *Negosh*, which is almost literally the pronunciation of the Welsh equivalent of *Nagoes*. On the other hand it must be conceded that in Catlin's time at least Mandan numerals bore no resemblance whatsoever to Welsh, but were very like the dialect of the tribes with which they had more recently been in contact.

Catlin, however, had no knowledge of Welsh other than what he was able to look up in reference books, and one imagines that in those pioneering days there were very few Welsh grammar books in America.

If La Chapelle discovered a harp among the Mandans, Catlin found something even more specifically Welsh – a coracle. He described the Mandan canoe as being unlike anything used by any other Indians and 'an exact replica of a Welsh coracle'. It was made with raw-hides (buffalo skins) 'stretched under a frame of willow, nearly round like a tub; which the woman carries on her head from her wigwam to the water's edge, and, having stepped into it, stands in front and propels it by dipping her paddle forward, and drawing it to her instead of paddling by the side.'[2]

This is exactly the technique employed by some coracle-men in Wales even today. When not fishing the coracle-man will paddle over the fore end of the craft, either with a figure-of-eight stroke, or by a scooping motion. Catlin also noted that the paddle had a claw at the top of its loom, which would have made it identical with the type of paddle used on the River Teifi in Wales today.

But it was the language associated with the coracle by the Mandans which showed the most astonishing affinity with that of Wales. Catlin did not, indeed could not have known this, and made no comment on it. But a few comparisons will suffice to confirm the similarity:

Description	Mandan	Welsh
Coracle	Koorig	Corwg
		(pronounced corrug)
Paddle	Ree	Rhwyf
		(pronounced reef)
A fishing area	Burra	Bwrw

It is a great pity that the early pioneers knew so little about the coracle, or else these similarities could have formed the basis for a thorough examination of the whole question. At one time there was said to be a Mandan coracle in the museum at Cincinatti, but alas there is no trace of it today. Thomas L. McKinney had heard of the 'unusual Mandan canoes which require a special skill to propel'. Incidentally, McKinney supplied an interesting footnote to the last days of the Mandans. He stated that there were two Mandan villages in 1804 on opposite sides of the Missouri River about four miles below the mouth of Knife River in the present North Dakota, adding that in 1837 – he put the date a year earlier than Catlin – 'the tribe was visited with smallpox', thus decimating a population previously estimated at about 1,600.[3]

When the Spaniards came to settle in Alabama in 1559 they discovered hidden in a cave some distance up the Dog River a number of derelict coracles. These were officially described as canoes, but from the name the Spaniards gave them – *las cáscaras* (the eggshells) – there seems little doubt that they must have been similar to the Mandans' craft. *Las cáscaras* must have been secreted by an Indian tribe, most probably by Madoc's followers, more than two hundred years previously. One of the craft was kept as a curiosity at Fort Serof, adjoining Fort Morgan, for many years.

Mr. Arthur Halliday, of Baltimore, has a copy of notes written by his great-grandfather, Jabez Halliday, compiled in 1803, on the subject of the 'White Indians'. This includes a description of a coracle found in an abandoned Mandan village near a tributary of the Missouri. 'Whether or not this is any further proof of the existence of the Welch Indians I do not venture to vouchsafe,' wrote Mr. Halliday. 'When I told Mr. Rhys about the discovery he paid little attention, saying that John Evans had made no mention of coracles in any report and had emphatically turned down the conception of there being any nation with Welsh antecedents.'[4]

Mr. Halliday not only personally inspected the coracle, but made a sketch of it and added a detailed description of the craft. It was, he said, 'like a scooped-out egg-shell, seemingly most fragile and light enough to carry on the back. It was somewhat less than five feet in length and about three feet five inches in width, made from the branches of willow which had been cut into frames, covered with buffalo hide, and was propelled by a single paddle which was rather more than five feet long'.[5] This description tallies almost completely with the dimensions of a Teifi coracle, except perhaps that the paddle was shorter.

Both Catlin and Halliday, as well as other writers, refer to the use of other and more orthodox craft by the Mandans. They not only had dug-out canoes, but, at one time, quite large boats. Catlin made sketches of some of these canoes, but not of the coracle, which is possibly why Stephens dismissed the idea of an Indian canoe resembling a Welsh coracle. Some few years later Mr. Halliday was introduced to a Mandan who explained to him that the coracle had enabled his tribe to fish more effectively than any other tribe, though when it came to making lengthy trips the craft was slow in comparison with the traditional Indian canoe. It was true, said the Mandan, that his tribe also used the larger canoes as well, but the coracle was an ancient tradition with the tribe, being easy to make and to carry with them. so it had always been retained.

When the Mandans went out to fish the custom was for the coracles to race to an agreed starting point. The first two craft to reach this point carried on and started fishing; the others held back until the two leaders had gone a specified distance. It may be coincidence, but in the *Transactions* of the Carmarthen Antiquarian Society this self-same code for coracle-fishing is mentioned as having been an unwritten rule for centuries.[6]

Of even greater interest were some of the words and phrases used by the Mandans in relation to the coracle. Apart from the terms already mentioned by Catlin, a big fishing-net was called

Ruydrat, which has a marked similarity to the Welsh *rhwyd rhwth*, used to describe the wide-meshed part of a coracle-man's net. Then again the Mandans referred to fish not by name, but as 'those ones' [Yrai Honah]. In Wales even today coracle-fishermen hardly ever speak of salmon, or of any other fish by name, but always speak of 'them', or 'they'. The Mandans said there was a name for fish, *pisg*, which they never used, as the very mention of the word was supposed to bring bad luck. The Welsh equivalent is *pysg*.

By Catlin's time the language of the Mandans had changed considerably, and various new elements had been introduced into it, presumably reducing the original affinities with Welsh. It must be remembered that the true tribal identity of the Mandans had been bastardized over the centuries, and it had undergone revolutionary changes in the previous fifty years as a result of dwindling numbers, inter-marriage, wars and closer contact with other tribes. Few authorities agree on their origins, or even on the later development of the tribe. They have been linked with their enemies the Sioux and actually termed a Sioux tribe, which is a completely inaccurate diagnosis. The *Encyclopaedia Britannica* states that they formed 'with the Hidatsa and Arikara the so-called Indians among the bison-hunting nomads', which is about as confused a picture as one can have of them. Some say their language allied them with the Hidatsa, while others declare equally emphatically that before 1800, when their numbers were reduced to 1,250, they had virtually lost any tribal identity with the Hidatsa. In Indian sign language they were known as 'the tattooed people'.

One man not only made a study of the Mandans, but helped a linguist to compile a vocabulary of their dialect. He was James Girty, of the renegade wood-runners, those Americans who became notorious at the time of the fight for independence when they allied themselves to certain Indian tribes and the British against their own people. James Girty, born near Harrisburg, Philadelphia, was the son of American parents. His father was killed by the Indians, but James and his two brothers threw themselves at the mercy of the natives and became to all intents and purpose part of the tribe. James was an interpreter for the

Indians at Fort Pitt in 1774, and later helped organize raids against the colonists with the collaboration of the British.[7]

Three things are certain about James Girty. He himself was not of Welsh descent and could not originally have known the language. He was a 'runner' between the British and the Indians for a considerable time and he talked about the 'Welsh Indians' and linked them with the Mandans. Finally, he met Francis Lewis, the signer of the Declaration of Independence and spoke Welsh to him. The last-mentioned detail is important. It is not certain whether this meeting was the origin of the story about Lewis's life being saved by a Welsh-speaking Indian; it might be quite a separate story. But Lewis himself related meeting James Girty the Renegade serving in the Indian mercenaries and recording that he spoke Welsh.

It will be seen from some of the findings of James Girty's 'Welsh Indian Vocabulary' that, while he confirms many of Catlin's discoveries, he also listed many words which were not apparently known or used in Catlin's time. This would appear to support Catlin's theory that in earlier days Welsh words were more evident in the Mandan dialect. Girty was compiling his vocabulary more than sixty years before Catlin visited the tribe and some twenty years before Governor Sevier's statements were made.

Unfortunately Girty only compiled a vocabulary. He was not a scholar and made no attempt at grammatical comparisons, or an analysis of similarities in sentence construction. Here are some of the words and phrases he listed:[8]

English	'Welsh-Indian'	Welsh
I	Me	Mi
You	Nehi	Chwi
He	Efo	Efo
She	Ea-ah	Hi
We	Noo	Ni
Water	Duah	Dwr
Bread	Bara	Bara
River	Nant	Nant

English	'Welsh-Indian'	Welsh
Father	Taid	Tad
Cow	Buch	Buwch
Partridge	Cluga	Clugjar
Woods-men	Coedig	Coed-wig
stone	kraig	carreg
old	hen	hen
dance	dansio	dawnsio
valley	koom	cwm (*koom*)
morning	borrah	bore (borra)
night	nostogr	nos
thanks	dyawf	diolch
I am	yr-effi	yr wyfi
He is	ym-eff	y mae ef
You are	Yor-iddich-ni	yr ydych chwi
in the boat	in y kook	yn y cwch
blue	glas	glas
milk★	faeth	llaeth
to cross	croesi	croesi
harp	tefyn	telyn
to be born	genni	geni
bridge	pont	pont
estuary	aber	aber
high	uchaf	uchel
to belong	pertin	perthyn
great	mawr	mawr
foot	troed	troed
disgusting	ake-e-Vee	Ach-y-fi
beautiful	prydfa	prydferth
sing	canu	canu

It is said that Girty's vocabulary of comparisons totalled more than 350 words, phrases and short sentences. Of many of these there is no longer any trace, and in the absence of the complete list one cannot draw any firm conclusions. But it would seem that in several instances the language must have changed in the sixty

★ The exact Welsh equivalent of *llaeth* would be 'nourishment'.

years between Girty's acquaintance with the 'Welsh Indians' and Catlin's encounters with the Mandans. For example in Catlin's time river in Mandan was *passah la*, not *nant*, night was *estogr* not *nostogr*, and foot was *shee*. The only distinguishable pattern appears to lie in the Mandan translation of the letter 'l' into 'f', which is fairly consistent throughout Girty's list. Girty made one commentary on his list: 'Names of animals were never of Welsh origin, and the commonly used "good" and "bad" bear no likeness to the Welsh tongue, being *shusu* and *k'he cush* respectively.'

The conundrum of the language similarities remains unsolved. There are undoubtedly sufficient likenesses to suggest a language link at some time or other, but too many dissimilarities for this thesis to be proved.

In making comparisons between the Mandan *koorig* and the Welsh coracle (incidentally, to show the distinction between the two, the Mandan word for canoe was *menanka*), I have so far only made reference to the better known coracles of the Rivers Teifi and Towy. Coracle-fishing in Wales today is almost entirely confined to those two rivers. But there are many references in the tenth to the fourteenth centuries to the use of coracles in that part of North Wales which was the kingdom of Gwynedd. Giraldus, Maredudd ap Rhys and even the *Mabiogion* mention coracles being used on the Dovey, the Conway and the Cheshire Dee. The Bala coracle in its day was as famous as that of Teifi, though it is now rarely seen outside of a museum.

That the coracle would have been an invaluable aid to the Welsh explorers is unquestionable. It would provide them with an ideal method for their actual landings and for exploring the shallowest creek. A coracle can float in two or three inches of water when towed, yet can be loaded to the gunwales and still handled well. On any average river at least five times as much water can be fished out of a coracle as by wading on the same length and stretch of water. It has the additional advantage of being easily carried on the back.

Catlin made no mention of any 'sacred books', or faded parchments in his evidence on the Mandans, and perhaps for this reason his testimony is all the more valuable. But he referred to their pottery, examples of which in the Cincinatti Museum show distinctly civilized traits in their design and resemble early Celtic pottery, though experts say such similarities as there are may be found in ancient Irish pottery. More interesting were the blue glass beads which the Mandans made. 'These people have an extraordinary art of manufacturing a very beautiful and lasting kind of blue glass bead, which they wear in great quantities and value above all others that are brought amongst them by fur-traders,' wrote Catlin. 'This secret is not only one that fur-traders did not introduce amongst them, but one that I cannot learn from them.'[9]

These beads were mentioned again and again by other explorers as being something unique among the Indian tribes. There is only one reason for regarding this as a remote clue to their ancestry. The history of Lundy Island records that a very similar blue glass bead was made in that island and was always used by the Icelanders when they made long voyages, presumably as a form of currency. Not only was it used as such in the Scillies, but the blue glass beads are described as being 'of a Hiberno–Danish origin.'[10] It could have been that some people from Lundy joined Madoc on his second expedition.

Robert Durrett in his study of the white Indians published in the *Filson Club Publications*, No. 23, 1908, told of six skeletons with breast-plates engraved with the Welsh coat of arms, found at the Ohio Falls in 1799. As this seemed to be either a practical joke, a monstrous piece of romancing, or a discovery of tremendous importance, I tracked down the origin of the story. It is contained in a letter, written on May 30, 1824, by Thomas S. Hind. A Mr. John S. Williams had inquired of Major Robert Armstrong, of Tennessee and an officer in the U.S. Army, what he knew or had heard of the 'Madoc expedition'. The inquiry was passed on to Hind, who replied:

> Your letter of the 17th. to Major Robert Armstrong was placed in my hands some days ago. . . . It is a fact that the Welsh in the twelfth century found their way to the Mississippi and as far up the Ohio as the Falls of that River at

Louisville, where they were cut off by the Indians and captured and sank into Indian habits.

Proof No. 1: In 1799 six soldiers' skeletons were dug up near Jeffersonville. Each skeleton had a breast-plate of brass with the Welsh coat of arms, the Mermaid and the Harp with Latin inscription in substance, "virtuous deeds meet their just reward".

One of these plates was left by Captain Jonathan Taylor with the late Mr. Hubbard Taylor, of Clarke County, and when called for by me in 1814 for the late Dr. John P. Campbell, of Chillicothe, Ohio, who was preparing notes on the antiquities of the West, I was informed that the breast-plate had been taken to Virginia by a gentleman of that state.

Proof No. 2: The late Mr. McIntosh, who had been for fifty or sixty years a western Indian trader, was in Fort Kaskakaska, prior to its being taken by General George Rogers Clark in 1778, and heard, as he informed me himself, a Welshman and an Indian from far up the Missouri speaking and conversing in the Welsh language.

The Mohawk Indians had a tradition among them respecting the Welsh, and of their having been cut off by the Indians at the Falls of the Ohio. The late Colonel Joseph Hamilton Davies, who had for many years sought for information on this subject, mentions this fact, and the fact that the Welshmen's bones were found on Corn Island.

Signed:

THOMAS S. HIND.[11]

Even if the breast-plates had been found and examined by experts, it is almost certain that they would have proved completely different from their description in this letter, not to mention a totally different explanation. But, like the 'sacred books' and parchments, the evidence is missing once again.

Nevertheless the *koorigs*, the fortifications, the iron utensils, the pottery and the linguistic similarities do on their own constitute formidable evidence in favour of the Welsh ancestry of these wandering Indians, driven from one site to another over the ages, never numerous enough to impose their civilization on other tribes.

Catlin, it is true, stresses the blue and grey eyes of the Mandans and their European features, but makes no mention of beards or whiskers. But he only saw the tribe in their last days when habits must have changed and inter-marriage completely altered their characteristics. But the most important testimony in favour of 'white Indians', as distinct from the purely native variety, is that which insists they wore beards, for this characteristic more than any makes them stand out from any known Red Indian tribe. Not only are there several references to the 'bearded Indians', but they invariably come from the Missouri area, Ohio, Illinois, Kentucky or Tennessee. The *Medical Repository* of 1805, Bruff's letter to Wilkinson in the *Territorial Press*, the *Gentleman's Magazine* and *the Magazine of History* all testify to the existence of the 'bearded Indians'. In an account of a journey by two men named Needham and Arthur in 1773 to the Alleghany region there is this description: 'Eight days' journey down this river (the Tennessee) lives a white people which have long beards and whiskers and wear clothing. Not many years since ye Tomahittans sent twenty men laden with beaver to ye white people: they killed tenn of them and put ye other tenn in irons, tenn escaped and one of them came with my man (Needham) to my plantation.'[12]

There can be no doubt whatsoever that the Mandans contained the few survivors of what must have been a much more unusual and distinctive tribe, and the Indians themselves knew the stories about their having descended from a people 'far across the ocean'. This tradition was very prevalent among the Cherokees, whose chieftains seem to have known rather more of the history of the 'Welsh Indians' than any other tribe. Benjamin S. Barton stated that when the Cherokee first arrived in Tennessee they found the land held by a pale-faced and 'moon-eyed people'.[13]

The fortifications remain the most positive evidence of their European ancestry dating from the pre-Columbus era. Colonel Bennett H. Young's expert testimony on Fort Mountain sums this up very well: 'A remarkable prehistoric stone fortification in the state of Kentucky is situated in Madison County about three miles east of Berea. This fort occupies what is known as Indian Fort Mountain. For the military skill displayed in the selection of this mountain as a stronghold and for the patience and labour expended in building the necessary walls to render it impregnable, too much cannot be said in praise of both the genius and the skill of the men who constructed the fortifications. The old forts in Kentucky were not built by Indians, but by a past people greatly skilled in arts.'[14]

With the Mandans now virtually extinct, it is almost impossible to believe that any further evidence will be produced, unless some systematic attempt is made at excavations in certain areas where their camps or forts are known to have been sited. No such attempt has yet seriously been made, nothing to compare with the Norse excavations in Canada. What is needed is an application to these ancient sites of the 'Carbon 12' method of dating, based on radioactive decay, now accepted as the most reliable method known to modern archaeology.

The case for the Welsh Indians thus rests upon evidence gathered from those claiming they encountered such a people. I have examined seventy-three independent testimonies, and of these forty-four seemed worthy of careful consideration, as well as having the merit of confirming the trek of the tribe from Alabama, through Tennessee, Georgia and Kentucky to the Carolinas, the Ohio. Missouri and Mississippi Rivers to the villages that Catlin found. Modern ethnological research does not help much because it is too rigid and precise in its approach and ignores all evidence which does not fit into its tabulated tribal categories, like, for example, the Bureau of Ethnology's historically inaccurate description of the Mandans as a Siouan tribe. Alas, there is no adequate history of many Indian tribes to enable the theories of science to be checked with the chronology of facts.

The chief weakness of the claims of similarities in Welsh and Mandan is that they cannot be substantiated on a grammatical basis or by any rules of syntax. Yet in this very weakness there may well be, if not an element of proof, at least a possible explanation. 'Secret languages' have existed for centuries, being used by special groups of people to preserve the identity of a language and to exclude outsiders from using it. Sometimes, as with the Romany tribes, the secrecy has occasionally been broken and trusted outsiders admitted to some, if not all, of the secrets. In the Philippines and among the West African Lucami in Cuba such secret languages have existed. There has always been one special feature about such secret languages: they have put the emphasis on the social function of such a speech form rather than any attempt at preserving or creating a language structure or syntax. That is to say, such languages have invariably consisted of a systematic substitution for individual words, without ever attempting to create a grammar. Thus, when necessary, the substitute words became taboo; they are remembered, but not spoken. Taboo words have been known to be guarded and recollected long after they have ceased to be spoken, whereas any attempt at grammatical construction would quickly be lost through lack of practice.

The impression gained by some travellers was that Mandan – Welsh was a secret language. Both Catlin and Girty – and for that matter some of the early French explorers – were given to understand that certain words resembling Welsh were taboo; they were almost passwords to safe conduct, or expressions of trust. Thus Catlin was told that among the Mandans legend had it that 'they descended from the first white man to come to this country', but that this was something they normally told nobody.

As far as evidence on the European side of the Atlantic Ocean is available, it seems undeniable that discovery of lands in the West was known long before Columbus's time and that this news reached France, Germany, the Low Countries and Italy, if not Spain or Portugal. Where such evidence obviously refers to Vinland, or the northern part of America, one might justifiably concede that it came from the Norse discoveries. But there is no indisputable evidence in the cartographical field to show that Vinland's existence was acknowledged by any chart-maker. Sir James Marshall Cornwall, former President of the Royal Geographical Society, summing up his own views of the Vinland map, has stated: 'I'm sure that the argument that it is based on an example of early Viking cartography is specious. If you ask me, the truth probably lies somewhere between all the claims. Some early cartographer heard of the Icelandic sagas – for instance, through a pilgrim – and just stuck it in.'[15]

All reputable and authenticated maps of the pre-Columbus area make no reference to Vinland, but to land in the Atlantic south-west of the British Isles, France and Spain. There is absolutely no suggestion that the Norsemen sailed south-west, and when this evidence points to the finding of the Sargasso Sea and the West Indies, or Florida and Alabama, it can only be linked with Madoc.

I will deliberately omit the evidence of maps previously mentioned, as it could be argued that some of them merely show hindsight, or give third-hand evidence, or even that they could be forgeries. But there is the anonymous Weimar map of 1424 which shows land to the far west of the Atlantic and marked as *Antillia*. This could not refer to any Norse discovery. The Genoese Bedaire made a map in 1434 which shows in the direction of the West Indies land marked as *Isola Nova Scoperta* (Newly Discovered Island). Two years later Andrea Bianco drew another map which shows a large stretch of land far out in the Atlantic Ocean also marked *Antillia*. These maps give no indication of actual evidence of discovery and there is every reason to believe that *Antillia* was a legendary name, based on travellers' tales. Yet the fact remains that there were at least rumours, or reports of land having been discovered which were seriously heeded by some cartographers quite early in the fifteenth century.[16]

Legends were the inspiration by which the New World was eventually found. Whether it was the 'Fountain of Youth', the stories of Sinbad the Sailor, the narratives of the voyages of St. Brandon, the fairy tales about the Sargasso, or the strange story of Madoc, the inspiration was sustained. It prompted the probing of exploratory minds in the fifteenth century and undoubtedly provided Columbus with the will to succeed. Even more remarkable, as has already been demonstrated in this narrative, scientific facts explain almost every one of these legends even down to that of the 'disappearing islands'.

An interesting feature of the development of cartography applied to the Atlantic Ocean in the fourteenth and fifteenth centuries is that there was a gradual tendency among all map-makers to site the legendary lands in the west farther and farther south. For example in the Catalan map of 1375 'Saint Brandon's Isle' is depicted as situated in the Atlantic Ocean parallel to the south-west coast of Ireland and relatively close to that country. As geographical knowledge increased – and this applies as much to Madoc as to St. Brandon – map-makers placed the mythical lands farther west and farther south. Thus by 1492 Martin Behaim's map shows Brandon's Isle near the Equator and beyond the Fortunate Islands. It would seem as though by the beginning of the fifteenth century the consensus of opinion veered away from the Vinland legends to those reports which spoke of land in the south-west.

History, not unnaturally, tends to be written by historians, but seldom by geographers, or seamen, or interpreters of legend, and much of the early history of the world has suffered in consequence. Fortunately, occasionally the record is put right by a seaman who is also a diligent researcher. Thus Thor Heyerdahl proved that the Peruvians could have crossed the Pacific in balsa-wood rafts. It may well be that only now, in the light of a more scientific and pragmatic approach to the possibility of the techniques employed by early discoverers allied to more constructive imagination in sifting legends, are we on the verge of learning how to find the missing link between history as we know it and the legends which provide the only clues to what transpired before documentation began.

BIBLIOGRAPHY AND SOURCES

THE SUPPLEMENTARY NOTES to Chapters at the end of the book will provide detailed information on sources, and for this reason it is not proposed to duplicate this here. The following list is of principal sources which are essential for any student of the subject, presented for convenience in alphabetical order of authors:

ARMSTRONG, ZELLA: *Who Discovered America?*, The Lookout Publishing Company, Chattanooga, Tennessee, 1950.

BOWEN, THE REV. BENJAMIN F.: *America Discovered by the Welsh*, J. B. Lippincott & Co., Philadelphia, 1876.

BROWN, JOHN P.: *Old Frontiers.*

BURDER, GEORGE: An article entitled *The Welch Indians* in *The Magazine of History*, vol. 20, Extra Nos. 77–88.

CATLIN, GEORGE: *Letters and Notes of the North American Indians*, Egyptian Hall, Piccadilly, London, 1842.

CRONAU, RUDOLF: *Amerika. Die Geschichte seiner Entdeckung von der altesten bis auf die neuste Zeit*, Verlag von Abel & Muller, 1892.

DE ROO, P.: *History of America before Columbus*, vol. 2, J. B. Lippincott & Co., Philadelphia, 1900.

DE VOTO, Bernard: *Westward the Course of Empire*, Eyre & Spottiswoode, London, 1953.

DRAKE, SAMUEL: *Indians of North America.*

FILSON, JOHN: *History of Kentucky.*

HAKLUYT, RICHARD: The third and last volume of *The Voyages, Navigations, Traffiques and Discoveries of the English Nation*, vol. 3, George Bishop, Ralfe Newberrie and Robert Barker, London, 1600.

HERBERT, SIR THOMAS: *A Relation of Some Yeares' Travaile*, William Stansby, London, 1634.

HOWEL, JAMES: *Epistolae Ho-Eloanae*, vol. 2, 1647.

LLOYD, SIR J. E.: *History of Wales.*

MACKAY, JAMES: His Manuscript Notes in the E. O. Voorhis Memorial Collection, Missouri Historical Society, St. Louis.

OLESON, TRYGGVI J.: *Early Voyages and Northern Approaches, 1000–1632*, Oxford University Press, 1964.

POHL, FREDERICK J.: *Atlantic Crossing before Columbus*, W. W. Norton & Co., Inc., New York, 1961.

POWEL, DR. DAVID: *Historie of Cambria*, a history of Wales in the English language, edited by Dr. Powel, translated into English by Humphrey Llwyd, and taken from the works of Caradoc of Llancarvan and other sources, London, 1584.

STEPHENS, THOMAS: *Madoc – an essay on the discovery of America by Madoc ab Owain Gwynedd*, Longmans, Green & Co., London, 1893.

STODDARD, MAJOR AMOS: *Sketches of Louisiana*. Philadelphia, 1812.

WEISE, ARTHUR JAMES: *The discoveries of America to the year 1525*, Richard Bentley & Son, London, 1884.

WILLIAMS, PROFESSOR DAVID: *John Evans and The Legend of Madoc*, University of Wales Press, Cardiff, 1963.

WILLIAMS, JOHN: *An Enquiry into the Truth of the Tradition concerning the Discovery of America by Prince Madoc ab Owain Gwynedd*, J. Brown, London, 1791.

Also consulted

1 The Cottonian MSS. in the British Museum.
2 The Hengwrt MSS.
3 The *Myvyrian Archaiology*.
4 *Archaeologia Cambrensis*.
5 The *Gwydir Papers*, containing the revised 1827 edition of *The History of the Gwydir Family*, interleaved with letters from the Wynne Family, various manuscript notes, pedigrees of Welsh families and handwritten memoirs and miscellanea.

6 *The Gentleman's Magazine.*
7 *The Cambrian Biography.*
8 *The Journal of the National Library of Wales.*
9 *Inventory of Ancient Monuments in Caernavonshire,* vols. I, II and III.

For all other sources see Supplementary Notes.

SUPPLEMENTARY NOTES TO CHAPTERS

SUPPLEMENTARY NOTES TO CHAPTERS

CHAPTER 1

[1] The Pillars of Hercules were traditionally situated between Tangier and Gibraltar.

[2] *Medea*, Act III, v. 375: '*Venient Annis Saecula seris, quibus oceanus Vincula verum laxit, et ingens Pateat tellus, Typhisque Novos Detegat orbes; nec sit terris Ultima Thule.*'

[3] *Sunday Express*, January 25, 1959.

[4] Cited by De Guignes.

[5] Hongkong newspaper *Wen Pei Po*, September 18, 1962.

[6] The Vinland map was published and reproduced in *The Vinland Map and the Tartar Relation*, Yale University Press, 1965.

[7] *Politiken* (Copenhagen), October 12, 1965.

[8] *The Times*, October 11, 1965.

[9] Below this inscription on the tablet are the words: 'Authority is – Encylopaedia Americana copyright 1918 – Webster's Encyclopaedia – Richard Hakluyt, 1552 to 1616, a Welsh Historian and Geographer – Ridpath's History of the World – ancient Roman coins found in Forts in Tenn. These Forts resemble the Forts of Wales of the ninth and tenth centuries and of the white Indians of the Tennessee and Missouri rivers.' It should be pointed out that Hakluyt was a Herefordshire man and there is no proof of Welsh ancestry, though his family had lived for generations on the borders of Wales. Above the inscription on the tablet is a 'Red Dragon Flag' in a white circle, representing the Welsh Flag of the twelfth century, which consisted of a Red Dragon embossed on a field of white and royal blue, the origin of which lies in a legend that tells how Uther Pendragon, father of King Arthur, had a vision of a flaming dragon in the sky, which his seers interpreted as meaning that he should ascend the throne. This was the second memorial to Madoc erected in U.S.A., the first being one put up by the State of Tennessee.

CHAPTER 2

[1] After Stephens's death his Eisteddfod essay was published in book form in

1893. This is *Madoc – an essay on the discovery of America by Madoc ap Owen*, Longmans, Green & Co.

[2] *Archaeologia Cambrensis*, 1894, p. 72.

[3] *The Courier*, October 17, 1818.

[4] *The Age of Owain Gwynedd*, Professor Barbier, Nutt & Co., London, 1908.

[5] *An Enquiry into the Truth of the Tradition concerning the Discovery of America by Prince Madoc ab Owen Gwynedd, about the year 1170*, by John Williams, J. Brown, London, 1791.

[6] See *History of the World*, by George Abbott, Archbishop of Canterbury, pp. 56–7.

[7] *The Journal of the National Library of Wales*, xiv (summer, 1965), pp. 122–4.

[8] From a paper by J. Morgan Lewis entitled *Brechfa: first critic of the bards*, Cincinatti Cymmrodorion Society, 1877.

[9] Cited in an article entitled *The Welch Indians*, by George Burder, *The Magazine of History*, vol. 20, Extra Nos. 77–80.

[10] See Stephens's *Madoc*. The ode referred to is stated in the *Myvyrian Archaiology*, vol. 1, p. 284, to be dedicated to *Rodri vab Ywein* (Rhodri, son of Owain), but this is not clear from the actual text.

[11] Cited by J. Morgan Lewis, who refutes Stephens's view and points out that the original text of Cynddelw is ambiguous and can be interpreted in at least three different ways. Either it is an ode addressed to Rhodri and refers to Daffydd and Madoc, or it may not have been addressed to anyone, and concerned Dafydd and Howel; or it might be ascribed to Dafydd and Rhodri. Brechfa, in Lewis's view, was a self-appointed interpreter of the bards 'in the light of historical fact', and he 'tidied up the ode' to take account of misinterpretations of certain phrases and known facts. He disagrees with Stephens's view that 'in the bosom of the vast ocean' means Anglesey by stating that the literal translation of this phrase is '*far o'er* the bosom of the vast ocean', whereas Anglesey is separated from the Welsh mainland only by a narrow channel. There is some substantiation of this view in the manuscript notes of the *Gwydir Papers*.

[12] *The History of the Gwydir Family*, by Sir John Wynn (1553). First published by Daines Barrington, then re-edited, with additional notes, and printed for private subscription by the Taliesin Press, Ruthin, 1827. The book contains a genealogical tree of the House of Gwynedd. It appears from this book and the MS. notes therein that the author was furnished with some materials 'which neither Powel, nor Sir John Wynne, had ever seen.'

[13] Ibid.

[14] *Historie of Cambria*.

[15] *Did Prince Madoc Discover America?*, a pamphlet by A. Rhys, Chicago, 1938.

Also cited by Kathleen O'Loughlin in *Madoc ap Owain Gwynedd*, printed in St. Catherine's, Ontario, 1947.

[16] Ibid.

[17] 'Munition' is the exact word used by Dr. Powel, but this must be interpreted as meaning simply weaponry in the twelfth century.

CHAPTER 3

[1] Cited by the *Dictionary of National Bibliography*.

[2] *The Age of Owain Gwynedd*, Barbier.

[3] *Archaeologia Cambrensis*, 1862, p. 150.

[4] Cited by J. Morgan Lewis: *Brechfa: first critic of the bards*.

[5] *The Age of Owain Gwynedd*, Barbier.

[6] *Prince Madog: Discoverer of America*, by Joan Dane, Elliot & Stock, London, 1909.

[7] *The Cistercian Abbey of Strata Florida*, by Stephen W. Williams, Whiting & Co., London, 1889. The Abbey was founded by Rhys ap Gruffydd.

[8] Cited by J. Morgan Lewis.

[9] Letter from Joan Dane to Mrs. Grafton S. Porter, Cincinatti, May 23, 1910.

[10] *Devonshire Records*, Exeter, 1893.

[11] *The Royal Tribes of Wales*, Yorke.

CHAPTER 4

[1] Thor Heyerdahl in an interview with the Oslo correspondent of *The Times*, January 15, 1954.

[2] Article entitled *Mystery River in the Atlantic*, by E. Griffiths, *World Digest*, March, 1956.

[3] *An Inquiry into the Discovery of America by Madoc*, John Williams.

[4] Statement by Dr. Bradford K. MacGaw in *Who Discovered America?* by Zella Armstrong, The Lookout Publishing Co., Chattanooga, 1950.

[5] Dr. Gerald S. Hawkins, chairman of the Dept. of Astronomy at Boston University, in his book *Stonehenge Decoded* (Souvenir Press, London, 1966), claimed that Stonehenge was probably an astronomical observatory of the Druids.

[6] *De Bello Civile*, Bk. I, chap. 4.

[7] Marcus Annaeus Lucanus, A.D. 39–65. Cited from *The Pharsalia of Lucan*, translation by H. T. Riley, London, 1853.

[8] *Mictis*, the Roman name for the Isle of Wight.

[9] *Naturalis Historia*, by Pliny (1st century A.D.), Bk. IV, chap. 30.

[10] *Collectanea Rerum Memorabilium*, by Caius Julius Solinus (3rd century A.D.), Bk. XXIII.

[11] Translation of Rufus Festus Avienus by W. F. Skene in *Celtic Scotland*, I, 168.

[12] *British Coracles*, by James Hornell, *The Mariner's Mirror*, Vol. XXII, No. 1, 1936.

[13] Cited by Stephens in Madoc – an essay *on the Discovery of America*.

[14] Triad 68, *Myvyrian Archaiology*.

[15] *A History of the Royal Navy*, by Sir Nicholas Harris Nicolas, Richard Bentley, London, 1887.

[16] *Cambro-Briton*, vol. II, p. 389.

[17] Cited by Stephens in *Madoc*.

[18] A *Relation of Some Yeares' Travaile*, by Sir Thomas Herbert, William Stansby, London, 1634.

[19] *Archaeologia Cambrensis*, 1862, p. 150.

[20] J. Morgan Lewis's *Brechfa: first critic of the bards*.

CHAPTER 5

[1] See *Cambrian Biography*, 1803, article about Madoc; *Cambro-Briton*, 1820, p. 57.

[2] Published in *The Public Advertiser*, May 25, 1787.

[3] *Myvyrian Archaiology*, 2nd edition, p. 401. The principal reference in the Welsh text reads:

'Tri Difancoll ynys Prydain: Cyntaf Gafran ab Aeddan a'i wŷra aethant i'r mor ynghyrch y Gwerddonau Llion, ac ni chlywyd mwyach amdanynt, Ail Merddyn Bardd Emrys Wledig a'i naw Cylfeirdd a aethant i'r mor yn y Ty Gwydrin ac ni bu son i ba le ydd aethant: y Trydydd Madawg ab Owain Gwynedd, a aeth i'r mor a thrichannyn gydag ef newn deg llong, ac ni wyddys i ba le ydd aethant.'

[4] Cited in a translation of Cynfric ap Gronow by Evan Williams, Carmarthen, 1674.

[5] The *D.N.B.* states that he was alive in 1489.

[6] Ibid.

[7] *Spanish Chronicles* of Cortes.

[8] *Historie of Cambria*.

[9] See Thomas Stephens's *Essay on Madoc*.

[10] Westward the Course of Empire, by Bernard de Voto, Eyre & Spottiswoode, London, 1953.

[11] The third and last volume of the *Voyages, Navigations, Traffiques and Discoveries of the English Nation*, by Richard Hakluyt, George Bishop, Ralfe Newberie & Robert Barker, London, 1600, vol. III.

[12] *Epistolae Ho-Elænae*, by James Howel, vol. ii, p. 71.

CHAPTER 6

[1] *G. H. De Originibus Americanis. libri quatuor*, Hegae Comitis, Lugduni Betavorum, 1652.

[2] *The First Voyage of Sir J. H. . . . made to the West Indies, 1562.* See Hakluyt's *Principal Navigations*, vol. III.

[3] See also *De Orbe Novo*, by Peter Martyr Anglieri, edited and translated by F. A. MacNutt, 2 vols., New York, 1912.

[4] Moscow Radio, October 11, 1959, reported by *The Times* and *Daily Telegraph* (London) of the following day.

[5] Ibid.

[6] *Piri Reis haritasi istanbul, Davlet Basimevi*, 1935. Folded coloured map, 35 × 25 in., English text pp. 12–16. A full-size fascimile, accompanied by a pamphlet in Turkish, German, English and French, was published in 1935 by the Turkish Government.

[7] The Antilles was the name then given to the West Indies generally. In the marginal note describing the shores of the West Indies Piri Reis stated that for these shores and islands he had made use of the map of Christopher Columbus.

[8] José Fernandez Martinez writes under the pen-name of Fermart. He has supplied Columbus's living descendant, the Duke of Veragua, with considerable documentation. Cited by Nino Lo Bello, in an article in the *Evening News* (London), July 8, 1964.

[9] Translation of Piri Reis's notes by Bay Hasan Fehmi for the Society for Turkish Historical Research, 1932.

[10] Ibid. The actual text refers to St. Brandon as 'Sanvolrandan, a priest'.

[11] *Rebus Factis*, Peter Martyr, Valladolid, 1508. It is believed that Cambrio was an unusual, half-Latin, half-Spanish phrase for Wales. Martyr appeared to be quoting the exact wording on the map, and it is quite clearly *cambrio* and not *cambio*, the Spanish for 'change' or 'exchange'.

[12] *Spiegel historiael, Rijmkronijk,* Jacob van Maerlant, Leyden, 1784–5.

[13] *Encyclopaedia Britannica*, 9th edition, vol. XII, p. 90.

[14] *Report of the United States De Soto Expedition Commission.*

[15] *Spain's Title to Georgia*, by Herbert E. Bolton.

CHAPTER 7

[1] Cited in the *Gwydir Papers.*

[2] *Corwc* or *corwg* is the most ancient of the Welsh words for coracle; this word was used to describe both river-craft and sea-going craft. It is less frequently applied to describe a drinking-horn. The modern Welsh word for this craft – *corwgl* is not to be found in ancient Welsh literature.

[3] Cited by E. D. Jones in *The Journal of the National Library of Wales, xiv* (summer, 1965), p. 123. The full text in Welsh is: '*Madauc ap Ouain Guyned oed vori | ur maur a chuannoc i drafel | ac am na ale o vod aral enkarvtrio | ir Sygned guneuthur ac adei- | lad a unaeth long heb hayarn | ond i hoylio a chyrn/rhac lyncku or mor hunnu hi ai ga- | lu oi guneuthuriad Guennan Gorn ac yn honno i nofiod y moroed urth i blesser ac i tra- | faeliod lauer o uledyd tra-| more yn diarsuyd on urth dymchuelyd adre ynn gyfagos at ynys yr yakyttiod phryd- | ie yno ynn greulon ac ai hamhared ymhel ac an hynny vyth hyd hediu i geluir y mann hunnu ar y mor Phrydie Kasuennann. Yr ystori honn a doeth o lau buy gilyd dann uarant gredad o hynny hyd hediu hediu | Vely i dyvod Eduart ap Sion uynn i mi 1582 y 13 Vis Maurth.*'

[4] Ibid.

[5] *Carloviana*, by G. D. Burtchaell, Dublin.

[6] *America Discovered by the Welsh*, by the Reverend Benjamin F. Bowen, J. B. Lippincott & Co., Philadelphia, 1876.

[7] From a letter to the author by Mr. D. G. Evans, Bristol, July 4, 1963. There was a Lundy Granite Company formed in 1863, and wound up in 1868.

[8] *Historie of Cambria*, Dr. Powel.

[9] *A Relation of Some Yeares' Travaile*, by T. H. Esquire (Sir Thomas Herbert), William Stansby, London, 1634.

[10] Ibid.

[11] Cited by Kathleen O'Loughlin in *Wele Madoc Dewr Ei Fron*, St. Catherine's, Ontario, 1942.

[12] *Epistolae Ho-Eloanae*, by James Howel, Bk. ii (1645–55), 4 vols.

[13] From an article entitled *Prince Madoc Discovered America* by John O. Morgans in the magazine *The Ambassador*, reprinted in *Little Gems from Fort Morgan*, No. 74, Fort Morgan, Alabama, October, 1965.

[14] *A Relation of Some Yeares Travaile*. Sir Thomas Herbert added to his account of the Madoc story in later editions of this book.

[15] Cited in a translation of Cynfric ap Gronow by Evan Williams, Carmarthen, 1674.

[16] *Manco Capac – The First Inca of Peru*, by the Rev. John H. Parry, V. Llewellyn Ellis, Pwllheli. The Rev. Theophilus Evans also wrote a book entitled *Mirror of the Chief Poets*, which contains some fact, but more fantasy.

[17] *Welsh Histories & Poets*, 1796. Also cited by George Burder.

[18] Pennant's *Tours of Wales*, vol. 2, 1784.

[19] *Carloviana*, by G. D. Burtchael, Dublin.

[20] Manco Capac, by the Rev. John H. Parry.

[21] Cited by 'Meiron' in *Welsh Histories and Poets*, claiming this to be a translation of Ieuan Brechfa.

[22] Cited by the *Cambrian Journal* as a translation of Ieuan Brechfa.

CHAPTER 8

1 Honourable Society of Cymmrodorion suppl.

2 *Transactions* of the Caernarvonshire Historical Society, *Afon Ganol Wall Fragments,* by Norman Tucker, 1956.

3 Quoted from the MSS. in the possession of the Rev. E. F. Synnott, formerly Rector of Iden, East Sussex.

4 See also *A History of the Royal Navy,* by Sir Nicholas Harris Nicolas.

5 Letter to the author by Mrs. O. M. Wilde, November 13, 1965.

6 Letter to the author by Mr. Norman Tucker, November 5, 1965.

7 Leland's *Itinerary,* ed. Lucy T. Smith, 1906.

8 See *Old Price's Remains,* cited by Mr. Norman Tucker.

9 *Transactions* of Caernarvonshire Historical Society, *Afon Ganol Wall Fragments,* 1956.

10 *A History of the Royal Navy,* Nicolas.

11 See further details of sources in Chap XIII: Duvivier.

CHAPTER 9

1 *Historie of Cambria,* Powel, and *General Historie of Virginian New England and the Summer Isles,* by John Smith, London, 1621.

2 *John Evans and The Legend of Madoc,* by Professor David Williams, University of Wales Press, Cardiff, 1963.

3 *Kosmos: 1845–1858,* vol. II, p. 274, by Alexander von Rumboldt.

4 *The Aboriginal Races in North America,* by Samuel G. Drake, revised by H. D. Williams, 1880.

5 *An Enquiry into the Truth of the Tradition concerning the Discovery of America by Prince Madoc ab Owain Gwynedd,* by Dr. John Williams, J. Brown, London, 1791.

6 Cited in *British Remains,* 1777.

7 Cited by Major Amos Stoddard in *Sketches of Louisiana,* Philadelphia, 1812.

8 Cited in *Explorers of the New World,* by Katherine and John Bakeless, G. Bell & Sons, London.

9 *Travels in the Interior of North America,* by Prince Maximillian of Wied-Neuwied, London, 1843.

10 Cited by Harry Toulmin, Judge of the Mississippi Territory, and also by *Palladium* (Kentucky), 1804.

11 *Sketches of Louisiana,* Stoddard.

12 Ibid.

13 *An Enquiry into Madoc,* Williams.

[14] Captain Stewart's statement was published in the *American Museum*, 1797.

[15] Cited from an extract of the log of H.M.S. *Scylla*, signed and witnessed by Capt. R. Lambert, R.N., 1861.

CHAPTER 10

[1] Cited by Burder, *The Magazine of History*, vol. 20, Extra Nos. 77–80.

[2] *Gentleman's Magazine*, London, 1791.

[3] This is wrong. French travellers did not refer to them as the Padoucas, but as the *Commanches*.

[4] Cited by Burder and quoted from the *Gentleman's Magazine*, vol. ii, pp. 1067, 1798.

[5] *History of Kentucky*, by John Filson, original edition, pp. 95–8.

[6] Stephens: *Essay on Madoc*.

[7] From an article entitled *They Signed Away Their Lives for Yours*, *Saturday Evening Post*, July 9, 1947, and Lossing's *Lives of the Signers*, p. 71.

[8] *History of Kentucky*, by John Filson.

[9] Cited by Stoddard in *Sketches of Louisiana* and Burder. The letter was dated August 24, 1753.

[10] *Who Discovered America?* by Zella Armstrong, Lookout Publishing Company, Chattanooga, 1950.

[11] *Gentleman's Magazine*, 1791.

[12] Cited by Zella Armstrong: *Who Discovered America?*

CHAPTER 11

[1] Letter from Mr. Halliday to the author, October 17, 1965.

[2] Article in the *Missouri Historical Review*, vol. 25.

[3] *John Evans and The Legend of Madoc*, Williams.

[4] James Mackay's Notes in the E. O. Voorhis Memorial Collections, archives of the *Missouri Historical Society*, St. Louis.

[5] *Missouri Historical Review*, vol. 25.

[6] Cited by Zella Armstrong in *Who Discovered America?*

[7] James Mackay's *Notes* in the archives of the Missouri Historical Society.

[8] Williams: *John Evans and The Legend of Madoc*.

[9] Ibid.

[10] Cited by Zella Armstrong in *Who Discovered America?*

[11] *Reglamentos de Don Manuel Gavoso de Lemos*, New Orleans, 1797.

[12] Cited by Zella Armstrong, who quotes a lengthy statement by Mrs. Penelope J. Allen.

CHAPTER 12

¹ *Westward the Course of Empire*, by Bernard de Voto, Eyre & Spottiswoode, London, 1953.

² *Early Voyages and Northern Approaches 1000–1632*, by Tryggvi J. Oleson, Oxford University Press, London, 1964. Chap. 14, p. 100.

³ Articles in the *Boston Evening Transcript,* January 3 and 10, 1891.

⁴ Ibid.

⁵ J. Morgan Lewis's *Brechfa.*

⁶ Extracts from the correspondence of the Smithsonian Institution in the *Annual Report, 1866,* pp. 126–7.

⁷ Ibid. Citing letter from Mr. George Gibbs, February 12, 1866. The Hon. John R. Bartlett was then Secretary of the State of Rhode Island; he published a paper touching on the Welsh Indians at the request of the Welsh citizens of New York.

⁸ *Palladium*, Frankfurt, Kentucky, 12 December 1804.

⁹ *History of Alabama*, by Albert J. Pickett, vol. I, p. 174.

¹⁰ *Handbook of American Indians North of Mexico*, by F. W. Hodge, Vol. 2, Bureau of American Ethnology, Smithsonian Institution, 1910. p. 282.

¹¹ Ibid. p. 286.

¹² Cited by Stoddard: *Sketches of Louisiana.*

¹³ Pages 113–14. See also Bruff's letter to Wilkinson, *Territorial Press*, VIII, pp. 56–61.

¹⁴ From *The Blond Mandan: A Critical Review of an Old Problem*, by Marshal T. Newman, *Southwestern Journal of Anthropology*, vol. 6, no. 3, pp. 255–72.

¹⁵ *Sketches of Louisiana*: Stoddard.

CHAPTER 13

¹ *Van den Vos Reinaerde*, by Professor Dr. J. W. Muller, Leiden, 1939. Issued by the Mij. der Ned. Letterkunde.

² *Van den Vos Reinaerde*, by J. D. Wolters, Groningen, 1959, issued by Dr. D. C. Tinbergen.

³ Letter to the author by M. Edouard Duvivier, December 20, 1965.

⁴ *Lundy, Bristol Channel*, by Anthony and Myrtle Langham, privately printed, 1960. See also *Transactions* of the Devonshire Association Index, compiled by A. A. Pursdon, British Museum.

⁵ *America Discovered by the Welsh*, by Benjamin F. Bowen.

⁶ See *Orkney Inga Saga: 1139–1148*, printed in the Rolls Series (No. 88) 'Icelandic Sagas', vol. 1, edited by Gudbrand Vigfusson, 1887, and *Icelandic Sagas*, translated by Sir G. W. Dasent, H.M.S.O., vol. 3, 1894. In these works there is confirmation of some of the Icelanders' navigational techniques.

[7] See *Bulletin de Géographie* (Paris), 1858.

[8] See *Orkney Inga Saga.*

[9] Log note by Columbus on 16 Sept., 1492. See *Enumeracion de Libros y Documentes concernientes a Cristobal Colón y Sus Viages,* published by the Royal Academy of History, Madrid, 1892.

[10] See *Lundy, Bristol Channel,* by A. and M. Langham; also *History of Lundy Island,* by John Roberts Chanter, *Transactions* of the Devonshire Association, vol. VI, 1871.

[11] *Orkney Inga Saga.*

[12] *Wright's Early English Ballads,* vol. XIV, Percy Society.

[13] Translation of Piri Reis's notes by Bay Hasan Fehmi for the Society for Turkish Historical Research, 1932.

[14] *Cambrobritannicae Cymraecaeve Linguae Institutiones,* 1592, p. 60. Dr. Jonathan Williams said Dee was a native of Bugaildu, near Knighton.

[15] *Her Majestie's Title Royal to Many Foreign Countryes, Kingdomes and Provinces,* Cotton MSS. Vitell. C. vii 3.

[16] *Inventio Fortunata,* a paper by Benjamin F. De Costa, read to the American Geographical Society at Chickering Hall, May 15, 1890.

[17] Noted in the margin of the Ptolemy Map, 1508, Rome.

[18] *The Strange Discoveries mayd by Doctor John Dee,* by Dr. John David Rhys, Raglan MSS.

[19] Cited by Hakluyt in *Principal Navigations,* vol. I.

[20] Another version of both Mercator's and Cnoyen's statements gives it as follows: '. . . a certain priest who came of that race famed in legend by King Arthur and who knew of his countrymen's voyage to a strange sea filled with weed.' Extracts from Cnoyen's lost book are to be found in the British Museum, Cotton MSS. Vittel. C. vii. Nicholas of Lynne composed an astronomical table in 1386 which was used by Chaucer in his *Treatise of Astrolabe.* Dee's mention of Cnoyen's *Fortunata* Map is cited in the *Spiegel Historiael* MSS. of Leyden.

CHAPTER 14

[1] *Wele Madoc Dewr Ei Fron,* by Kathleen O'Loughlin, Ontario, 1942.

[2] *A Relation of Some Yeares' Travaile,* by Sir Thomas Herbert.

[3] Cited by Peter A. Brannon, of the Alabama Department of Archives and History.

[4] *Old Frontiers,* by John P. Brown.

[5] *Natural and Aboriginal History of Tennessee,* by John Haywood, Chap. VII.

[6] Judge Samuel Cole Williams stated that the name of this man was Francis Budwine, saying that about the year 1730 or 1735 a party of Cherokee on an expedition in the Mississippi River took as prisoners the crew of a French boat.

Among the French prisoners was Francis Budwine, who afterwards lived among the Cherokee. Certainly Governor Sevier knew Budwine, but the name may be an American corruption of François Baudouin.

[7] *Nineteenth Annual Report* of the Bureau of Ethnology to the Smithsonian Institution, p. 22.

[8] *America Discovered by the Welsh*, by Benjamin F. Bowen. See also Chap. 13 of this book.

[9] Letter to the author by Mr. Coles J. Pearman, dated December 17, 1965.

[10] *Precursors of Jacques Cartier*, by H. P. Biggar, published by the authority of the Minister of Agriculture, under the direction of the Archivist, Ottawa, Government Printing Bureau, Ottawa, No. 17.

[11] Letter by Elizabeth Sevier to James Farson, undated.

CHAPTER 15

[1] *A History of the United States*, by Edward Channing, vol. I, p. 59.

[2] *Who Discovered America?*, by Zella Armstrong.

[3] *The General History of the Vast Continent and Islands of America*, by Antonio de Harrara.

[4] *Manco Capac*, by the Rev. John H. Parry.

[5] *A Relation of Some Yeares' Travaile*, by Sir Thomas Herbert.

[6] *Old Frontiers*, by John P. Brown.

[7] *Precursors of Jacques Cartier*, by H. P. Biggar.

[8] Cited by Hatchett Chandler in *Little Gems From Fort Morgan*, The Christopher Publishing House, Boston, 1961.

[9] Ibid.

[10] *American Antiquities and Discoveries*, by Josiah Priest, 1833.

[11] Letter to the author by Mr. Arthur F. Griffith, November 12, 1965.

[12] See *History of Alabama*, Pickett, and *Who Discovered America?*, Armstrong.

[13] *Civil and Political History of Tennessee,* by John Haywood.

CHAPTER 16

[1] Judge Haywood confirmed the treaty between the Indians and the 'white people', though he did not call them Welsh. See Haywood's *Civil and Political History of Tennessee*.

[2] Col. Robert Durett made a special study of the Welsh Indian stories. He also confirmed the treaty between the Indians and the 'white people' after which, he said, the latter moved to the Missouri River. See *Filson Club Publications*, No. 23.

[3] *Journaux de la Sieur de la Verendrye*, Paris.

[4] See *The Aboriginal Races in North America*, by Samuel G. Drake.

[5] *Journaux de la Sieur de la Verendrye.*

[6] *Travels in the Interior of North America*, by Maximillian, Prince of Wied, London, 1843.

[7] *Letters and Notes of the North American Indians*, by George Catlin, 2 vols., Egyptian Hall, Piccadilly, 1842.

[8] Ibid.

[9] Ibid.

[10] *Oldest Native Document in America*, by Hjalmar Rued Holand, in the *Journal of American History*, 1910, p. 184, note.

[11] *Contes et Voyages*, by Pierre la Chapelle, Paris, 1774.

[12] *Letters and Notes of the North American Indians*, Catlin.

[13] Ibid.

[14] *The Indian Tribes of North America*, vol. I, p. 424, and vol. II, p. 210, by Thomas L. McKinney and James Hall. As a matter of interest the census of Indian tribes in 1946 gave the total number of Mandans still existing as 396, though it can be categorically stated that these so-called survivors cannot be considered either ethnologically, nor historically, as belonging to the original Mandan tribe.

CHAPTER 17

[1] *Letters and Notes of the North American Indians*, Catlin.

[2] Ibid.

[3] *The Indian Tribes of North America*, by Thomas L. McKinney and James Hall, vols. I and II.

[4] Letter from Mr. Halliday to the author, October 17, 1965.

[5] Ibid.

[6] *Towy's Fishing Pools*, by M. H. Jones, in *Transactions* of the Carmarthenshire Antiquarian Society, 1905–6.

[7] *Westward the Course of Empire,* by De Voto.

[8] *A Welsh-Indian Vocabulary*, by James Girty. Extracts made by Thomas C. Pritchard, of Harrisburg, 1789, and included in the *Gwydir Papers.*

[9] *Letters and Notes of the North American Indians*, Catlin.

[10] See *Lundy, Bristol Channel*, by A. and M. Langham, and *Some Account of the Island of Lundy*, by G. Steinman, in *Collectanea Topographica et Genalogica*, Vol. 4, published by J. B. Nichols, 1836.

[11] *American Pioneer*, vol. I, p. 373. Little is known of Welsh heraldry in early times, except that it was very different from that of England at the same period. The ordinary charges of chevron, fess, bend, etc., are not to be found in Welsh coats, which were either those of families or tribes. The usual charge is that of animals

and birds with which they were acquainted, such as wolves, eagles, ravens, etc., for it was not until the thirteenth century that lions came into fashion.

[12] Cited by Zella Armstrong in *Who Discovered America?*

[13] *New View of the Origin of the Tribes and Nations,* by Benjamin S. Barton, 1797.

[14]*Prehistoric Kentucky,* by Col. Bennett H. Young. Undoubtedly there is much scope for excavations and more detailed exploration of archaeological remains throughout North America. Mr. J. Kr. Tornöe, with the support of the Nansen Foundation, has published conclusions of his own researches in *Norsemen Before Columbus,* Allen & Unwin, 1966. He confirms that Vinland means 'Vine-Land' by referring to the text of the Norse Sagas: *vinvio ok vinber* meaning 'vines and grapes'. The author states wild grapes still grow in various parts of North America. Also the *Furdustrandir* (Wonder Sands) of the Sagas appears to locate a stretch of about 37 miles of unbroken sand from the north point of Cape Cod to Monomoy Point.

[15] Statement made by Sir James Marshall Cornwall in an article entitled *Is the Vinland Map a Forgery?* in the *Sunday Times,* March 6, 1966.

[16] The land most frequently named in pre-Columbus maps, apart from the Antillia, was the Fortunate Isles, *Insulae Fortunatae* of the cartographers and Isles of the Blest of the story-tellers. According to the Greeks these islands were situated at the western edge of the known world. Homer appears to identify them with the Elysian Fields, while in later ages they were identified with islands further distant, first the Canaries and Madeira, then with Bimini in the West Indies. The Avalon of the King Arthur cycle is also a homologue of this classic myth.

SUPPLEMENTARY NOTE ON THE HILL-FORT ON CARN FADRUN AND THE FORTIFICATIONS AT DUCK RIVER, TENNESSEE

The plan of the fortifications at Carn Fadrun includes part of a pre-Roman fortification of about twenty-six acres in area, but the summit fort can almost certainly be identified with the 'Castle of the sons of Owain' mentioned in *Giraldus Cambrensis* in 1188 as newly built. It derives most of its strength from its position, for the east wall, 8 ft. thick, still retains its rampart walk in places and cannot therefore have stood much above its present height of 3 ft.

There has been no scientific excavation and the amount of disturbance by casual visitors is fortunately rare. Carn Fadrun is a hill of igneous rock which forms the dominating feature of the western Lleyn. The sides rise steeply for more than 200 feet. Ascent is difficult but not impossible. The top of the hill has a large level area, defended by two strong stone walls. There are stone huts of irregular shape of unmortared rubble, the walls being ten feet thick.

There are marked similarities in construction and planning to the fortifica-cations at Duck River, most notably in the rampart walks, the arrangement of materials, measurements of entrances and the thickness of walls, and evidence of a triangular design in each site. The difficulty, of course, of any positive identification of Madoc's followers in America on the sole basis of structural similarities is that there is only a limited possible repertoire of types of structure in dry stone.

INDEX

INDEX

A

Abbott, George, 13
À Beckett, Thos., Archbishop of Canterbury, 37, 42
Aberffraw Castle, 39, 58, 86
Aber Kerrik Gwynyon, 97, 99, 100, 102, 103
Adam of Bremen, 166
Afon Ganol, 92, 102, 103, 104
Allen, Mrs. Penelope J., 144, 148
Alexander the Great, 1
Amerycke, Richard, 7
Anaximander, 8
Anarawd, 35
Angharad, 23
Annesta, 24, 40, 41
Antillia, 76, 78, 236
Apaches, 155
Aranquiz y Votes, d'Alonzo de, 81
Arikaras, 145, 227
Aristotle, 2
Armstrong, Major Robert, 231
Armstrong, Zella, 130, 131, 194
Arthur, King, 13, 57, 68, 164, 165, 178
Arthurian Legends, 65, 79, 164–6
Ashe, Geoffrey, 4
Astronomy in ancient Wales, 48
Athapascans, 155, 160

Atlantis, 2, 3, 5, 8
Avienus, Festus, 50
Aztecs, 5, 58, 65, 151, 196, 197, 208

B

Baldwyn, Archbishop of Canterbury, 42
Barbier, Prof., 13, 24, 38, 39, 51
Bartlett, John R., 155
Barton, Benjamin S., 233
Basingwerk, Book of, 63
Beatty, Chas., 113, 117, 118, 119
Bedaire, 236
Behaim, Martin, 4, 78, 237
Benfras, 34
Bermuda, 177
Bernard, Bishop of St. David's, 34
Bianco, Andrea, 236
Bienville, Sieur de, 191
Biggar, H. P., 190
Big White Man, 145
Bimini, 198, 199
Binon, Mr., 131, 132
Black Book of Admiralty, 99
Black Cat, 145
Blest, Isles of the, 3
Boone, Daniel, 132
Bouganville, 212

Bowen, Rev. Benjamin F., 86, 153, 170, 189

Bowles, William, 132–6, 137, 138

Brandon, St., 3, 4, 43, 48, 50, 53, 78, 79, 80, 85, 86, 105, 106, 167, 174, 178, 236, 237

Brannon, Peter, 200

Breccan, son of Niall, 84

Brenda, of Carno, 24

Brown, John P., 160, 183, 197

Brynjulfsson, Gisle, 36, 53

Burder, George, 210

Burtchaell, G. D., 84

C

Cabot, John, 7, 190

Cadwaladr ap Cynan, 33, 34, 35, 36, 37, 86

Cadwaladr, John, 109

Cadwallon, 58

Caedfan ab Cadwaladr, 37

Caesar, Julius, 32, 49, 125

Camden, William, 27

Campbell, Dr., 66

Campbell, John P., 232

Canedda, 37

Caradoc of Llancarfan, 29, 39, 62, 63

Carondelet, Baron, 140

Cartier, Jacques, 190

Catlin, George, 121, 207, 212, 213, 214, 215–19, 222, 223, 224, 225, 226, 227, 230, 231, 233, 234, 235

Channing, Edward, 194

Chaplain, Capt. Abraham, 128, 220

Charles IV, King of Spain, 144, 145

Charlevoix, Father, 114, 156

Cherokees, 130, 148, 154, 155, 158, 159, 185, 186, 187, 191, 204, 205, 208, 209, 214, 218, 233

Choctaws, 118

Chrochan, George, 128, 130, 189

Chrisiant, 2nd wife of Owain Gwynedd, 24, 37, 40, 42

Cincinatti Museum, 218, 225, 231

Claiborne, Governor, 185

Clark, General George Rogers, 232

Clark, Capt. Wm. (later General), 156, 213, 217

Cnoyen, James, 72, 177

Columbus, Bartolomé, 72

Columbus, Christopher, 4, 6, 7, 8, 21, 25, 28, 43, 47, 60, 67, 71–78, 173, 183, 194, 196, 198, 236

Conway, Robert, 97, 98

Coracles:
  early history of, 49, 50, 83
  use of in Wales, 224, 226, 227, 230
  evidence in America, 224, 225, 226, 227

Cornwall, Jas. M., 235

Cortes, Hernando, 64, 65, 68, 73, 180, 196, 197

Corvenor, bard, 52

Cosa, Juan de la, 76

Creek Indians, 134, 159, 199

Crone, G. R., 75

Curraghs, 49, 50, 83, 85, 86

Cynan ab Owain Gwynedd, 24, 36, 37

Cynddelw Brydydd Mawr, 14, 15, 16, 17, 18, 27, 34

Cynddilig, 51
Cynfric ap Gronow, 63, 91, 95, 102, 173, 182, 195
Cynoric ap Owain Gwynedd, 35

D

Dafydd ab Owain Gwynedd, 18, 19, 23, 24, 28, 87, 88, 89, 97, 100, 107, 174, 181
Dafydd Ddu Eryri, 137
Dane, Joan, 39, 40, 41, 106
David, John, 120
Davies, Col. Joseph H., 232
Davies, Rev. Walter, 11, 12
Daughters of the American Revolution, 10, 184
De Costa, Rev. Benjamin F., 10, 152, 153, 162, 165, 176
Dee, Dr. John, 62, 175, 176, 177, 178
Deio an Ieuan Du, 28
Delawares, 159
De Luna Arellano, Don Tristan, 200
De Soto, Hernando, 80, 184, 201, 203, 204, 205
De Voto, Bernard, 67, 152
D'Iverville, Sieur Pierre le Moyne, 182, 200
Didorus Siculus, 2
Dinwiddie, Governor of Virginia, 128
Doegs, 11, 112, 132, 136, 159, 160, 209
Dolwyddelan Castle, 86, 87, 203
Drake, Samuel, 112, 113, 117, 118, 119, 127
Durrett, Robert, 209, 231
Duvivier, Edouard, 168, 171

E

Edwal ab Owain Gwynedd, 88, 92, 93, 94, 181
Edward, Lewis, 223
Einion ab Owain Gwynedd, 88, 92, 93, 94, 181
Einion Sais, 25
Eleanor of Aquitaine, 39
Elizabeth I, Queen, 60, 68, 175, 176
Epejo, Antonio de, 195
Eriksen, Leif, 6, 54, 55, 162
Erik the Red, 4, 6, 43
Evan, Rev. Evan, 21
Evans, John, 9, 10, 137–50, 212, 214, 225
Evans, Rev. Theophilus, 69, 92, 124

F

Farson, James, 191
Filson, John, 127, 128
Fort Morgan, 10, 184, 188, 200, 225
Fort Mountain, 183, 204, 205, 206, 233, 234
Flemings, in Wales, 166–9
Franklin, Benjamin, 46
Fraser, Lady, 126

G

Gabota, Sebastian, 73
Gachupines, 197
Gardar, 4
Gayoso de Lemos, Don Manuel, 149, 150
Geoffrey of Monmouth, 165
Geraint of Devonshire, 51

Gibbs, George, 155
Gilbert, Bishop of St. Asaph, 35
Gilbert, Sir Humphrey, 60, 62
Giraldus Cambrensis, 13, 33, 50, 51, 131, 230
Girty, James, 227–30, 235
Goeral, 24
Gomara, Francisco Lopez de, 58, 60, 62, 73
Greal, 157
Griffiths, Arthur F., 203
Griffith, Maurice, 116, 117, 156
Gruffydd ap Conan, 20, 22, 29, 33, 34, 36, 51, 53, 85, 106
Gruffyd ap Rhys, 33, 87
Gruffyd ap yr Ynad Coch, 34
Guiot de Provins, 172
Gwalchmai, 20, 28, 34, 37, 89
Gwalltir Mechain, 12, 14
Gwenllian, 24, 25
Gwerdonnau Llion, 177, 178, 199
Gwennan Gorn, 83, 84, 92, 95, 99, 100, 172
Gwladys, 1st wife of Owain Gwynedd, 37
Gwynedd, history of, 33–42

H

Hakluyt, Richard, 9, 27, 66, 67, 68, 70, 91, 176, 180, 181, 194, 195
Hall, James, 127, 219
Halliday, Arthur T., 138, 148, 225
Halliday, Jabez, 207, 225, 226
Ha-Na-Tah-Nu-Riah, Chief, 215
Hanno, 1, 2
Haro, Biud de, 72, 74, 75, 196
Hawkins, Sir John, 60, 71

Haywood, John, 183, 188, 203, 205, 206
Henry I, King, 33, 79
Henry II, King, 36, 38, 39, 41, 86, 88, 89, 95, 100, 105, 168, 170
Henry VII, King, 21, 25, 64, 67, 72, 73, 97
Henry VIII, King, 67
Henry of Portugal, Prince, 48
Herbert, Sir Thomas, 22, 30, 53, 64, 88, 89, 91, 92, 93, 94, 100, 104, 153, 163, 175, 181, 182, 193
Hercules, Pillars of, 1, 2
Herjolfson, Bjarni, 6
Herrara, Antonio de, 194
Heyerdahl, Thor, 43, 45, 237
Heylin of Bodorgan, 25, 109
Hicks, Lewis, 119
Hidatsa, 227
Hind, Thos, S., 231, 232
Hodge, F. W., 159
Holand, Rued Hjalmar, 217
Hopi tribe, 159
Hornell, J., 50
Hornius, 70, 71, 72, 196
Horsford, Prof. E. N., 152
Howel ab Owain Gwynedd, 19, 23, 24, 35, 36, 37, 87, 88
Howel ap Maradudd, 33, 35
Howel, James, 30, 68, 90
Hudd, Arthur, 7
Hurons, 159
Hywel Dda, 33

I

Ieuan Brechfa, 16, 19, 20, 37, 38, 40, 53, 86, 95, 96, 153, 170, 175, 181

Ingram, David, 60, 67
Ingstad, Helge, 53, 54, 55
Inventio Fortunatae, 174–7, 199
Iolo Morganwg, 12, 30, 56, 57, 58, 59, 60, 133, 136, 137
Iorwerth Drwyndwn, 23, 37, 87, 88
Iowas, 114
Isabella, Queen of Spain, 75
Isypernik, Prof., 75

J

Jefferson, Thos., 109, 150, 156
Jenkin ap Meredith of Tywyn, 29
Jessaume, 144, 147
Johnson, Dr. Samuel, 59, 133
Jones, E. D., 14, 17, 84
Jones, Merfyn, 189, 190
Jones, Rev. Morgan, 110, 111, 112, 113, 119, 124, 132, 138, 159, 220
Jones, Owen, 133, 136
Jones, Dr. Samuel, 138, 147, 150
Jones, T. Gwynn, 85

K

Knight, Lucian Lamar, 183, 205
Knowles, Edwin B., 73
Knuth, Count Eigil, 6
Kon-Tiki, 44
Kutenai Indians, 153, 154, 221

L

La Chapelle, 207, 217, 224
Leland, 103
Lewis, Andrew, 109

Lewis, Francis, 109, 127, 128, 220, 228
Lewis, J. Morgan, 53
Lewis, Capt. Merriwether, 150, 156, 213
Lewis, Morgan, 109
Llewelyn ap Heylin, 25, 109
Llewelyn ab Iorwerth, 20
Lloyd, Charles, 113
Lloyd, Sir J. E., 9
Lloyd, Thos. of New York, 110
Llwyd, Edward of Oxford, 110
Llwyd, Humphrey, 22, 29, 62, 67, 91
Llywarch Prydydd y Moch, 14, 15, 16, 19, 20, 34, 40, 41, 89, 94, 107, 171
Lookout Mountain, 183, 201, 205, 206
Louis VII, King of France, 39, 170, 173
Lowery, George, 191
Lucan, 49
Lundy Island, 41, 50, 51, 82, 86, 87, 92, 94, 96, 106, 107, 166, 169, 170, 172, 173, 174, 231
Lynn, Rev. Humphrey, 125
Lyttelton, Lord, 49, 95

M

Mabiogion, 15, 169, 230
Mabon, priest, 85
MacGraw, Dr. B. K., 47
Mackay, James, 141, 142, 143, 144, 146, 147, 148–50, 159, 212
Madoc ab Gruffydd, 12
Madoc ab Llewelyn Gruffydd, 12
Madoc ab Meredydd, 12, 13, 28

Madoc ab Owain Gwynedd:
  his origins, 11–31
  early life, 39–42
  as a seaman, 82–96
  as an ambassador, 41, 170
  his voyages, 97–107, 169–73,
    180–2, 193–5
Madocks, W. A., 90
Madoc's Creek, 221
Maelgwyn, 24
Maerlant, Jacob van, 78, 79, 166
Mah-To-Toh-Pa, 215
Malory, Sir Thos., 164, 165
Malte-Brun, 77
Manco Capac, 195
Mandans: 144, 161, 207–19
  their discovery by early ex-
    plorers, 114, 115, 117, 145,
    210, 213
  their customs, 115, 210, 217
  their villages, 115, 116, 146,
    210, 211
  their language, 190, 221–35
  Catlin among the, 213–19
  Welsh associations, 15, 122, 123,
    138, 141, 148, 149, 150, 159
  their extinction, 219
Man-To-Tom-Pa, 219
Map, Walter, 166, 167, 168
Marana, Paul, 112, 159
Maredudd ap Rhys, 20, 22, 25, 26,
  28, 39, 68, 230
Marriott, John, 66
Marisco, William de, 87
Marston, Thos. E., 6
Martinez, Jose Fernandez, 77
Martyr, Peter, 71, 74, 75, 78, 196,
  199
Matthew of Westminster, 52
Mauvillians, 191, 209

Maximilian, Prince of Wied, 115,
  212
McKinney, Thos. L., 127, 219, 225
McMorrough, King of Leinster,
  84
Meilir, 34
Meiron, 16, 22, 24, 40, 92, 93, 94,
  153, 170, 181
Me-Nwek-E-Sunk-To-Ca, 215
Meredydd ab Llowarch ab Bran,
  25
Meredydd of Bodorgan, 25
Merrick brothers, 108
Missouri Company, 142, 147
Mobile Bay, 10, 80, 182, 184, 187,
  188, 191, 192, 193, 199, 200
Modoc tribe, 159
Mohawks, 232
Monta Norumbega, 68
Montezuma, Emperor, 64, 65, 69,
  73, 197
Moqui tribe, 152, 197
Moravian Mission in America, 127
Morgan ab Seissyl, 23
Morgan, Daniel, 109
Morgans, John O., 90
Morison, Samuel, 76
Mormon, Book of, 110
Morris, Lewis, 109
Morris, Roger, 83, 84
Mound Builders, 205, 207
Muller, Prof. J. W., 166, 167
Muscle Shoals, Battle of, 186, 209
Muscogee tribe, 160, 208

N

Narvaez, 199
Nastair, A. P., 140, 143, 148
Navajo tribe, 155, 159

Necker Abbott of Cirencester, 172
Newman, Marshall T., 161
Nicholas of Lynne, 7, 72, 176, 177

O

Ocaloosta, 191
Ochuse, 200
Oconostota, Chief, 186, 187, 188, 191, 192, 203, 208, 209, 214
Old Stone Fort, 183, 204, 206, 207, 209
Oleson, Tryggui, 152
O'Loughlin, Kathleen, 152, 162, 181, 182
Omans, 114, 159
Ortelius, 62
Osage tribe, 158, 159
Osborn, Jas., 73
Owain Gwynedd, 11, 12, 13, 14, 15, 19, 20, 21–31, 32–42, 86, 87, 88, 95, 105, 169
Owen, Gutyn, 22, 27, 30, 39, 60, 63, 64, 68, 91, 195
Owen, Rev. N., 113
Owen, William, 125, 134, 144
Owen-Pughe, Dr. Wm., 17, 30, 56, 57, 58

P

Padoucas, 125, 126, 136, 138, 141, 146, 147, 159, 209, 212
Padrón Real, 190
Pagitt, 66
Palfrey, John G., 9, 162
Parry, Rev. John H., 92, 95, 195
Pearman, Coles J., 189
Peckham, Sir George, 60, 67

Pedr Sant, 99
Peepy, Joseph, 119
Pennant, Thomas, 86, 136
Percy, Dr., Dean of Carlisle, 21
Periplus, 1
Pickett, Albert James, 156, 183
Pineda, 184, 199
Piri Reis, 76, 78, 174
Piri Re s Chart, 76, 78, 174
Plato, 2, 5, 8, 53
Pliny, 48
Ponce de Leon, 46, 180, 184, 193, 199
Porter, Capt. David, 121, 123
Powel, Dr. David, 23, 29, 30, 60, 61, 62, 63, 64, 65, 66, 68, 84, 91, 110, 144, 153
Prescott, 9, 69, 196
Price, Sir John, 91
Price, Dr. Richard, 109
Price, Rev. Thos., 63
Priest, Josiah, 201
Pritchard, John (of Invermere), 153
Pritchard, William, 138
Ptolemy, 3, 96
Pueblós, 197
Purchas, Samuel, 9, 66, 91, 197
Pyfog, 24
Pytheas, 3

Q

Quaritch, Bernard, 72
Quetzalcoatl, 52, 197

R

Raleigh, Sir Walter, 66, 114, 195
Rees, Morgan, 127

Reese, James, 109
Reynolds, Hughes, 204
Rhodri ab Owain Gwynedd, 18,
    19, 20, 24, 28, 88, 89
Rhodri Mawr, 33, 42
Rhys, Arthur, 24
Rhys ab Gruffydd, 41
Rhys, Morgan John, 141, 143, 225
Ribeiro, Diego, 190, 191, 198
Ricarees, 218, 219
Richard I, King, 52
Rien ab Owain Gwynedd, 24, 36
Riryd ab Owain Gwynedd, 24,
    85, 88, 92, 94, 95, 96, 99, 100,
    181
Roberts, Lt. Joseph, 157, 158, 220
Robinson, Nicholas, Bishop of
    Bangor, 21, 22
Rogers, Major, 126
Rojas, de Luis Governor of
    Florida, 80
Rome, Map of 1508, 172, 176
Ruysch, John, 172, 176

S

Salinas, Governor, 80
Samwel, David, 133
Sargasso Sea, 63, 172, 173, 177,
    178, 236, 237
See-pohs-ka-nu-mah-ka-kee, 217
Seneca tribe, 154, 155, 158
Seneca, 2, 53, 163, 169
Sevier, Elizabeth, 191, 192
Sevier, Governor John of Tennes-
    see, 185, 186, 188, 189, 191,
    203, 204, 206, 214, 228
Sevier, Joseph, 191
Sevier, Ruth, 186

Shawnees, 116, 117, 159
Shoshonees, 156
Sioux Indians, 115, 116, 145, 212,
    219, 227
Skelton, R. A., 6
Smith, Capt. John, 110
Smith, Joseph, 110, 151
Solinus, Caius Julius, 49
Southey, Robert, 39, 57, 58, 59,
    86, 133
Starnes, 213
Stephens, Thos., 9, 10, 11, 13, 14,
    16, 17, 18, 47, 48, 49, 50, 51,
    52, 53, 54, 61, 63, 65, 70, 91,
    96, 127, 130, 147, 156, 157,
    159, 160, 182, 213, 218, 219,
    221, 222, 223
Stewart, Capt. Isaac, 120, 121,
    125, 156
Stoddard, Major Amos, 117, 156,
    160, 161, 185, 186 203
Stone, Gilbert, 183
Strabo, 3
Strata Florida, 39, 40
Stuart, John, 191, 192
Sutton, Benjamin, 117, 118, 119
Sydney, Sir Philip, 29, 62
Synnott, Rev. E. F., 98, 99, 100

T

Taliesin, 34, 53, 82, 165, 169, 170,
    171, 173
Tappan, Lt.-Col. Samuel, 155
Taylor, Prof. Eva, 7
Taylor, Hubbard, 232
Taylor, Rev. Isaac, 90
Taylor, Capt. Jonathan, 232
Theobald, Archbishop of Canter-
    bury, 34

Theopompus, 5
Thomas, John, 109
Thompson, David, 212, 213
Timothy, Rev. T. E., 103
Trahaiarn of Powys, 51
Trudeau, Don Zenon, 140, 141
Tucker, Norman, 102, 103, 104
Turner, Prof. W. W., 155
Tuscaroras, 110, 111, 158, 159, 209

U

Ultima Thule, 3

V

Van Velthem Lodewijk, 79, 166
Varshavsky, Samuel, 7
Vaughan, Robert of Hengwrt, 21, 22
Veragua, Duke of, 76
Verendrye, Sieur de la, 114, 115, 126, 207, 209, 210, 211, 212, 217, 218
Vespucci, Amerigo, 8, 9, 60, 184
Vinaver, Eugene, 164
Vinland, 5, 6, 7, 53, 162, 163, 166, 235, 236
Vinland, Map, 5, 6, 43, 70, 235
Von Rumboldt, Alexander, 112

W

Wahletka, Princess, 154
Walsingham, Sir F., 60, 67

Watkins, Patrick, 121–3
Weimar, Map of, 1424, 236
Welsh Port Books, 97, 100
Whitney, Jock, 108
Wilde, Mrs. Victor, 102, 103, 206
Willem the Minstrel, 79, 107, 164–74, 199
Williams, Prof. David, 111, 112, 141, 147
Williams, Edward, 56, 57, 59, 60, 131
Williams, Dr. John of Sydenham, 13, 46, 70, 96, 113, 117, 118, 119
Williams, John S., 231
Williams, Joseph, 109
Williams, Roger, 108
Williams, Sir Thos. of Trefriw, 21, 22
Williams, William, 109
Williams, Rev. W. Venable Williams, 97
Winsor, Justin, 10, 162
Wolters, J. D., 167
Wynne, Sir John, 20, 22
Wynne, Morice, 22

Y

Ynys Hir, 90, 170
Ynys Wair, 169, 170
Ynys Yr, 170
Young, Col. Bennett H., 233
Young, Brigham, 151